Fallen S

A biography of Gail Russell

By Steven Glenn Ochoa

JC Publications
Sacramento, Ca

Fallen Star

A biography of Gail Russell

By Steven Glenn Ochoa

(ISBN-13): 978-0-692-63771-5
Includes, index, bibliography and chapter notes.
©2016 Copyright by Steven Glenn Ochoa

Cover design by Williams writing, editing, and design©

Manufactured in the United States.

JC Publications
Sacramento, Ca
JCPublication.com

This Book Is Dedicated To
Gail Russell
In Loving Memory

Table of Contents

Introduction

There was never anyone, ever, quite like her. Her name was Gail Russell (1924-1961), the beautiful actress from Paramount Studios during the 1940's, who had those incredibly, moving eyes of sapphire blue, along with hair that was the hue of midnight. Gail always spoke in a low, whisper-like tone, as soft as a warm, summer breeze. It was said that Gail spoke as if the sound of her own voice frightened her. In a strange way, many things in her short life did. She was so afraid of life in general, of what it had to offer, both good and bad. Her beauty was legendary, and like most beautiful things, not destined to last. There have been many actresses as lovely as Gail Russell in the history of Hollywood, but there has never been one more beautiful.

When you met her, you were always taken aback at her natural beauty. It is the same feeling people get when they see a lovely rose, a rainbow after a winter storm, or any sunset at end of day. Yet it was Gail's eyes that caught your immediate attention. Those lovely, blue eyes, clear and searching, and yet her lovely face, when in repose, always had a haunting sadness. It was as if Gail possessed some secret sorrow that she alone knew, and which she never found some kindred soul with whom she could, or would confide in.

Gail Russell was the only actress who had that unique quality of beauty and vulnerability. She was like those lovely animals in a glass menagerie, so beautiful to look upon, and yet so delicate and fragile.

Yet there was that other side to Gail's character, that strange combination of half light, half shade, of joyfulness and melancholy. That was why there was always this air of tragic sadness about her demeanor, why those eyes were always so lovely, yet so sad. It was always this struggle for Gail to endure in a career she never truly learned to love, and which she entered in only to help her family out financially. It was primarily the main reason she turned to alcohol to get her through the tremendous ordeal of performing before the movie camera. It was a natural consequence of the struggle between her inherently shy nature, and the need to perform in a public arena. This in turn led to an addiction to alcohol that ended Gail's career in Hollywood, and her young life in 1961 at the age of thirty-six.

Gail Russell had an amazing life. She was known as Hollywood's Cinderella Girl who rose from obscurity to movie fame with the release of the supernatural thriller "The Uninvited" in 1944 at the young age of nineteen. She only made 25 films over a period of eighteen years. Gail was a bright star that shinned all too briefly in the Hollywood Heavens. She was a talented artist, and a much underrated actress who was just too beautiful to last. Gail was so like the rose. I am reminded of that line of poetry by the French poet Francois de Malherbe, "But she was of the world where the fairest things have the worst fate. Like a rose, she has lived as long as roses live, the space of one morning."

Chapter 1
The Girl From The Windy City

Gail Russell was born on September 21, 1924, in Chicago, Illinois. She was the second child of George Russell Sr. and Gladys Barnett, and the younger sister of her brother George Jr., who was five years older. Gail Russell was her real name. Gail's mother, Gladys, came from a small rural town in Pike County, Illinois, one of seven children who were later orphaned at the age of nine. When Gladys was old enough, she later moved to Chicago where she sold California fruit in a small store. She was on her own then, and had to take the first job that would pay her a living. She wore a black dress with a white cap on her head, and with her coal black hair and blue eyes, attracted a lot of attention. One day a man from the old Essaney Studios in Chicago saw Gladys, and suggested she accompany him to the studio for a screen test. She was afraid of losing her job if she asked for some time off, and was leery of a simple country girl getting involved with the worldlier movie crowd. Gladys politely declined the offer, but often later regretted what she might have missed.[1]

It was at a dance that Gladys met Gail's father, George, who was a member of the dance band. He was a very talented musician who could play several instruments – guitar, clarinet, even the piano. George Sr. later left the band when he married Gladys, and started a family. He became an insurance salesman to provide better security for his family. The family later moved to the South Side of Chicago, in the Hyde Park District.[2] This is where Gail grew up, and later attended Kosminski Grammar School.

It was during these early years of Gail's childhood that she began to develop her extreme shyness towards other people. At first her parents thought that it was just a normal childhood reserve at meeting new people. Later, however, it became apparent that this fear of meeting new people could develop into something more serious. It was as if Gail would deliberately go out of her way to avoid people, and desired to be alone. Gail also developed a curious habit of hiding under the family's grand piano whenever they had visitors over. She wouldn't come out and meet them until she had studied them for a while, and then would eventually come out and play. Her mother's friends would laugh at such childish behavior, but some were afraid that little Gail would never grow out of this strange habit. "How terrible for Gail," they would say. "She will be miserable all her life unless she gets over it." Such comments were well intentioned, yet I cannot but believe that this was the start of Gail's inferiority complex, and her low self-esteem. Children hear such words, and even at an early age, understand, and are easily hurt by unthinking adults. This was to be the genesis of Gail's lifelong fear of meeting new people, and performing in public.

As her mother told writer Kate Holliday in a movie magazine article in 1945 – "Ever since she was a baby, you see, Gail has been painfully shy. As a child she never wanted to meet guests who came to our home in Chicago.

Instead, she would back away from strangers until she was hidden from the shadows under the piano. She would stay there despite all our coaxing, and it was only when she had studied the people in the room for some time that she would timidly reappear. I don't think that she was at all abnormal in this. She was just like thousands of children who cannot face new situations until they have been accustomed to them. What was responsible for this in Gail's case, I do not know for sure. Perhaps it was the fact that her brother, who is five years older than she, was a gregarious youngster who always loved people. Gail may have felt, even as a baby, the difference between them. Whatever the cause, she remained almost tortuously shy. She was never afraid, but she wanted to be alone, to escape parties if she possibly could, to play with only one child instead of a dozen, to live her own life. Time after time, when she was in grade school, I brought her pretty dresses to wear to parties, and found Gail completely disinterested in them. She insisted that any clothes she wore be simple to the point of plainness, to keep her from being conspicuous. Time after time, she demanded that her father or her nurse or I walk behind her on the street, that she be allowed to be alone, and again, and again, she went through moods when she would say nothing for a whole day, after which she'd simply spout to her father or me."[3]

It was also during this time that Gail's appetite for art began to express itself. Even during babyhood, at five years old, she started sketching. At seven, she was drawing cartoons. At ten, she wanted oil paints, and began to work in that medium. At eleven, she began doing fashion layouts that were well beyond her years. Art became an escape for Gail, a necessary release from the stress of relating to the other children at school. She did all the things normal adolescent girls do, especially roller skating, and ice skating.[4]

Those early years in Chicago were happy for Gail. Her father made a good living as a bond salesman, and the family lived in a big, spacious apartment on the South Side, Hyde Park District, furnished in Early American, with a grand piano, maid service, and a big Buick parked in a garage.[5] Gail soon developed a passionate regard for chop suey at the age of four, and had a fur coat to wear in kindergarten class. Then there was the time she had stolen the colored pencils, crayons, and paper at art school, had been found out, and forced to return them. There was also the incident with David, the red-headed boy next door, who invited Gail over to play a game of Tarzan. She was supposed to swing on a rope attached to the tree limb, and land on a nearly pile of hay. Unfortunately, Gail missed the hay, and landed on the hard ground, breaking her arm. She went home where her brother George, who was five years older, poured a bottle of Sloan's Linement on her arm, and wrapped it in a bed sheet. Since there was a circus in town, Gail was afraid she wouldn't be allowed to go, so it was nearly a week before she told her parents the truth.[6]

A favorite pastime for Gail was riding her bike in Hyde Park on many an afternoon with a little wooden box on her handlebars that carried Chip, her

Angora cat. She also kept scrapbooks of her favorite actress, Ginger Rogers, and would often see her movies after school. Sometimes Gail would watch her films time after time, until the theater closed. Many a time her father had to find her, and bring her home. Summer was especially fun for Gail when she would go swimming in Lake Michigan every morning until all the curls were gone from her hair. She was only eleven that March day in 1935, while roller skating down Michigan Boulevard with Johnny Powell, that they entered the Episcopal Church to escape the cold wind blowing off the lake. They were the only people there at the time, and it was there, in the second pew, that Gail Russell received her first kiss from a boy.[7]

Gail spent much of her vacation time from school on her uncle's farm in Michigan. It was here that she grew to appreciate the simple things in life, the timeless value of honesty, and the character that were to be the solid foundation of her young life. As she explained in an article she wrote for Movie Stars Parade Magazine in October, 1950 – "I was born in a large city – Chicago – but spent much time on my uncle's farm in Michigan. I'm grateful for those years because I believe they gave me a better sense of values than I would have had otherwise. Somehow you learn more about people in the country. In the city, people seem to be on the defensive, 'putting on a front' as they say. The country strips pretense away; people are themselves. I think I acquired my appreciation of honesty on my uncle's farm – and that has been the basis for my life since. Honesty is the most important word in my book. Also, it was there I learned to love nature and the outdoors."[8] Despite this seemingly normal childhood, Gail was still troubled by her extremely shy nature. She was supposed to be in a play in grammar school about the Pilgrim Fathers, and had only about four lines of dialogue to speak. However, Gail was so terrified to speak on stage in front of an audience, so in consequence, her speech was canceled. She was moved to the rear of the stage to be part of the background where she could gaze at the audience without being seen.

This was to be the basis of Gail's lifelong struggle with stage fright, or as the psychologists call it – glossophobia – the fear of speaking in public. If young Gail Russell had been properly counseled, by her parents, as well as her teachers, she would never have been plagued throughout her career by this problem. This failure to prepare her to perform in public, in essence to interact with people, would later be repeated by the executives at Paramount Studios in Hollywood. This fear of speaking in public, especially performing before a movie camera, indirectly led to Gail's psychological dependence on alcohol to endure acting in front of the movie camera. This later led to an actual physical dependence on alcohol to continue in her career as a Hollywood star.

It was to be a life-long struggle for Gail to conquer her extreme shyness. In a 1950 movie fan magazine article for Motion Picture, Gail told writer Helen Weller – "I can't remember the time I wasn't painfully shy. I don't mean the garden variety shyness most people have. Mine was a thousand times worse. I was possessed with an agonizing kind of self-consciousness where I felt my insides tightening into a knot, where my face and hands grew clammy, where I couldn't open my mouth, where I felt impelled to turn and run if I had to meet new people ... I was always shy. I remember when I was twelve, and invited to my first party. Mother, knowing I would try to back out of going, had me dressed up early in the afternoon, believing that my new organdy dress would give me the courage to go. But as the hour for the party drew near, I sat at home trembling, wishing I could disappear. I became so panicky that I began to cast about for an excuse not to go. Suddenly, I saw a blind man down the street selling pencils. I ran to him and offered to help him. For the next few hours, I walked with the blind man. By the time he was through, the party was almost over, and I sauntered in as everyone was leaving, with my very noble excuse for not having come earlier. It was that way through my teens. During the years when most girls are interested in parties, proms, sororities, and boys, I stayed by myself through a positive fear of meeting people. I tried, several times, to free myself to attend school affairs, but at the last minute my legs would turn to water. Once I got as far as the door of a party – but when I heard the music and laughter inside, panic seized me. I turned and ran home, locking myself in my room.[9] Another time a friend took me by the hand and forced me to attend a party. I sat in a corner all evening absolutely petrified, wishing in my heart that I could get up and mingle with the others. But the simplest act of saying 'Hello' to any of the guests was torture. I felt that everyone was staring at me, that my slip was showing, or there was a run in my stockings. I would look with envy at the groups of girls who gathered after school, walking home together, or stopping in at the ice cream parlor, a gay, laughing bunch. I could no more bring myself to join them than I could fly. So I used to walk home alone."[10]

In an earlier magazine article in May, 1945, Gail also told writer Gladys Hall – "Until I was twelve years old, I was so shy you couldn't get me to open my mouth! When my parents had guests, I would run, get under the piano and hide there. Whenever I had to recite lessons or speak pieces in school, I behaved like an imbecile. Or, I didn't show up. During my first interview, in a producer's office at Paramount Studios, I just sat there with my teeth in my mouth. The first time I ever danced with a boy in my life was with Henry Blees in a scene we did for 'Henry Aldrich Gets Glamour,' my first picture. That was the first time I ever wore high heels, too. I'd never been to a dance before. When someone would ask me, I'd lock myself in my room with a book, and eat graham crackers. I didn't care for clothes. I had them, but I didn't want them. Naturally I didn't, since I didn't go anywhere, except the movies. Otherwise, I always came home straight from school, went to my room and read or drew. I was a sad character. I was sad because of myself. I didn't have any self-confidence. I didn't think I was pretty. I didn't believe I had any talent. I didn't know how to have fun. I was afraid. I don't exactly know of what – of life, I guess. I didn't even know how to talk about fun. I'm not very good at it now."[11]

Yes, it seems that Gail was in many ways a normal, little girl. Yet she was also a strange, troubled little girl. Afraid of strangers, afraid of people, even when they were trying to help her. So what do little girls do to escape the every day challenges that life has to offer? They try to escape to a safer world, and what better world was there during the 1930's Great Depression Era of Chicago, Illinois, than the movies. For Gail, the movies meant Ginger Rogers. She was her all-time screen idol. As Gail told Screenland Magazine writer Gladys Hall in 1945, "I've always loved the movies. When I was a child, at home in Chicago, there would be weeks when I'd go every afternoon, every single afternoon, to the movies. I'd walk blocks to my favorite picture house, and sit there often right through dinner, seeing a film two or three times, forgetting time. My father would have to come and find me. Once – I'd just seen a Ginger Rogers' picture – my father met me dancing through the streets, singing, speaking lines. Ginger was my idol, and I'd sat through the picture three times, and had memorized the dialogue and the lyrics of the songs. It may seem odd that anyone so shy could dance and sing in the street, make a spectacle of herself. But when I felt I was not me, you see, I wasn't afraid. I suppose that really explains why I am in pictures, for on sound stages, I don't have to be me."[12]

Between the movies and her art, Gail was content to use these two mediums of expressions to counterbalance the uncertainties of everyday life, and to help her cope with meeting people.

The year 1936 came, and it was a pivotal year for Gail and her family. The Great Depression was at its height, and her parents had decided to either move to Florida, where they had relatives, or go to California to better their circumstances. Gail's mother asked her which state she preferred. Gail chose Florida because of the beautiful beaches and the palm trees. Then her mother told her she had a better chance of meeting Ginger Rogers if the family moved to California, the home of Hollywood, the Glamour Capital of the World. That settled it for Gail. She chose California and the chance to finally meet her all time movie idol.[13] That decision to come to California was the first "fork in the road" that would change Gail's Destiny, and would later bring her fame and fortune as a Hollywood star. Who would have thought that twelve year old Gail Russell's love for Ginger Rogers would eventually determine her fate, and make her wildest dreams come true? Little did that shy, little girl know that eventually she would join her all-time movie idol on the Silver Screen, and add her name to the list of Hollywood Stars.

Chapter 2
California

For Gail Russell, California was a god-send to a twelve year old girl who was used to the harsh winter seasons of the Midwest. As Gail told Gladys Hall in Screenland Magazine in 1945 – "When I was twelve, we moved to Glendale, in California, and lived in a little apartment, and I went to school at the dark feet of a mountain. I loved California. The sunshine took away so many shadows. I loved the lovely smells of lemon and orange blossoms. We went to all the missions, did all the things tourists do."[1]

Gail truly loved her new lifestyle in sunny California, but she was still plagued by her terrible shyness, as well as those "black moods" that seemed to strike her on occasion. These traces of melancholy would compel her to seek isolation, to cut her off from family, and any social contact. She would withdraw in her room where she would read or draw, or go for long, lonely walks in the rain until the mood would pass. Then Gail would suddenly emerge from her isolation and talk, laugh, with her family, as if nothing were wrong. It was a recurrent problem that was to haunt Gail all her life. As she recalled to writer Gladys Hall in 1945 – "We lived in Chicago, my mother and father and brother and I, until I was twelve. But I might as well as lived in limbo for, excepting for the movies, where I wanted to go, and for school, where I had to go, I didn't have any contacts or interest there. And no friends. No friends of my own age, that is. Not a single girlfriend in whom I would, or could confide. My brother is five years older than I, and we were not really companionable until I went into pictures. My mother and I were close, but my Dad was, in a way especially our own, my best friend. Dad was an insurance salesman during the day, but in his heart, he was a musician, and at night, he played the clarinet in an orchestra. When he'd come home, late, after everyone was in bed, he'd often tap at my door, and I'd sneak out, and we'd raid the ice box, and talk about music, mostly, and art, and poetry. Edgar Allan Poe is my favorite poet. I must have looked funny, perched on the kitchen table, in my long, outing, flannel nightgown, solemnly reciting 'The Raven'. Dad used to tell me that I could be anything, anything I wanted to be, but I thought he was saying that because he loved me."[2]

Gail was particularly close to her father mainly because as artists, he in music, and Gail in art, they possessed a common bond of affection for the beautiful things in life. George Sr. was a bond salesman by day and a musician by night, and having to hold two jobs to support his family must have put a tremendous strain on his relationship with his children. Especially Gail, who he must have realized, by now, was a lovely girl who spent too much time by herself. Don't forget, it was 1936, and the Great Depression was still going on in the country, with one quarter of the population out of work. People still don't realize, even today, how hard it was back then.

Gail's mother, Gladys, was also concerned about her daughter's desire to be alone a great deal of the time. Like all loving mothers, she was desirous of having only the best for her children. After the family had settled in Glendale, and Gail was attending Wilson Junior High School, Gladys noticed that Gail was getting taller and slimmer, but with the height came a new problem. Gail began to walk with her head down. Her mother asked her one day, "What are you trying to hide, with your head down like that?"[3] Her mother already knew the answer. Gail was becoming aware that she was getting to be very pretty, and the boys were beginning to notice too. With all the newfound interest in Gail by the boys in junior high, and later in high school, Gail would deliberately lower her head in order to avoid the stares of those adolescent males. For Gail's mother, it was a far cry from what her young daughter used to be. As she recalled to Modern Screen Magazine in 1948 – "The setting is a Chicago restaurant where we have taken her for a meal with a group of our friends. We are no more than seated when Gail is begging for our butter pads. Her father and I give her a flat, no. But she is so cute and appealing. She soon has seven pads of butter lined up in front of her waiting for the bread and potatoes. 'Gail, seven butters! One is too much,' I say. 'Oh, mother,' she complains, 'you never understand. A girl's got to have weight to play on the boy's football team.' Anyone who caught that scene would never have made a bet that the chubby, little ten year old at our table – who wore a size 14 skirt, mind you – would one day become a tall, slim, 110 pound movie star."[4]

Gail's mother now made a concerted effort to try and bring her daughter out of her "shell", and begin to socialize more with her classmates. To try a new look, different clothes, make-up, even use a little perfume. She knew that young girls at Gail's age were judged, perhaps unfairly, by their looks, even more so than boys. So it soon became a minor tug-of-war between Gail and her mother to look more feminine. However, Gail was insistent on looking and dressing as inconspicuous as possible. She still preferred to use only lipstick for make-up, and one day walked into her mother's room and calmly announced she would no longer wear earrings any more. Being taller, slimmer, and more beautiful with her black hair and blue eyes, she was being noticed more, especially by young boys. It was more of an annoyance to Gail rather than a compliment. She preferred not to be the center of attraction, rather to be left alone to read or draw, possibly as an unconscious fear of people. For a shy person, beauty could be a curse as well as a blessing. As Gail's mother recalled in a Modern Screen Magazine article in 1948 – "I don't think Gail knew she was beautiful until after we'd come to California to live, and she was going to Santa Monica High. Her classmates began to call her Hedy. She told me about it and I said fine, why not part her hair in the center and make it inescapable? She though I was out of my mind. However, from that day forward, she began to take more interest and pride in her appearance. Locked herself in her room and worked with her hair from morning till night.

Though I must say that the results were almost imperceptible. She wasn't then, and never has been, a glamour girl."[5]

Gail, even in high school, continued to dress, and act, as plainly as possible so as not to attract attention to herself. Her mother, however, still tried to get her to socialize more often. The problem with Gail, however, was that she was "young" for her age, or perhaps even naïve. She simply didn't know what to do when boys made a fuss over her at school. Being naturally shy, she didn't know what to do with all the added attraction her beauty produced. Her mother tried to coax her to attend more parties and dances. As she recalled to Modern Screen Magazine, "I'd hear about school dances from other girls. Never from Gail, because she never went. 'How about a little party before the next dance?' I'd say, hoping this might break the ice, and get her started. 'Now mother, don't push me,' she'd say, 'I don't like dances.' I never did learn whether she was afraid nobody would cut in on her or whether too many would . . . She didn't even start going to dances until three years ago (when she was 19), and never felt she needed a formal evening dress until last year."[6]

It wasn't as if Gail's mother was being too controlling, it was just a loving parent's desire to see her daughter get more out of life, and not miss out on what life had to offer a beautiful young girl of her generation. Yet Gail had her own personality, and her extreme shyness would never allow her to become more outgoing, no matter what the benefits. There is that one episode concerning Gail, and her desire to remain out of the limelight that her mother, Gladys, vividly recalled to Modern Screen Magazine – "There is the story of the time she entered a waltzing contest at the Pasadena Ice Rink – she had taken prizes in previous contests – and I discussed with her beforehand what she would wear. She shrugged; the whole question was of no importance. But I went out shopping anyway, thinking that something showy was in order for a waltz contest. I bought a beautiful full skirt and went over to a friend's house in Pasadena, and we worked up a blouse and some other things. Then I telephoned Gail to meet us at the rink a half hour early. We waited and waited. That little devil came in at the last moment – on purpose – too late to change into our dazzling creation. She took the prize wearing a plain little number made of calico."[7]

A few years later, Gail's mother was asked if perhaps after being established as a famous actress for Paramount Studios, perhaps she had become too obsessed with her extraordinary beauty. Gladys replied – "People sometimes ask me how I've managed to keep a very pretty girl from having her head turned. My answer is made simple by the fact that Gail is not the kind that is affected by her looks. She doesn't invite attention, and is actually plain, both in the way she dresses, and in the way she acts."[8]

The Russell family lived in Glendale for a while when for some reason they decided to return to Chicago to live. Perhaps it was for a better business proposition that Gail's father was determined to go back to his home state to work, and to live. However, it proved to be short lived, and within a year the Russell family returned to California, in the San Fernando Valley, in the City of Van Nuys. Gail later recalled that first day she enrolled in a new school – "On my first day at Van Nuys High School, being the shy type, I was quite bewildered by all the new faces, all the activity, at the last roll call, the name Russell was announced, and a firm young voice answered, 'Here'. The Russell who owned the other voice turned out to be Jane. I can remember how she looked that day – healthy, wholesome – even then wearing her future husband Bob Waterfield's sweater – which incidentally, reached almost to her knees! She was so different from me – extroverted, confident, friendly. She took me in tow, taught me the ropes, and helped me as much – in ways she never knew. I wouldn't have missed her friendship for the world!"[9]

The Russell family soon gained a reputation for being "movers" as Gail attended five more high schools – Glendale, Fairfax, Hoover, University, and ultimately, Santa Monica.[10] It was here, in the coastal city of Santa Monica, that Destiny had a further role to play in the life of young Gail Russell.

Chapter 3
The Budding Of A Young Star

It was November, 1940, and Gail Russell was now sixteen and attending University High School in West Los Angeles, California. In Europe, the Second World War had been raging for a year. In America, President Franklin Roosevelt had been elected for an unprecedented third term due to an improving economy, and the successful attempt of keeping the United States out of the war.

Gail Russell, as a sophomore in 1940, was in her first year of high school. Back then, in Los Angeles, there were only three year high schools. There were also two graduating senior classes – one class in March, and one class in June. Gail's graduating class would have been in June. She was by now a little more mature, and starting to emerge from her shell, yet there was within her a still ever present reluctance to socialize openly with her classmates. That shyness, which so plagued her during grammar school, was still robbing her of the chance to enjoy life more fully. It was also a feeling of inferiority which Gail developed early in childhood due to her unnatural fear of strangers who came to visit her parents at home. She could still remember quite vividly how they used to tell her parents that their young daughter would be miserable all her life unless she grew out of her annoying habit.

Then there was the unfair comparison with her older brother George Jr., nicknamed "Russ," who was five years older, and more open and friendly with people. Russ was already, at twenty one years old, an accomplished musician like his father, who could play several instruments, especially the guitar. He found work in a band which he organized, and was contributing to the family income. Gail must have felt so inadequate compared to her older brother, even though she loved him very dearly.

Gail's social life was beginning to improve as she entered her junior year in high school at University High in 1941. She started to join in school activities, even joined the staff at the art department that produced the school yearbook, "The Chieftain". Yet she still struggled to associate with other kids her own age. As Gail told Screenland Magazine in 1945 – "At Uni High and at Santa Monica Tech, where I went, afternoons, to study art, for I was planning to be a commercial artist, I began to have a little fun. I still didn't go to dances or have dates, but I did make some friends, joined in the school activities, began to laugh, and I had my first crush on a boy. It was, decidedly, "unrequited love', however, for he was a senior, and he went with an upper class girl. I was not a vamp in his life. Which didn't crush me, really, nor surprise me, for I had such a healthy inferiority. I didn't expect anything. I never thought about my looks, one way or another. And most of the time I was working too hard to have thought or time for other things. I was hoping for a job at Bullocks-Wilshire when I graduated."[2]

Yet for all her shyness, Gail was typical teenage girl in the 1940's. She liked to dress casually, usually in slacks or a blouse, occasionally in blue jeans. She was fond of midriff pajamas, of which she owned eight pairs in every color and print. Gail was often seen in a red or blue peasant skirt and blouse, and a pair of bright play shoes.[3] She owned just four pieces of jewelry, all of them gold – an anklet, a baby ring (which she always wore on the little finger of her left hand), a cross, and a St. Christopher's medal.

Gail also collected toy dolls in all shapes and sizes, dressed in individual costumes from different countries. Her favorite color was blue, her favorite actors were Ginger Rogers and James Stewart. Favorite books were "Ramona" and "Seventh Heaven," and she was very fond of crossword puzzles. Her taste in music ranged from classical to Broadway tunes, big bands like Glenn Miller and Tommy Dorsey, singers like Bing Crosby and Jean Sablon. Gail rarely ate breakfast in the morning, however coffee was a must every day. She usually skipped lunch, and settled for one large meal at dinner time. Gail's favorite meal was roast lamb, mashed potatoes, and creamed broccoli. A close second was hamburger steak smothered in ketchup sauce.[5] She also had a strange habit of eating her evening meals alone in her room, rather than together with the rest of the family. Her mother disapproved of this annoying habit of hers, but she seldom insisted that Gail eat with the family.[6]

Gail would always read the morning and evening newspapers, glancing at the crossword puzzles and the comic strips, either "Lil Abner" or "Prince Valiant". "I like the way those two funnies are drawn," she said.[7]

For Gail, that junior year at University High School in 1941 was the first time she even really started to emerge from her self-imposed isolation, and start to socialize with her fellow classmates. Maybe it was due to her maturing at seventeen years of age, or it could have been her artistic nature responding to the beautiful campus Uni High was at that time. The school stood on a high hill with tall trees, and a running, fresh water spring that ran through the campus. It was originally the home of the Gabrieleono Tongua Indian Tribe, and the ancient village once stood on the hill. While doing research on Gail's life, I happened to visit University High School in 1973. In their school library, I came across a 1941 University High School yearbook. Inside were two pictures of Gail. One picture shows her among her A-11 junior class on page 47. The second photo shows Gail among the art staff of the Uni High yearbook called "the Chieftain", standing timidly in the center back row on page 77. Gail was using her creative art skills to help illustrate the yearbook. If you happen to view the last end pages of the yearbook, you will see her rather funny, clever caricatures of her fellow classmates, you will also see her signature clearly printed on the bottom of the right hand page. It was a banner year for University High in 1941. Among the graduating class were actors Freddie Bartholomew, Anne Baxter, Jimmy Lydon, and Linda Darnell (named Monetta in the yearbook).

By the time September had arrived in 1941, Gail was officially a senior in high school, and with her art classes she was preparing to become a commercial artist after she graduated. She was looking forward to a job at the Bullocks-Wilshire Department Store, and a quiet, normal life. Gail was beginning to blossom into young womanhood, and the boys were beginning to take serious notice of her on campus. They began to call her "Hedy" because she drew a remarkable resemblance to Hedy Lamarr, the glamorous movie star from Metro Goldwyn Mayer Studios in Hollywood. Gail, with her lovely blue yes, and luxurious, raven black hair, could have been her stand-in, or at least her younger sister. Gail was embarrassed with all the fuss the adolescent boys were making over her, and discouraged the rest while settling on just one boyfriend at a time. For this reason, as well as others, Gail was looking forward to 1942 when she could begin to grow up, and be out on her own. However, little did she realize what Fate had in stone for her, not only a young girl's "Dream Come True, Chance of a Lifetime" Cinderella tale, but one of the greatest, if not the greatest, Hollywood Discovery Stories of all time.

Chapter 4
The Hedy Lamarr Of Santa Monica

By March 1942, the world of seventeen year old Gail Russell had completely changed. With the attack on Pearl Harbor on December 7, 1941, by the Japanese, the United States had been unexpectedly thrust into the Second Word War. The Russell family fortunes had also taken a turn for the worse. Gail's father had started his own business, but when the war started, the company couldn't make it financially, and refusing to stay afloat through the black-market, the company folded.[1] Gail's mother soon had to work to help support the family, and then the second blow fell. Gail's older brother, Russ, was drafted into the army, and his much needed income was soon lost. Now came another disaster for the Russell family. Their home, which was half paid for, was repossessed by the insurance company. Soon the family car was gone, then the furniture began to disappear, piece by piece. The remaining family soon moved into a tiny, three room apartment. When Gail was discovered by Paramount Studios, she was sleeping on newspapers instead of a normal bed.[2]

It was at this inopportune time that the famous "Meiklejohn Incident" occurred. The story of Gail Russell's "discovery" by Hollywood has got to rank a one of the greatest "Cinderella" stories of all time. You have heard of Lana Turner being spotted in the Top Hat Café in Hollywood,[3] or Ava Gardner's portrait being seen in Larry Tarr's Showcase Studio in New York City.[4] Yet Gail's tale of discovery has to rank as one of the best in Hollywood history.

William Meiklejohn, then head of Talent at Paramount Studios in March, 1942, was driving home from San Diego one day in his maroon sedan along the Pacific Coast Highway in California. He soon spotted two teenage boys hitchhiking beside the road, and being in a good mood, decided to pick them up, and give them a ride. They told him they had played "hooky" from Santa Monica Tech that day, and had decided to spend the day at the beach. One of the boys, Charlie Cates, noticed the Paramount "A" parking sticker on the windshield of Meiklejohn's car, and asked him if he was in the movie business. Meiklejohn said yes, and began to tell the boys of his association with such top stars such as Dorothy Lamour, Paulette Goddard, Veronica Lake, and the "discoveries" he had made. The boys said if Meiklejohn thought Veronica Lake was pretty, he ought to see one of their classmates at school, Gail Russell. "The prettiest girl in school," they told him, the prettiest girl he had probably ever seen, even in his life as a talent finder. The kids in school called her the "Hedy Lamarr of Santa Monica."[5] "No kidding, Mister," Charlie Cates said. "You ought to see this girl. She's the most beautiful thing I've ever seen. She ought to be in the movies. No kidding. Not only is she beautiful, but when she starts talking, wow, what a voice! Every boy in Santa Monica Tech is turning handsprings just to get her to look at them."[6] The boys kept going on and on, praising Gail's eyes, her face, her voice, her trim figure. The boys should have been car salesmen, for by the time Meiklejohn dropped them off at the side of the road, he made a mental note of this Gail Russell, and intended to look her up. Meiklejohn was always on the lookout for new and promising starlets to bolster the Paramount roster.

You have to think about this incident for a minute. What are the odds for this to happen to Gail? On that particular day, on that particular road, two boys from her class to run into William Meiklejohn, head of talent at Paramount Studios. What were the chances? One hundred million to one? Such are the vagaries of Destiny.

By the time Meiklejohn got around to getting in touch with this young beauty that the two boys raved about, he had forgotten her first name. He instructed his head of testing at Paramount, Milton Lewis, to locate this Russell girl, and arrange a screen test. Lewis began to call several local high schools, but it was always the wrong Russell. He finally called the local Santa Monica newspaper office, and asked if they ever heard of the "Hedy Lamarr of Santa Monica"? "Oh, you mean Gail Russell," he was told. They instructed him to call University High School where she was enrolled. After calling Uni High, Lewis was told Gail only attended Uni High in the mornings, and that she was currently enrolled in the art school at Santa Monica Tech in the afternoons. He asked the front office to leave a note for Gail at her desk in class, and ask her to come to Paramount Studios for a screen test. The note read as follows –

"4-8-42

GAIL RUSSELL:
PLEASE CALL MILTON LEWIS AT PARAMOUNT STUDIOS REGARDING SCREEN TEST.
HOLLYWOOD 2411, EX. 642,
PLEASE CALL AS SOON AS POSSIBLE.
          L.G."

Gail Russell had quite a surprise in store for her as she went to art class that memorable afternoon in April. As Gail later recalled to writer Gladys Hall in a Screenland Magazine article in 1945 – "So when, one day, I came into class at Santa Monica Tech, and found a note on my desk which said, 'Call Milton Lewis concerning a test at Paramount,' I thought it was a joke someone had played on me, and threw it in the wastebasket. All the kids tried to tell me it wasn't a gag, but I couldn't be told. Just the same, just the same, after school was over, and all the kids were gone, I crept back into the classroom, and fished the crumpled note out of the wastebasket. I can't say I had a premonition that I was retrieving my Destiny. I think it was a perfectly normal curiosity that prompted me. Or was it? Was it a wild hope, submerged in my subconscious until that moment, stirring its wings in my heart? Whatever the impulse may have been, it sent me delving into that wastebasket, then running, teeth chattering to the nearest telephone. I called the Paramount Studios, and asked for Mr. Milton Lewis. Sure enough, he asked me to come to the studios that day. Then I tore home. My folks were getting ready to go out. I sat there, grinning foolishly, tongue tied again. Finally I said, very off hand, and sort of doing a Zasu Pitts with my hands, that if they were not doing anything very important, perhaps they would drive me to Paramount Studios – then there was excitement going off like fireworks all over the place, my mother telling me what to wear, Dad at high pitch saying that he'd always 'known' it. I think we all knew that we'd come to a fork in the road."[7]

Gail's discovery could not have come at a more opportune time. Her family's financial fortunes were at their lowest, and you could understand her parents' desire, especially her mother, to convince Gail to help her family. You can imagine the struggle between Gail and her mother trying to decide what clothes to wear at the meeting at Paramount Studios. Her mother trying to convince her to wear something elegant and formal, with all the necessary make-up and jewelry. However, that just wasn't Gail's style. She eventually arrived at Paramount, wearing a sweater, slacks, some flat shoes, and no make-up. However, eager as Gail was to help her family, and at the same time realize her wildest dreams, she really had no idea about the dream world she was about to enter. This naïve, shy little girl from Santa Monica had no clue as to what she was about to let herself in for. As Gail told Gladys Hall in Screenland Magazine in 1945 – "I went into Mr. Lewis office like a sleepwalker. He told me to meet Mr. Bill Russell, the studio's dramatic coach. For two hours they sat there, those two patient men, trying to get something more than monosyllables out of me. I don't know why they didn't put me down as mentally deficient. I don't know why they didn't send me home. I don't understand how they could have had any hope of or for me. But they did. After a while, they took me to see Mr. William Meiklejohn, head of talent for Paramount, who had to put the final okay on tests. Three days later I made the test. I had a scene from "Love Finds Andy Hardy." Mr. Russell, my guiding and guardian angel, made the test with me. He took hold of my hand as the cameras started to click, and I wouldn't let his hand go. I was signed to a term contract within the next few days. But for months after I'd signed, Mr. Russell would have to meet me at the front gate of the studios when I arrived in the morning, or I wouldn't go in."[8]

The local newspapers next week were filled with the news of Hollywood's latest discovery, Gail Russell, the newest "Cinderella" girl who was known as the "Hedy Lamarr of Santa Monica". On July 17, 1942, Gail Russell appeared before Santa Monica Superior Court Judge Emmet H. Wilson, who approved her agreement with Paramount studios for a seven year contract starting at $50 a week, with future bonuses and final options at $750 per week during the final year.[9] Gail later admitted that her first check came to only fifty cents after deductions for Screen Actors Guild fee, social security, hospitalization, old age pension, etc. Nevertheless, her father had that first check framed, and Gail had it hanging on the wall of her West Los Angeles apartment when she died on August 26, 1961.

One of the first things Gail's family did with her salary was to move out of their cramped three room apartment, and move into a more spacious bungalow in Santa Monica. Gail now had to endure Paramount's rigorous course for potential starlets in pursuit of movie stardom. Her frail ego was in for a rude shock. Her Paramount coaches informed her that everything was wrong with her in every way, and that everybody expected her to correct it. Gail hung her head, and she must learn to hold it up high. She toed in, and must learn to walk correctly. Her grammar was awful, and must learn to speak properly. Nervous and trembling, Gail would twist her hands so much that her first directors would tie her hands to her sides with handkerchiefs during scenes until she was broken of the habit.[10] Gail's diction was impossible, and had to make it flawless. Then there was the matter of her dress. Gail was most at home in casual clothes such as slacks, skirt, and loafers. Often she preferred to go barefoot, especially at the beach. Paramount said all that had to go while at the studios. Gail was a glamour girl now, and she must look the part. So what if the clothes were too tight she couldn't breathe or sit comfortably. She was a movie star now, and had to dress like one. Other stars such as Ava Gardner, Lana Turner, or Hedy Lamarr, loved the glamorous dresses because it made them feel more feminine. It also gave them greater poise, beauty, and self assurance.

However, for Gail, all these changes just made her more unhappy. She had an inferiority complex to begin with, and that combined with an extreme shyness made an almost insurmountable barrier to overcome. Yet Gail was determined to make her career choice a success, no matter what the cost. Since Gail was still underage at seventeen, she was required to attend the school at Paramount until she became eighteen on September 21, 1942. There in class she was joined by Diana Lynn, Elena Verdugo, Helen Walker, Jean Heather, and Yvonne De Carlo.

Bill Russell (no relation) became her drama coach, and her closest confidant at Paramount. He stood by Gail as she drowned in her tears and fears while trying to memorize her lines of dialogue. Her old fear of appearing in public to speak resurfaced, and caused her endless amounts of fear and doubt. Don't forget, Gail had only one previous acting experience in her entire life. It was that Thanksgiving Play in grammar school in which she had only four lines of dialogue to speak. However, at the last minute she was so terrified to speak them before a live audience that her lines were removed. "I just couldn't say them," Gail would later say. "They just put me in a corner of the stage, and I just sat there afraid to look at the audience."[10]

Still, Bill Russell stood by her side, always encouraging Gail to believe in herself, that she would be a good actress. It was Bill himself who ruined her first screen test when he knocked over a bucket in nervous anxiety for Gail as the camera started to roll.

New starlets were expected to work every day at training for stardom. There were everyday meetings in the publicity office of the PR chief, posing for cheesecake photographs. Here again, the shy Gail had a hard time posing before strangers in a bathing suit. More than one photographer was annoyed to have to spend at least half an hour convincing Gail to agree to pose. There were also workout classes in the gym by head instructor Jim Davies. The elaborate diction and acting classes were under Bill Russell, head of the drama school. When Gail was thought ready to be tested for acting potential, she was furnished old Paramount movie scripts from which she was expected to rehearse on her own, and when the time came, was scheduled to perform in the room known as the "Glass Cage," or the "Snake Pit." It was about the size of a small radio station, with a large window on the far side behind total darkness. Young actresses were expected to perform in front of various producers, directors, or Paramount executives who were unseen while observing the starlets' rehearsal. It was intimidating, to say the lease, especially for someone as shy as Gail. Yvonne De Carlo, in her 1987 autobiography, "Yvonne" with Doug Warren, recalled an episode in the "Glass Cage" with a surprising revelation regarding Gail. She wrote, "Another contractee was the shy and sensitive Gail Russell. I felt I had much in common with her, but she was much more vulnerable than I. She confided in hushed tones how she wished her mother, Gladys, had never dragged her to Paramount for her screen test. She despised acting, and everything it entailed, especially being put on display before executives and film crews. I sympathized with her misery, but had no soothing words for her. My great concern was holding on to my contract, not getting out of it. There was an actress on the lot, however, who would show Gail how to cope, the good natured but tough talking starlet Helen Walker. She took Gail under her wing, and introduced her to the tranquilizing benefits of vodka. Poor Gail was only thirty-six when she died in 1961, surrounded by empty liquor bottles."[11]

Yes, it was a great blessing that Gail was chosen to become a movie star. Yet it was also a terrible curse. For it was through the tremendous struggle to become, as well as remain, a Hollywood star, that Gail became addicted to alcohol that eventually shortened her career, and ended her young life.

Chapter Five
Henry Aldrich Gets Glamour

It must have seemed like a dream to Gail that September of 1942, to be actually considered a candidate to become a movie star for Paramount Pictures. She still couldn't believe they actually thought they could make an actress out of her. Her screen tests were not sensational by any standards. Yet Milton Lewis, and even William Meiklejohn, saw a quality in Gail that was uniquely hers. A soft, gentle manner, together with a fragile, haunting beauty that was utterly enchanting to behold. Gail's low, whisper of a voice, along with her raven black hair and sapphire blue eyes, proved irresistible to the movie camera, let alone a potential movie audience.

Gail soon caught the eye of director Hugh Bennett who was then in the process of making "Henry Aldrich Gets Glamour" at Paramount with Jimmy Lydon. Lydon was, like Gail, an ex-alumnus of University High School. Director Bennett had seen Gail's screen test, and was impressed with her exotic beauty and childlike manner. He decided to cast her in the part of Virginia Lowry, the high school vamp in Henry Aldrich's history class. Thus, with only one week's training, Gail was scheduled to be in her first motion picture. She could hardly believe it, and neither could her drama coach, Bill Russell. He told Bennett that Gail wasn't quite ready yet to star in a movie, that they were pushing her too fast, that one week of training wasn't enough. Yet Bennett persisted, and the Paramount executives agreed they had to see what Gail was capable of, and that they had to see a return of the investment of time and money that Paramount had spent on her training.

As Gail later recalled to writer Gladys Hall in Screenland Magazine in 1945, "It happened so fast. I never played extra. I had only one week's training before I went into "Henry Aldrich Gets Glamour!" So very fast – I didn't know what I was getting into. I felt like someone walking in a maze. I was scared stiff. I think I stuck it mainly because of my Dad. He was so thrilled. The minute I'd get home, after work, he'd back me in a corner and say, 'What happened today? What did you do today?'"[1]

Needless to say, Gail was amazed to get such a key part in her first movie, and a little overwhelmed at all the work and effort necessary to act in pictures. Rehearsing by herself was one thing, rehearsing before a live movie set was another. Gail's shy nature and extreme stage fright were again brought to the surface. That first day of shooting was an eye opener for Gail. As she told the New York Herald Tribune in 1944, "My first part was in one of the Henry Aldrich Pictures. I can hardly remember it. When I went over the scenes with Mr. Russell, it seemed possible – well almost possible. But on the set, with the director shouting, and the lights blazing, and the cameras threatening, I'd go deaf. Really. They'd tell me what to do, and I simply couldn't hear. I'd try desperately to listen, and all I did was wish I were dead."[2]

Director Bennett soon became aware of Gail's extreme stage fright, and her reluctance to perform in front of a movie camera before cast and crew members on a set. On the first take Gail completely froze and stumbled over her lines, breaking down into tears, and running to her dressing room. Fellow co-worker Jimmy Lydon remembers how Gail couldn't even get through the first rehearsals, that after three or four attempts at a scene, she would forget her lines, and break down and cry. They would baby her, and try and comfort her in her dressing room. After regaining her composure, and re-applying her make-up, she managed to finish the scene. Lydon later admitted that it was only a so-so take, but the director and cast were just satisfied to get through one complete scene.[3]

Yet with all the trouble director Hugh Bennett had in trying to get a performance out of Gail, he still decided to give her the part of Virginia Lowry in the movie. Bennett saw in Gail another cinema quality that other Paramount executives had overlooked. Behind that shy, gentle nature, and fragile beauty, there was underneath an alluring, exotic glamour that appealed to male audiences. It was Bennett who had helped create that legendary movie phrase, "come hither look," and applied it to Gail.

At first, it was a major struggle for Gail to complete the filming of the Henry Aldrich picture. She had trouble remembering her lines, especially with all the onlookers on the movie set – the stagehands, the grips, the prop men, and most of the people behind the movie camera. Gail said as much to Hugh Bennett. So the director decided to limit the number of people Gail would have to see while shooting a scene. Only essential movie technicians were allowed on the set. This seemed to do the trick. Yet it took many "takes" for Gail to get the scene right. Gail seemed to have an unnatural fear of the movie camera which was hard to explain. Later, Frederick Othman, in a 1944 newspaper article, quoted Gail as saying there was always a "wall of eyes" behind the camera that always unnerved her, "hundreds of eyes, gleaming in the dark, staring at me. Boring holes in me. Giving me the heebie jeebies." The camera would move in on her for a close-up shot, and her own eyes would stare at her. Writer Eileen Geelman, in a New York Sun newspaper article on February 28, 1944, asked Gail if she were frightened while performing before the movie camera. "Frightened? Of course I'm frightened. Did you ever stand up on a set with everyone looking at you? All those electricians and grips and everyone. It's terrifying."

Despite all Gail's shortcomings as an actress, with all the retakes, worry, and frazzled nerves, she managed to finish the film on time. "Henry Aldrich Gets Glamour" was the latest in a series of films by Paramount Pictures depicting the everyday adventures of the typical American teenager in the form of Henry Aldrich, played by popular actor Jimmy Lydon. It was supposed to be Paramount's counterpart to rival MGM Studios "Andy Hardy" series starring Mickey Rooney. The movie also starred John Litel, Frances Gifford, and a very young Diana Lynn. It was to be Gail's first meeting with Diana since they first met while attending school at Paramount.

Diana, at sixteen, was two years younger than Gail, and the exact opposite in temperament. While Gail was sometimes shy, moody, and withdrawn, Diana was friendly, happy, and bubbling over with confidence. Unlike Gail, Diana came from an upper middle class background, and was a trained concert pianist. Born Dolores Loehr on October 7, 1926, in Los Angeles, California, to a well-to-do oil supply concern executive and a concert pianist. Diana was child prodigy on the piano, and a "Quiz Kid" on the radio.[4] At first, Gail wasn't eager to make friends with Diana, knowing the vast difference in temperament between them. She politely rebuffed the friendly overtures of the younger Diana. They were later to become lifelong friends, and Diana was one of the few stars to attend Gail's funeral in 1961.[5]

"Henry Aldrich Gets Glamour" turned out to be a big hit with movie audiences in 1943, and was considered to be the best in the series. The plot concerned Henry trying to date the prettiest girl in class, Virginia Lowry (played by Gail), while winning a fan letter contest to movie star Hilary Dane, played by Frances Gifford. Henry is later mistaken for Hilary's boyfriend, and later gains a reputation as the local "wolf" to all the girls in Centerville. Henry goes through all sorts of adventures as he tries to set the record straight. It is a delightful comedy, and did well at the box office. There is one memorable scene in the movie when Henry has taken Virginia Lowry, played by Gail, on a moonlight ride at night, and Virginia tries to get Henry to get romantic with her. Poor Henry is very inept, and ends up dropping Virginia while carrying her over a fence. It was ironic that Gail's character in the film was the exact opposite of Gail when she was in high school. The Hollywood Reporter stated in its film review that "A flash that will count is registered to Gail Russell as the town belle... you'll be hearing from Gail Russell."[6] Variety, in its film review on December 30, 1942, wrote – "Gail Russell makes a sufficiently seductive high school co-ed, who finds that Henry's Hollywood experience still makes him run away from a girl's embrace."[7]

Shortly after completing filming "Henry Aldrich Gets Glamour," Gail was invited by William Meiklejohn to attend a luncheon for the Mexican Ambassador on September 17, 1942, just four days shy of her eighteenth birthday. She had only been a Paramount star for five months, and already she was attending celebrity events. Also in attendance at that event were stars Gary Cooper, Ruth Hussey, Betty Hutton, Joel McCrea, Ingrid Bergman, Cesar Romero, Dick Powell, director Cecil B. DeMille, and Paramount Studios' head Buddy De Sylva.

1942 proved to be a momentous year for Gail Russell, and she was looking forward to next year to be even better. Little did Gail know that she was soon to meet her all-time idol, Ginger Rogers, in a way she could never have imagined.

Gail at the age of two, 1926.

Gail at four with her older brother George in 1928.

Gail at the age of five with a neighbor's child 1929.

Gail at the age of five with Santa Clause, 1929.

Gail at 17, when the local newspaper announced to the world
Hollywood's newest discovery, "The Hedy Lamarr of Santa Monica."

Gail chats with co-star Ginger Rogers while
filming "Lady in the Dark," 1943.

Gail takes a short break between scenes with director Lewis Allen and co-star Donald Crisp, while filming "The Uninvited." 1943.

Gail shown clutching a movie script. 1944.

Gail after Judge Emmet Wilson grants third option
on her Paramount contract, January 29, 1944. Gail was 19.

Gail with actor Peter Lawford at Ciro's nightclub, July 6, 1945. Gail was 20.

Gail and John Wayne take a break while filming
"Angel and the Badman," 1946.

Gail at the Trocadero nightclub on March 7, 1946 with good
friend Diana Lynn, and steady boyfriend Guy Madison.

Gail visiting the set of "The Virginian" in 1946 with stars Joel McCrea and Barbara Britton.

Gail wearing the hat of actor Robert Mitchum at a Hollywood party in 1947. Accompanied by Diana Lynn, Loren Tindall, Guy Madison.

Gail shows Gary Cooper her quick draw on the set
of "Variety Girl," 1947. Co-star William Demarest watches.

Gail gets a surprise visit from Jane Russell on the set of
"Night has a Thousand Eyes," 1948.

Gail with co-stars, Luther Adler, Henry Daniell and director Edward Ludwig, rehearsing a scene for "Wake of the Red Witch," 1948.

A light hearted moment on the set of "Wake of the Red Witch," as Gail and "The Duke" try and determine who has the bluest eyes, while hair stylist Peggy Grey looks on. 1948.

Gail takes acting advice from director Frank Borzage
on the set of "Moonrise," 1948.

Gail and co-star Dennis O'Keefe relax between
takes on the set of "The Great Dan Patch," 1949.

Co-star John Payne suprises Gail with a birthday
cake on the set of "El Paso," Sep 21, 1949.

Gail and Guy taken at the time they announced
their plans to marry, July 31, 1949.

Newlyweds Gail and Guy enter their new home at 11742 Chenault
Street in Brentwood California, shortly after returning from
their honeymoon. October, 1949.

Gail and Guy in the living room of their new home in Brentwood, Ca, October 1949. The picture above the fireplace was painted by Gail from a poster she saw while vacationing in Mexico.

Gail is rushed past reporters by jailer Robert Mildrew in the early morning of November 25, 1953.

Gail reluctantly talks with jailhouse reporters after being released on bail in the early morning hours of November 25, 1953.

Gail pleads not guilty to misdemeanor drunk driving at Santa Monica court. November 27, 1953.

Gail is escorted by police matron Irene Locker after being released on bail. November 25, 1953.

Gail is released on $250 bail, accompanied by Guy Madison's business agent, Charles Trezona Jr., 1953.

Gail outside L.A. superior court after posting bail for drunk driving, May 6, 1954.

Gail leaving court with her brother George Jr.,
January 28, 1954.

Gail shows off her black toy poodle "Peanuts"
in front of her Westwood apartment, 1957.

Gail goes over a scene with co-star Jeff Chandler and attorney Jerry Geisler on the set of "The Tattered Dress," 1957.

Gail crashes her new convertible through the front window of Jan's Coffee shop. July 4, 1957.

Gail tries to touch her nose while undergoing a sobriety test by Sgt. C.H. Specht. July 4, 1957.

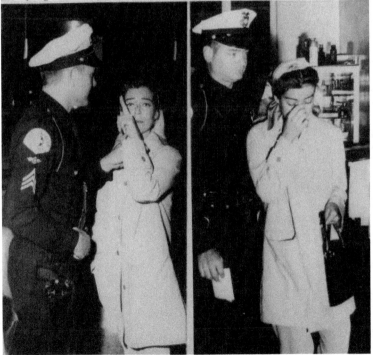

While being given a drunk driving test by Sgt. C.H. Specht, Gail refuses to tap her nose. Instead, she tries to touch the officer's nose telling him "Your cute." Later Gail is escorted by officer H.A. Wharmby and breaks down in tears. July 4, 1957.

Gail taking the drunk driving test, while Sgt. C.H. Specht watches.
July 4,1957.

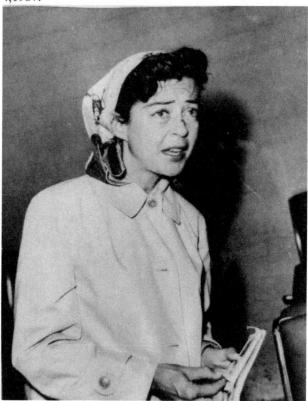

Gail tries to show her drivers license to
officers after crashing her car. July 4, 1957.

Gail is calmed by ambulanceman Harry Vaughan when informed that she is being taken to jail for drunk driving. July 4, 1957.

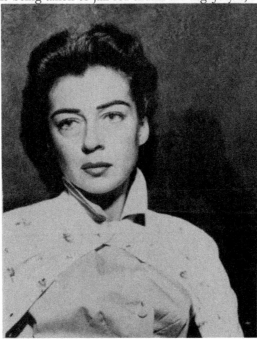

Gail outside superior court in Los Angeles after posting bail for drunk driving, July 19, 1957.

Gail with attorney Rexford Eagan outside
superior court los Angeles, February 3, 1958.

Gail and actor Nick Adams on the set of "The Rebel"
T.V. series reminding shoppers that there are only 7
days untill Christmas. December 17, 1959.

Chapter Six
Lady In The Dark

It was now June of 1943, and Gail still was not used to being a movie star. However, her drama coach, Bill Russell, no longer had to meet her at the gate before she would enter for work. Gail had signed with notable movie agent Myron Selznick, brother of famous movie producer David O. Selznick of "Gone With The Wind" fame. She was now making $75 a week with a signing option that provided a $1,500 bonus for next year. She was still taking those acting and dance classes at Paramount, although Gail no longer had to attend traditional school after she had turned eighteen back on September 21, 1942.

Paramount executives were very pleased with Gail's performance as the high school vamp in "Henry Aldrich Gets Glamour." While viewing the daily rushes with director Hugh Bennett, and later the finished product, producer Buddy De Sylva and director Mitchell Leisen were wondering if this young starlet could play another high school beauty. Leisen was filming "Lady In The Dark" with Ginger Rogers and Ray Milland, and there was the small part of Barbara that was still not cast. He asked fellow director Bennett if Gail Russell could play the part. When Bennett gave a qualified "yes," Leisen asked Gail's drama coach Bill Russell to offer her a copy of the script.

To say that Gail was overjoyed would be an understatement. She could not believe her good fortune. Here was an opportunity to co-star with her all time movie idol, Ginger Rogers! It was the culmination of her wildest dreams. As Gail recalled to writer Gladys Hall in Screenland Magazine in 1945, "It's strange, isn't it, that I should have been cast in 'Lady In The Dark,' my second picture, with Ginger Rogers, who had been my all time idol all my life? When I first saw her on the set, I stood there with my mouth open. The first day of actual shooting, when I came on the set, I was told I would have to learn the Charleston in fifteen minutes flat. I had a broken toe, and my best friend, Bill Russell, dramatic coach at Paramount... who had literally held my hand on every scene I'd made, was away with the flu. I was frantic with fear. I thought I am going to faint; I thought, I will run away and hide. Then Ginger Rogers came over to me, put her arm around me, took me into her dressing room, gave me tea, and went over the script with me. Best of all, she told me how scared she had been when she first got into pictures. That was the warmest thing she could have done for me. And she taught me the Charleston! After that, we used to talk about art, Ginger and I, between scenes on the set. And about music. And books. I drew cartoons of Ginger and she put them on the mirror in her dressing room. Ginger was, so to speak, the turning point in relaxing me."[1]

Ginger Rogers was touched by Gail's unabashed worship of her. On the first day of shooting, Gail told Ginger how she first saw her at the race track at Santa Anita in 1941, describing in detail the very dress she wore.

That first day of filming was not an easy one for Gail. Her stage fright returned as the camera moved in for her close-up scene with Ginger and actor Rand Brooks. In addition to her normal fear of performing before a crowded set, there was the added stress in trying not to disappoint her favorite actress. After a few blown takes, director Leisen finally got the shot he wanted. He wasn't too impressed by Gail's performance, and thought of replacing Gail. However, Ginger Rogers was insistent that he keep her young co-star. Leisen reluctantly agreed, mainly as a favor to Ginger. As David Chierichetti wrote in his book about Mitchell Leisen, "Hollywood Director," the director said, "Ginger insisted we use Gail Russell as Barbara, the girl who steals Liza's boyfriend right after she sang 'My Ship." The poor girl was gorgeous, but she had hysterics every time the camera started to turn. She only had a couple of lines, but it took us almost two days to get them shot. Ginger felt so sorry for her that she tried to work with her and help her as much as she could. She was really a neurotic character, and I'm not surprised she became an alcoholic."[2]

The part of Barbara was not a big part for Gail, in fact was only about five minutes of screen time, and a lesser role than Gail had in the Henry Aldrich picture. Yet it was one of the few pictures Gail made in color, and it was a rare glimpse of her fragile, haunting beauty at the young age of nineteen.

Gail's one scene was the end of the film, and it was technically a night shot, and cinematographer Ray Rennahan used subdued lighting which failed to enhance Gail's unique coloring. Her blue eyes and black hair was a stark contrast to the blonde hair and blue eyes of Ginger Rogers. "Lady In The Dark" was based on the Broadway play by Moss Hart, with music by Kurt Weill and Ira Gershwin. It was a lavish, Technicolor musical with colorful costumes and opulent sets, and a budget of nearly two million dollars.

New York Times Film critic, Bosley Crowther, who called the film an "overpowering display of splash and glitter, yet the story which Mr. Harts' play originally told of a lady with an active psychosis becomes somewhat offset in this film. Also the authors of the screenplay have chopped the original in such a way that much that was wistful and tender in it has been curiously left out."[3]

Crowther went on to praise Ginger Rogers' performance, yet there was no mention of Gail Russell, in fact, Gail received no mention in either the opening or closing screen credits. Gail's scene involved Ginger Rogers as Liza Elliot, at the high school dance with Ben, played by Rand Brooks, the estranged boyfriend of Barbara, played by Gail. The plain and shy Liza has her prom date stolen by the more beautiful and aggressive Barbara. In real life, it would be hard to imagine that the shy and innocent Gail would ever be able to steal any man from the glamorous and vivacious Ginger Rogers. Most critics, however, liked "Lady In the Dark," and it was a successful hit with the public. The fans of Ginger Rogers also got a fleeting look at the young Gail Russell, which could not help but further her budding career.

It was during filming of "Lady In The Dark" that Gail developed her first close friendship while in Hollywood. Diana Lynn happened to drop by on the set one day, and noticed Gail drawing cartoon caricatures of her fellow cast members. She noticed the picture of Ginger Rogers, and asked Gail if she really admired the actress. When Gail revealed that Ginger was her favorite actress since childhood, Diana found they had something in common. Diana had long been a admirer of Ginger since she co-stared with her in "The Major And The Minor" in 1942. She had played the part of the smart, younger sister of Ginger's rival for the affections of the Army Major in the movie, played by Ray Milland. With their mutual like for Ginger Rogers, Gail and Diana soon became close friends, and Diana was a good remedy for Gail's introverted nature, being her exact opposite in temperament, open to people, and friendly as a puppy. She suggested to Gail that she should send one of her caricatures to Ginger in a thank you note for all her help in preparing Gail in the role of Barbara in "Lady In The Dark." When Ginger got the note and the clever drawing, she quickly wrote Gail a thank you note in return. It said:

"My Dear Gail,

"How's my favorite pupil? You're the right kind of pupil to have as I don't have to do anything about it but address you as such – anyway we can pretend – can't we? I just love the drawing you enclosed in your note – you are a darn clever girl – and if you aren't careful, you're going to have so many accomplishments you aren't going to know which one to enjoy.

"As for that laugh, you are definitely going to get one – my nose is sunburned and I have so many freckles I look like a bowl of cornflakes. You tell those people at Paramount they had better treat you right or I shall conjure up such thunder they'll never forget. Tell them they should give you a pretty dressing room as they should start spoiling you right away – after you work too hard it then becomes difficult to appreciate spoiling. Be good – and Bless you.

Affectionately,

Ginger[4]

Gail continued to perform the duties of a star in the making by giving interviews to reporters, although Paramount executives were careful not to have too many people thrust at her at any one time. She was still hesitant to speak before total strangers. Gail still had to endure the mandatory "cheesecake" or pin-up photo sessions even though she detested them.

There was an incident that particularly embarrassed her. It was while she was still filming "Lady In The Dark," and outside the set at Paramount. It took the publicity people a half hour to convince shy Gail to pose in a bright red, one piece bathing suit, covered by a see through plastic raincoat. She was told to walk toward the photographer wearing boots, and carrying an umbrella. It had been raining, and Gail was to walk through a big puddle of water while smiling and waving her hand. At that precise moment, the

Paramount commissary had just opened for lunch, and people started to walk by, and noticed Gail in the photo shoot. She was mortified as Paramount executive William Meiklejohn, and stars such as Alan Ladd and Bing Crosby spotted Gail in her bright red bathing suit. She later said she felt like pulling that large puddle of water over her head, but it just wasn't deep enough.[5]

Gail had always been shy about exposing her body, even at the beach. She was also very self-conscious about her knees. Needless to say, it would be almost four years before she would agree to any more pin-up photos.

Gail continued to study hard with her acting and diction classes at Paramount. She also eagerly attended courses in dancing, ballroom, and tap. Gail felt she had deprived herself out of so much in life by not knowing how to dance or socialize more with young people. She continued to save most of her salary by depositing it in the bank, hoping to help her parents buy a new home. Gail didn't spend a lot of money on clothes like most girls her age, yet she did have four nice dresses for evening wear.

By the end of 1943, the war news was getting better for the United States and for the Russell family. The tide of victory for the war effort was turning favorably for the Allied nations cause in North Africa, and in the South Pacific. Gail's brother, George, was still safe while stationed in the Aleutian Islands in Alaska. He still couldn't believe it when Gail wrote telling of her miraculous discovery by Paramount Studios, and that she was actually a movie star. She had to send him an actual movie script, along with some publicity portraits, before he was actually convinced. Gail was still looking forward to an even better year for her, career-wise, but had no idea that 1944 was to be her banner year for movie stardom.

Chapter 7
The Uninvited

In late 1943, Paramount Pictures obtained the screen rights to Dorothy Macardle's bestselling mystery romance novel, "The Uninvited," and started production with a cast headed by Ray Milland and Ruth Hussey. Paramount had also hired British-born Lewis Allen to film the production in his directorial debut. However, producer Charles Brackett and director Allen were stymied in their choice of who was to play the key role of Stella Meredith around whom the whole story unfolds. Lewis Allen had searched the Paramount roster of new starlets, and had as yet not made a final choice. Ella Raines was at the top of the list, with Veronica Lake, Helen Walker, Jean Heather, and June Lockhart having been tested. Allen thought they all seemed too American, as Stella Meredith in the story was from Cornwall England, and had the dark, exotic beauty of a young girl who was unknowingly the illegitimate daughter of the Spanish model, Carmel.

David Rose, Allen's good friend, and head of Paramount productions in England, was walking on the Paramount lot one day when he spotted Gail in the studio commissary. He was impressed with her raven black hair and sapphire blue eyes, and asked who she was. He informed Allen of his discovery, and told him he thought Gail fit the physical profile of Stella Meredith. Allen then asked Gail to come to his office for an interview, and after a half hour was convinced he had finally found his girl. He then marched into Paramount head Buddy De Sylva's office, and calmly announced, "This is the girl I want for Stella."

Later, Gail walked into the office of her drama coach, Bill Russell, and casually asked him to glance at the movie script she had been asked to audition for. Bill glanced through the pages, and asked Gail which minor part she had been offered. Gail said, "Stella Meredith." Bill Russell couldn't believe his ears. He quickly called casting. "What's this stuff about Gail being cast of 'Stella' in Ray Milland's new picture?" he asked. When Paramount head Buddy De Sylva's secretary assured him Gail had been chosen for the part, "Hell's Bells," Bill Russell replied. "That's a lead part. She's only a green kid. You're going too fast."[1]

Yet, despite Bill Russell's misgivings, Lewis Allen decided to schedule an audition for Gail to try for the part of Stella Meredith in "The Uninvited." Gail studied the audition scene with Coach Russell, and two days later made the test in the infamous "Glass Cage" rehearsal studio. Behind the two-way glass to observe the test were director Allen, producer Charles Brackett, and lead executive Buddy De Sylva. As the camera started to roll, Gail could hear Bill Russell slowly whisper while he gently held her hand, "You can do it. I know you can do it!"[2]

The test was good, but not great. However, it was enough for Lewis Allen. He gave Gail the part of Stella Meredith, with one catch. Gail had to learn an English accent within twenty four hours because the entire film crew was scheduled to travel up north to Northern California, near Santa Rosa, to shoot some exterior scenes.

Paramount hired English Coach Miriam Greene to tutor Gail at her home, and for the next few hours they watched "Young Mr. Pitt," "Pygmalion," and "Rebecca" to develop Gail's English accent. By the time midnight arrived, Gail could hardly keep her eyes open, and more than once had to be shaken by the shoulders by Miss Greene to stay awake. Moreover, Gail wasn't given anything to eat until she asked for it in the proper English accent. Needless to say, it was a sample of what Gail had to endure in order to play the role of Stella Meredith.

The next day they returned to Paramount, and made a record of Gail's accent, and later played it for producer Buddy De Sylva. He ok'd the voice, but thought the accent too thick. Nevertheless, Gail had the accent good enough to join the production crew on location in Santa Rosa, at the Little River Inn. As Gail later recalled in a magazine article in 1945, "When, during the production of "The Uninvited," we went on location for the scenes laid on the Cornish Coast, that helped me too, I'd never been on location before. It was my first experience of working with people, eating with them, working so closely together. I began to feel one of them."[3]

Back on the Paramount lot for interior scenes, Gail began to run into more serious difficulties. Her old nemesis stage fright, resurfaced to trouble her once again. Director Allen noticed that whenever the camera zoomed in for her close-up scenes, Gail would stiffen in fright, stumble over her lines, and begin to cry. She knew her lines, but when she saw the camera lens come closer for her scenes, and all the people behind the camera who were working on the set, she would go deaf, and not remember a single line of dialogue. In exasperation and remorse, she would dissolve into tears, and run into her dressing room. Allen was patient, recognizing her youth and inexperience, but was troubled by the numerous retakes and production delays. One of Gail's drama coaches from her old Paramount days recalled those early years, saying "That kid is amazing. She's so damned shy I spent my entire time just keeping her from a stage of shock every time she went in front of a camera. She'd freeze at the mention of direction. She didn't know what it's all about, and I'm scared to death that one of these days we'll carry her off the set in a trance."[4]

Director Allen was at his wits end. He wanted his first film to be finished on time, and within the budget allowed.

Tom Weaver, in his book, "Science Fiction and Fantasy Film Flashbacks," interviewed the then 92 year old Lewis Allen, and asked him about his troubles with the young Gail Russell. He said, "I wasn't enthusiastic about taking Gail Russell, because she'd only done one small part in a picture before this. And when she read for me, it was pretty bad (laughs)." When Weaver told him Gail was good in "The Uninvited," the veteran director replied, "That was a performance that was 'manufactured.' She could only do about five or six lines, and then she'd burst into tears. Well, Ray Milland and I coaxed her along, and we made the picture in bits and pieces. We'd do half a page ... and so on. So we 'manufactured' a performance. Unfortunately, when the picture was a success and I was given my next picture (Our Hearts Were Young And Gay, 1944), Buddy De Sylva said to me, 'You did such a good job on "The Uninvited", you're gonna be stuck with Gail Russell again!'" (laughs). When Weaver asked if Paramount executives were aware of how tough it was for Allen to get a performance out of Gail, the director replied, "Oh, De Sylva was, yeah. But he just said, 'Lew, you can manager her!' (laughs) As I say, she used to burst into tears and go to her dressing room. Things didn't get better until the head of make-up and the hairdresser started taking her over to the bar across the street and they introduced her to liquor – which she eventually died of. At the time we did the 'The Uninvited,' she'd never had a drink in her life. You see, she was a very sad character – her parents treated her abominably. They had a son and they doted on this boy, and Gail was sort of an afterthought. At any rate, the poor girl finally drank herself to death." Weaver then asked if the make-up person and the hairdresser were trying to be helpful. The director again replied, "Sure, they wanted to give her confidence, and after she started going with them and having a drink at night, she had a little more courage during the day (laughs). She was looking forward to the drink in the evening, I guess." Weaver then asked if the reason she would burst into tears was due to nervousness. Allen replied, "She was scared to death!"

The conversation then turned to Ray Milland. Weaver asked if he was helpful in getting a performance out of Gail Russell. Allen replied, "Right. Between takes he'd take her aside and rehearse her and rehearse her and rehearse her. He was excellent with her; in fact, thanks to Ray Milland, Gail Russell became a star. The only person who was unkind to her was Donald Crisp, who played her father (actually, Donald Crisp played her grandfather). He thought it was sort of 'amateur' night, working with this unknown actress. You see, Donald Crisp was very much a professional, and he didn't agree with all this motion picture business of bringing young people in and giving them a break. He thought they should only employ 'pros'. He was just brusque with her, that's all." Weaver then asked if Allen recalled the budget and shooting schedule. Allen said, "I think it was 40 days or 48 days. We made it for about a million and a half – that's what Paramount was spending on its 'A' pictures in those days. Buddy De Sylva, the boss of Paramount, was very pleased with 'The Uninvited'."[5]

If what Lewis Allen said was actually true, he should have been ashamed of himself. Gail was only nineteen years of age at the time she made "The Uninvited," just one year out of high school. To allow liquor to be given to a minor, for any reason, was surely illegal, and beneath contempt. Whatever happened to Gail afterwards, her later alcoholism, her loss of career, her unhappiness at being an actress, a large part of the blame could be put at the feet of director Lewis Allen and the Paramount executives who allowed this to happen.

However, a very different view of Gail on the set of "The Uninvited" was given by actor and fellow co-star Ruth Hussey. She recalled that "She was fine on the set and there was no carrying on or histrionics. She just played her scenes and played them beautifully." It was hard to believe that Ruth Hussey and Lewis Allen worked on the same film.

Lewis Allen soon found a real problem filming Gail's scenes. Sometimes Gail would arrive on the set at 8 a.m., and not get a single scene shot until 4 p.m. Finally, Allen solved the dilemma by creating huge screens to block Gail's view of onlookers who were around the set. Then he ordered no one but essential personnel to be present when Gail's scenes were to be shot. This seemed to do the trick, as well as drama coach Bill Russell's constant presence and support for young Gail. However, Gail's closed sets soon gained her the reputation of been too vain, sometimes being referred to as "Sara" or the "Baby Bernhardt". It was a reputation she didn't deserve, considering her extreme shyness and stage fright.

Despite these improvements, it was still a struggle for this shy, little girl from Santa Monica who was only nineteen years old at the time, and barely out of high school. She remembered as much to Screenland Magazine in 1945, "Back at the studio again, I saw the rushes. Some of them were good and I thought, well, maybe I can do it, for up to that time, up to the middle of 'The Uninvited," Bill Russell had to stand by in every scene and, just before cameras rolled had to say to me, 'You can do it. I know you can do it!'"[6]

Yes, Bill Russell was one of the main reasons Gail became a star. He became sort of a mother hen where Gail was concerned. He constantly worried over her performance on film or at rehearsals. It was Bill who ruined Gail's first screen test when he kicked over a bucket, nervous over whether Gail would successfully pass it.

Gail also received added support from co-star Ray Milland. Like a true gentleman, he came to the rescue of a "Damsel in Distress". Gail remembered fondly in 1945, "After 'Lady In The Dark,' in which I had a very small part but learned a very great deal, I was cast in 'The Uninvited.' So big a part and in my third picture, and again I felt like running away, hiding, but again I found out that the big people are the friendly people, and kind, and unscary. For Ray Milland, took me under his wing. He was so kind to me, so helpful, that I could feel confidence growing on me like something warm. He taught me about camera angles. He'd actually muff scenes so as to give me a chance to do them again, and better. When I was underplaying a scene, he'd whisper, 'Keep your face in that camera! or 'This is your scene, take it!'"[7]

So by trial and error, many retakes, scenes where Gail had to endure artificial rainstorms, and walking up and down long staircases, she continued to do her part in the film. Yet it was not without a cost. For it was during the filming of "The Uninvited" that Gail was introduced to alcohol. A waiter who worked in the café across the street from Paramount Studios recalled the party for the press the day the picture got underway. "There'd been other parties here, lots of them. Miss Russell had often attended. And always she'd drink lemonade. But this time the reporters surrounded her and started asking her questions, and after a while she called me over and asked me to bring her a drink. I said to her, 'But you don't drink.' She said, 'Aw c'mon, bring me something strong. Don't worry. It's just for today. I need it to help me relax, to help me think better.'"[8]

The man who put her in a cab after the party remembered, "Everybody laughed. They thought, 'How sweet, little Gail on her first drinkee.' They thought she's so grateful and happy and excited she's just got to celebrate with a little drinkee or two'. They laughed. But I didn't laugh. There was something so heartbreaking about her as she sat in that cab, hiccupping away, a desperate look about her, trying to smile but not smiling really, looking desperate, her hands clenched, fear in her eyes. I didn't laugh."[9]

Then there came the day when Gail was tired of struggling to remember her lines, of being afraid of the looming camera lens, of all those stagehands staring at her while she worked. Her screaming nerves and nervous tension begged for some relief, any relief. So that day at lunch break, she put on a coat over her costume, walked out across Western Avenue gate, and entered the café across the street. As Gail recalled, "And this is the way it began … Lunchtime in the café across the street. Then the bottle in the dressing room. Then, every morning, the drink before breakfast. It helped relax me, me who felt in my heart I was a fake, a failure floating on hoak and trickery. All this – it wasn't a dream coming true. It was a dream becoming a nightmare."[10]

Gail had fallen into the great appeal of alcohol. It could make a public speaker out of a timid person, a confident actress out of an insecure one. Her nervous tension was now gone, and she could return to the movie set and finish her scene. It was the start of her psychological dependence, and later the physical dependence, on alcohol. It would eventually shorten her movie career, and inevitably her young life at the young age of thirty-six in 1961. Yet that was still in the future, and Gail only used alcohol occasionally during the filming of "The Uninvited."

After over four weeks, filming was finally completed on "The Uninvited." The film was released nationwide on February 26, 1944, and was a critical as well as a commercial success. Critics were generous with their praise of the film, the cast, especially the young starlet, Gail Russell. Even the usually stoic Bosley Crowther was impressed with Paramount's supernatural thriller. He wrote, "For such folks as like ghost stories – just the plain, haunted house at midnight sort wherein wailing is heard in the darkness and bugbear phantoms emerge from the gloom – Paramount has turned a little number called 'The Uninvited.'… Proceed at your own risk, we warn you if you are at all afraid of the dark … For this fiction about two young people who buy an old seaside house in England … is as solemnly intent on raising gooseflesh as any ghost story … Ray Milland and Ruth Hussey do nicely as the couple who get themselves involved. . . Gail Russell is wistful and gracious as a curiously moonstruck girl. . ."[11]

Paramount went all out in publicity to promote the new film and its new star sensation, Gail Russell. Magazines and newspapers were flooded with movie ads promoting Paramount's new, exciting star. Gail was referred to as Paramount's "exciting" new discovery, the lovely Gail Russell, whose beauty will excite you, the "Mystery Girl of 1944." Gail had become a star overnight. She was overwhelmed by newspaper reporters and magazine writers for interviews. Paramount was careful not to thrust a lot of reporters at her all at once, but granted only one interviewer at a time. Her mother wholeheartedly agreed with this policy, saying, "The men at Paramount have been magnificent. They realized her problem and have been extremely thoughtful about it. That was why the set on 'The Uninvited' was closed when she was working. That was why the publicity department arranged for her to be interviewed gradually, and didn't thrust a lot of people on her at once."[12]

Gail wanted to be interviewed in order to please the publicity department, but her old childhood fear of meeting strangers resurfaced. One of Gail's co-workers at Paramount recalled, "Interviews with Gail weren't difficult, they were impossible. She was hyper shy. She became so nervous in an interview that she could scarcely speak. After a while, we had to give up. They were too painful an experience for her."[13]

Now Paramount sent Gail off to New York City for the premiere of "The Uninvited," accompanied by publicity head Lindsey Durand, who later suffered an appendicitis attack, and had to be hospitalized. Gail openly wept at the audiences' enthusiastic reception of her performance.

Gail was swamped with requests for interviews which she still dreaded. She asked for one day off where she kept to her room, and read or drew, a necessary need to relax and unwind, to relieve her anxiety and nervous tension. Next day she was ready for anything, and later indulged in a 2 a.m. horse and buggy ride in Central Park, which proved to be the highlight of her trip. She took in the usual plays and Broadway shows, buying souvenirs for her family and her new friend, Carmelita Lopez.

By the time Gail returned home, she was totally exhausted. The filming of "The Uninvited" had taken an enormous emotional, as well as physical toll. When Gail started the film, she weighed 125 lbs. By the time production and the publicity tours were ended, she weighed only 106 lbs. She had lost all that weight in just six weeks. In addition, she suffered a nervous breakdown. The official Paramount publicity release simply stated Gail was suffering from "melancholia."[14] Paramount executives felt partially responsible for Gail's relapse in trying to schedule so many interviews and publicity trips. They arranged to give Gail and all expense paid vacation to the Camel Back Inn in Phoenix, Arizona, accompanied by one of her best friends, Carmelita Lopez.

When Gail returned home from vacation, she found that she was now a famous Paramount star. "The Uninvited" had changed everything, and Gail's life was never to be the same. The film proved to be a smash hit for Paramount. Though it was shot in 1943, it wasn't released until February of 1944. It was, and still is, one of the greatest ghost stories ever filmed. It starred Ray Milland, Ruth Hussey, Donald Crisp, Cornelia Otis Skinner, and introduced Gail Russell to film audiences. Although it was actually her third film, it was her first starring role. It told the story of music critic Roderick Fitzgerald, played by Ray Milland, his sister Pamela, played by Ruth Hussey, who purchased Windward House, an old mansion on the Cornish Coast of England. They soon discover the house is haunted by two ghosts, and soon discover a mystery involving the owner of the mansion, Commander Beech, played by Donald Crisp, and his granddaughter Stella Meredith, played by Gail. The film is beautifully photographed in black and white by cinematographer Charles Lang Jr. (who received an Academy Award nomination), an excellent screenplay by Dodie Smith and Frank Partos, plus an unforgettable music score by famous Paramount music composer Victor Young. He composed a haunting movie theme for Gail's character, Stella Meredith, called "Stella By Starlight." It has now become a famous movie theme and popular jazz melody, and is forever associated with Gail Russell.

It was hard to believe that in 1944, a shy, timid little girl from Chicago, Illinois, who used to dance through the streets pretending she was Ginger Rogers, was now a full fledged movie star. Who could have imagined this very same girl was now up on the Silver Screen with her all time idol, and could now see her own name shinning on the bright lights of the theater marquee?

Chapter 8
Our Hearts Were Young and Gay

Paramount Studios was now eager to cash in on Gail's sudden rise in popularity. Movie magazines couldn't get enough of this bright, new star on the Paramount roster. Publicity portraits were created with the caption proclaiming that Gail Russell was the new "Cinderella Girl" who had been discovered in high school, and was now a new movie star. The tale of the two teenage classmates of Gail who had been given a ride by Paramount talent head William Meiklejohn was now part of the folklore of Hollywood legend.

Still, with all her new found fame and notoriety, Gail still struggled with her shyness. Her timid nature still shrank from all the attention from the adoring public. Then there was always her extreme stage fright. It seemed a strange paradox that a movie star should have a fear of the movie camera.

Robbin Coons, the veteran writer for Screenland Magazine, recalled Gail quite vividly. She wrote, "Gail Russell was one of the most thoroughly, painfully frightened youngsters who ever faced a camera – or life… I met her four years ago on the day she made her first movie scene. She had been discovered – 'the Hedy Lamarr of Santa Monica,' they called her – a short while before. Now she sat, a slim, fragile, exquisite little girl in a party dress, waiting for her camera call. She had the beauty a princess might envy, and she was still the most miserable, scared little creature I'd ever met. It was more than the usual stage fright. It was deep, acute, dry-throated fear – real illness."[1]

Not only was Gail still uncertain about her talent, but she was still puzzled by why anyone would think she was pretty. Newspaper columnist Joyce Allen, in a 1945 interview with Gail, was quite impressed with her beauty. She wrote Gail "combines large, blue eyes with a tanned, fair complexion. Yet, one of Gail Russell's best features is her jet black hair, which under certain lights, will glow a blue shade," and imagine, Gail insists, 'I'm not really beautiful'." Charles Lang Jr., the cinematographer on "The Uninvited," was quite generous with his praise of Gail's physical beauty. He said, "the bone structure of her face is as nearly perfect, in a classic balance of features, as he had ever seen." He compared her cheekbones to Marlene Dietrich, her nose to Veronica Lake, her oval face to Ingrid Bergman, and her soulful eyes to Loretta Young.

Yet with all her talent and beauty, Gail was still at heart a shy, frightened little girl, even when being interviewed for a movie fan magazine. Gladys Hall, in a 1945 magazine article, remembers vividly her talk with Gail at Paramount. Gail said, "My life has been funny. Or I have been funny in my life. Or perhaps everybody's life is funny, strange, I mean, mysterious – in a frightening sort of way. That's why I liked doing "The Uninvited." I felt at home in the character of that lost, little girl, in the eerie atmosphere, because

I believe there are 'more things on land and sea' . . . You have to be sort of autobiographical when you talk about yourself for publication, don't you? Gail asked me, then, at my nodded 'Yes' her blue eyes, the blue of sapphires, darkened with earnestness and anxiety until they looked as black as her black hair and her low pitched voice, with its whisper of velvet, was so low that I had to lean across the table (we were lunching together at the Paramount commissary) in order not to miss, what she was saying. Noticing, Gail smiled, said, 'I do whisper when I talk, don't I? I've been told that I speak as though the sound of my own voice frightens me. Well, it does, a little. So many things do.'"[2]

Gail's next film assignment came to her quite by chance. While visiting Diana Lynn in her dressing room at Paramount, Gail noticed her reading a new movie script. Diana explained that she was studying for the part of Emily Kimbrough in Paramount's forthcoming movie, "Our Hearts Were Young and Gay," based on the bestselling book by Cornelia Otis Skinner and Emily Kimbrough. She asked Gail to help her with the dialogue so she could audition for the part. Gail agreed, and before long had memorized the part of Cornelia Otis Skinner. By now Diana was eager for them both to try and audition for the picture. As Gail recalled in the May 27, 1950 edition of the Saturday Evening Post, "Diana Lynn practically pushed me into the role of Cornelia Otis Skinner on "Our Hearts Were Young and Gay." Having read the book by Emily Kimbrough and Cornelia Otis Skinner, and fallen in love with the part of Emily, she decided that I must play Cornelia. Awed by the prospect, I asked my drama coach, Bill Russell, if he thought I could swing it. 'Of course you can,' he said. 'But you'll have to be willing to make an awful fool of yourself.' Bill was right. I thoroughly enjoyed the role, but at times I certainly felt silly."[3]

Gail and Diana were eventually chosen for their respective roles. It was ironic that Gail got the role of Cornelia Otis Skinner. She had co-starred with the noted stage actress in "The Uninvited," and now she was playing her in the new film. It was also ironic that Gail had robbed Ella Raines of another plum role. Ella had been in the lead for the role of Cornelia, as well as the lead for the top role of Stella Meredith in "The Uninvited." Ella wasn't chosen for the role of Cornelia because she was considered too "sophisticated" and mature.

Paramount had decided to select Lewis Allen to direct the picture, and knew he was able to handle the difficulties in working with Gail and her stage fright, having solved her problem while working on "The Uninvited." Shooting began on time, and the set was closed to all but essential personnel while Gail's scenes were being filmed. There were the usual number of retakes where Gail was concerned, yet by and large she sailed right through the production, and seemed to endure movie making with a lot less anxiety. Maybe it was because Gail was nearly a year older, and more mature, or perhaps it was the fact that she was getting used to the way movies were made. The large lens of the movie camera, and the bright klieg lights were not so terrifying as before. Then there was the simple fact that Gail was making a film with her best friend, Diana Lynn. Diana was the perfect antidote for Gail's shy, withdrawn, timid nature. Diana was always cheerful, friendly, happy-go-lucky, with her blonde hair, blue eyes, and dimpled cheeks. As Gail recalled to Screenland Magazine in 1945 – "Our Hearts Were Young and Gay" was my second big picture, second big part. "Our Hearts" was fun to make, it was a gay picture. Diana Lynn, who has been my best friend ever since the Aldrich picture, was in it. Our mutual interest in Ginger Rogers is what really made us friends. Diana saw me once, on the set of "Lady in the Dark," making some sketches of Ginger, came over and talked with me and we've been chums ever since."[4]

While filming "Our Hearts Were Young and Gay," Diana and Gail asked Paramount if they could share a dressing room, and became a big joke around the set with all their clothes strewn about the dressing room like a couple of adolescent school girls at play. One day the crew decided to teach them a lesson in neatness, and while they were shooting a scene, they emptied their dresser drawers and scattered their belongings all over the floor. When Gail and Diana returned to their dressing room, they got the message. However, within one week, they were at their old habits once again.

It was also at this time that Gail had her first serious romance since coming to Paramount. Bill Edwards, Gail's co-star in "Our Hearts Were Young and Gay," and Diana's boyfriend in the film, became Gail's steady date. Bill was very similar to Gail in temperament, quiet and shy, despite being six feet, five inches in height. He was 4F and ineligible for the draft, having hurt his back in a riding accident. Gail had a surprise birthday party on the set, and Bill gave her a gold ring with the inscription, "Forever and Forever." It had been a long time since Gail had let anyone get emotionally close to her. It was rare when Gail would open up to any magazine writer, and share her private life. However, she told Gladys Hall about her relationship with Bill Edwards in 1945 – "Now and again, we double-date, Diana and Dick Balkany, Bill Edwards (who played opposite me in "Our Hearts") and I. Usually we go to the Biltmore Bowl because Diana is underage, and that is the only place she can get in. The other day I overheard someone saying, 'I wonder what in heaven's name Gail Russell and Bill Edwards talk about when they have dates, they are both so quiet.' We talk. Or sometimes we don't talk, because it isn't necessary. Not to have to talk is one of the nicest things about being friends. Silences that are shared say things too…"[5] Suddenly Gail got very serious, and in her voice there was a tinge of sadness. She went on – "Being friends. That is all I want, now, being friends. I have never been in love. I don't want to be in love. I don't want to get married, not for a long, long time. I have too much to do. I have a lot of people to repay for all they've done for me. Mr. Russell, the first and most important. He sweated blood to get me the breaks. He stayed up nights worrying about my next day's scenes. He held my hand when I was drowning in fears and tears. He helped me believe in myself."[6] Suddenly, Gail perked up and smiled. She continued – "Besides, now I enjoy my job, I really do. Now I want what every actress wants, good parts in good pictures. Now I am taking diction lessons. English lessons, dancing, ballroom, and tap. Someday I want to be a dancer, too. I think I have a little flair for it, and I'd like to do the kind of things Ginger Rogers did with Fred Astaire. Now Gail became serious again, and said, "This is about as far as I've come in my thinking and planning and dreaming. Glamour, fame, money, all the perquisites success on the screen often brings to a girl. I haven't had enough of them yet to know whether I really want them, or not. We've saving for a home, Dad and Mother and I, so that every penny goes into the bank. We had our home taken away from us once, when it was half paid for. That fear come true must never happen again. So we are still living in our little rented bungalow in Santa Monica. I've brought just four dresses, but very nice ones, since I signed my contract with Paramount… And I'm still afraid … I'm still afraid – but not in the same way or for the same intangible reasons. Now I am only afraid of the kindness of people lest I am not able to repay them in like measure."[7]

With the release of "Our Hearts Were Young and Gay," Paramount had its second smash hit film starring Gail Russell, just a few short months after the opening of "The Uninvited." It was one of the biggest box office hits of 1944, and a much welcome relief from all the war news coming out of Europe and the South Pacific. Today, it is a much underrated comedy, and a major joy to behold. Gail and Diana portray Cornelia Otis Skinner and Emily Kimbrough in a true story about two college classmates who travel unchaperoned through Europe during the 1920's. They go through many hilarious situations and misadventures while appearing to be sophisticated and knowledgeable adults. In addition to Gail Russell and Diana Lynn, the cast was composed of Charlie Ruggles, Dorothy Gish, Beulah Bondi, James Brown, and Bill Edwards. It is one of the best comedies ever made, and it was the first film in which Gail Russell had top billing. Gail later admitted that of all her films, "Our Hearts Were Young and Gay" was her personal favorite.

Gail had been much impressed with the noted stage actress, Cornelia Otis Skinner, and recalled how much in awe of her she had been while filming "The Uninvited." On the first day Miss Skinner's scene was to be shot, Gail didn't dare speak to her. "Usually, you know, as they're getting ready for a scene, the crew bangs around and everybody shouts at everybody else, and its all confusion and clatter. When Miss Skinner appeared, there was sudden quiet. It showed the respect we all had for her, but it also overawed me entirely – until, one day, she said something funny – I'd forgotten what – in a comic little cockney voice. Everybody howled. After that, I worked up the courage to talk to her a little, and I discovered how silly it was ever to have worried."[8]

The film critics loved "Our Hearts Were Young and Gay," including the New York times Film Review, when it stated, *Our Hearts Were Young and Gay, Paramount's film version of the Cornelia Otis Skinner – Emily Kimbrough book of remembrance of things past, lives up to its title… its story is as light as a marshmallow and as cloyingly sweet… the producers have fused the effervescence of youth with rosy-tinted nostalgia to make an amusing and satisfying entertainment… Diana Lynn and Gail Russell are excellently cast in the roles of the ingenious and young Misses Kimbrough and Skinner."[9]

It was at this time that Paramount asked Gail and Diana Lynn to volunteer and help serve the American servicemen twice a week at the famous Hollywood Canteen, then located at 1451 North Cahuenga Boulevard near Sunset, in Hollywood, California. It was here that Gail finally met her famous namesake, Hedy Lamarr, the famous star of Metro Goldwyn Mayer Studios, back in 1943. Harrison Carroll, noted newspaper columnist of the Los Angeles Examiner, wrote in his article, "Meeting of Hedy Lamarr and Paramount starlet Gail Russell is the town's current chuckle. The two actresses are look-alikes, and the other night at the Hollywood Canteen, the Russell gal's soldier dance partner insisted on introducing her to Hedy. 'Don't you think she looks just like you?' he said to the MGM star. 'I wish I were as pretty,' replied Hedy, graciously. 'Do you know,' she added to the embarrassed starlet. 'You ought to be in pictures.' Whereupon Gail, very fussed, blurted out, 'Thank you, so should you.'"

Even though Gail had finished four films, and was now considered an established actress, those who interviewed her were aware that she didn't seem happy with her life as a movie star. Along with the nickname of the "Cinderella Girl," Gail was also given the title of the "Girl with the Tragedy Air." Her eyes, which were so lovely to behold, always seemed to be so sad. When asked about it, Gail always referred to her early days in films, especially "The Uninvited." Gail said, "The truth is that I was simply petrified. Though I knew my lines and felt the scenes, when I stood up there before the camera and opened my mouth, nothing would come out. I just froze stiff. Then I would get hysterical and cry. Eventually we got the picture finished, and maybe it was a good thing that I played a neurotic heroine, for I was just that way myself."

Director Lewis Allen would also echo those thoughts. He recalled later in an interview that "She's going to be a great actress when she loosens up. Naturally a serious, thoughtful girl, she is emotionally impacted. When we began our first scenes, she was so scared that her eyes glazed even if only the cast and crew were on the set. It took psychology, combined with understanding and patience, to cure her of her fear. But she is gradually gaining self-confidence."

Gail approached her problem from another angle when she said, "I take picture work too seriously to really have a good time at it. Though I'm acquiring some ease before the camera, I'm still very nervous, so afraid I won't make good. Never having had any dramatic training – I never was even in a school play. I had to start from scratch. Now I am studying with the studio coach, but I'm too tense, too key-up about it to relax."

Gail also discovered that there was an additional drawback to being a movie star. She was losing her old high school friends to the aura of being a Hollywood celebrity. Gail recalled, "I've noticed these days that I don't have as much fun anymore when I go dancing on Saturday nights with some of the boys I used to double date with during school. They treat me with so much respect. I have to kid them out of it. I guess they've figured I've changed, and that a girl who spends time on the set with Ray Milland and Ginger Rogers in "Lady in the Dark," couldn't be the identical Gail they cut classes with to run down to the ocean for a swim." Gail was now realizing that she had entered a new social class when she became a Hollywood star. Her old friends, dear as they might be, were no longer a part of her world. The American Ideal of no social classes were no match for the fame, glamour, and wealth a Hollywood career could offer. Gail would soon leave her old school friends behind, and soon only those involved in the entertainment industry would be numbered among her friends.

Another disturbing trait that Gail exhibited in her childhood would resurface again in 1944. Gail would occasionally experience inexplicable changing moods of behavior. These were dark and depressing periods where she would suddenly talk to no one, and retreat into her room. As Gail recalled to a reporter, "I have black moods. They come down on me without warning. Then I have a good cry, and run off to walk around the block." However, just as suddenly as they appeared, these same moods of depression would quickly fade away.

One of these deep moods of depression came upon Gail late in 1944. On December 31, 1944, Edwin Schallert wrote in the Los Angeles Times that Gail "has had a speedy career, and she recently ran into the shoals of despond about it all, because things happened so fast, and not according to her preconceived visioning. 'A case of nerves, I guess,' she told me, 'which struck about six weeks ago. I'm just beginning to come to life again. I think I can take it better now.'"[10]

Yes, Gail Russell was a strange, complex young lady, and definitely not your average movie star. However, she had decided to become a movie star, and for better or worse, her Destiny was set.

Chapter 9
The Unseen

By the start of 1945, Gail was now earning $200 a week under her standard Paramount contract. She would earn the minimum salary only when not working on a scheduled film, and then her contract would stipulate a larger sum for the duration of the production, which usually lasted from four to six weeks. Gail also had various bonus clauses in her contract, varying from $1,500 to $2,000 per option, but this was solely on the discretion of the Paramount front office. Still, Gail was earning a very good salary considering she had only a high school education, and was making far more than the rest of her family. She continued to put most of her earnings in the bank, hoping to help the family purchase a home for the first time in their lives. Gail hoped the nightmare of losing the family home would never be repeated. That was one of the main reasons she decided to continue being a movie star, to help her family out financially. It was certainly not because she loved making movies. It just took too much out of her emotionally, as her extremely shy nature reacted adversely to the demand of performing in public before the movie cameras.

It was a constant struggle for Gail. There would be times when she would perform beautifully one day on the set, and the very next day, forget her lines and dialogue. Yet there was also an added incentive why Gail endured the hardship of acting in films, a reason not solely based on helping her family. A reason newspaper reporter Chapman Dale wrote about in his column in 1944 entitled "Gail Russell." He wrote, "From all of which you may gather that Gail is 'different' – a girl who takes a little knowing. She combines a little girl sort of naiveté and charm with a sometimes impenetrable aloofness that makes impulsive people throw up their hands and say: 'Oh nuts! It isn't worth it. She won't even try to give.' But look below the surface and you will find the reason for it all … her older brother, now in the Aleutians, was always the one who received the attention. He was the one who was going to amount to something. 'Whatever I do now,' confides Gail 'is to show the people who didn't believe I would ever amount to much. I've simply got to show them.'"[1]

Gail certainly kept her vow. By 1945, she was well on her way to become a major star. Despite her notoriety, she was still a small town girl at heart. With her new found financial independence, she was now the proud owner of a horse named Kelly who was kept at a stable in the San Fernando Valley. She was also the owner of a cocker spaniel also named Kelly, a half-dachshund, half cocker named "Hank," a miniature schnauzer called "Emily," and a Maltese terrier named "Cornelia." Gail drove to the studio in a small convertible she affectionately called "Jezebel." She was also the proud owner of a leather saddle which was monogrammed with her initials G.R.

Gail was now more mature enough to go out socially, and all those studio dance lessons were finally paying off. She went to parties and dates on her days and nights off with the likes of actors Freddie Bartholomew, Jimmy Lydon, and Bill Edwards, who, like Gail, was fond of horseback riding and art. Many a movie fan magazine had a photo of Gail with new star Peter Lawford dancing at Ciro's Nightclub, and afterwards eating a romantic dinner at Romanoffs' Restaurant. On occasional weekends, Gail could be seen with good friends Diana Lynn and Carmelita Lopez going bowling, ice skating, or moonlight horseback riding. Gail was making up for all the years she deprived herself of so much fun in life by keeping to herself due to her shyness.

Gail's next film assignment was in the mystery thriller "The Unseen," which was supposed to be similar to "The Uninvited," but lacked the plot and script that supernatural tale had. The film was to be directed by Lewis Allen, and it was the third film in a row that Gail worked with him. It was to be their last film together, and Paramount executives hoped that their success together would continue at the box office. The film also starred Joel McCrea and Herbert Marshall, with a screenplay co-authored by famous mystery writer Raymond Chandler. Gail played Elizabeth Howard, a young governess hired to teach the young children, played by Richard Lyon and Nona Griffith of widower David Fielding, played by Joel McCrea, who is living in London, England. Gail's character soon becomes involved in solving an old and new murder, with a creepy old house as a backdrop to her many adventures. Even with a good cast and director, "The Unseen" proved to be a major disappointment with the public. Perhaps it was due to the fact that flesh and blood antagonists were not as frightening as supernatural spirits.

It was while filming "The Unseen" that Gail became seriously ill for the first time in her life. The fact that she was struggling with the flu, and still extremely nervous in front of the camera, made the filming of the movie a sometimes unpleasant experience. Director Allen also noticed that Gail had a difficult time wondering what to do with her hands during a scene. She had a nervous habit of wringing her hands in nervous anxiety, ever mindful of the all seeing movie camera and the numerous sound stage technicians around the set. It was due to Gail's sensitive nature that while all her scenes were being filmed, the set was always closed to visitors.

It was at this time also that Gail became friendly with actress Helen Walker, who coincidently happened to be shooting a move with Fred MacMurray. "Murder, He Says," in a sound stage next door. Helen had also tested for the role of Stella Meredith in "The Uninvited," which was eventually given to Gail. She lived in an apartment close to Paramount, and was alone now that her husband was in the army. She was more mature and less naïve than Gail, and like an older sister tried to protect her from the harsh realities of the daily "Hollywood grind" of making movies. Helen frequently dined with Gail, and would often visit her in her dressing room. For shy Gail, it was good to have a sympathetic ear to hear her troubles, and know that somebody understood what she was going through. It was probably at this time that Helen introduced Gail to the tranquilizing effect of alcohol, particularly vodka. Being odorless and colorless, it wasn't easy to detect on the breath.

"The Unseen" was not the critical and commercial success that "The Uninvited" had been. Film critics gave it mixed reviews. The New York Times stated "Early last year Paramount introduced chiller devotees to a classy congress of spirits in "The Uninvited," a spooks-and-shivers item directed by Lewis Allen and featuring Gail Russell. The studio has fashioned in "The Unseen" as tenebrous a tale as come along in some time… For this terror filled saga of sudden death surrounding a young governess… is superior mystery fare. Gail Russell is perhaps, miscast as the children's guardian. As the nervous, juvenile mistress of the mansion, her delineation lacks conviction."[2] The critics went overboard in their praise of the young child stars Richard Lyon and Nona Griffith. In fact, in their opinion, they thought they stole the movie from the more adult co-stars, Gail Russell, Joel McCrea, and Herbert Marshall.

Despite the critical review of her performance, Gail was satisfied with her work as well as her career. Especially her mother who diligently kept scrapbooks of Gail and her movie career. They were filled with every newspaper article and magazine story she could find on her daughter, including candid and movie photographs. Even foreign magazine covers were not exempt. Her mother also included letters and thank you notes, as well as the original note from Milton Lewis inviting Gail for a screen test at Paramount Studios on April 8, 1942.

"The Unseen" proved to be a minor setback in Gail's career, but her next film would team her with one of her all-time idols, and the biggest male star at Paramount, Alan Ladd.

Chapter 10
Salty O'Rourke

By January, 1945, Gail had matured into full womanhood at the age of twenty. She had grown to her full height of 5 feet, 4 ½ inches, weighed about 111 lbs., and with her black hair, long eyelashes, and her lovely sapphire blue eyes, was turning heads wherever she entered the Paramount commissary, or walked the Paramount lot.

It was around this time that Gail moved out of her parents' home to live with the family of her good friend, Carmelita Lopez. She thought it would be more convenient to live closer to the studios, and away from home where she thought there were too many distractions. It was all an attempt on her part to exercise her independence. Her mother wasn't too thrilled with the idea, and hoped that Gail would soon return home. She confessed as much to writer Sara Hamilton of Photoplay Magazine, "I never left off doing for her in those days. I never let her know how desperate we were at losing her. I still mended her clothes when I had the chance, and despite her tears I'd plant the seeds that I hoped would bring her back one day. It took six months for Gail to realize the truth that as a united family they could pull and work for the good of all. One day she told her mother her clothes were at the studio, 'We'll go get them tomorrow,' her mother said. 'No, let's get them now,' Gail responded. By that afternoon, Gail was back living at home.[1]

Paramount at this time scheduled Gail to appear with their top male star, Alan Ladd, in a race track drama entitled "Salty O'Rourke," directed by veteran Raoul Walsh. Ladd was incredibly popular with the movie public during the early 1940's, and for Gail it was a major boost to her career to be co-starring with him. It meant she was now on equal footing with the other actresses on the Paramount roster, and it was a thrill for her to see her name with Alan Ladd above the movie title during the film's opening credits.

Director Walsh had heard of Gail's shyness and extreme stage fright, and agreed with Paramount executives, along with some possible advice from fellow director Lewis Allen, to keep a closed set while Gail was filming her scenes. Gail still struggled with her lines, yet not nearly as severe as when she worked on "Henry Aldrich Gets Glamour" or "The Uninvited." Gail worked well with Alan Ladd, and her black hair and blue eyes contrasted well on screen with Ladd's blonde, blue eyed looks. She later became good friends with his wife Susan, and was frequently invited to attend celebrity parties at their home.

The atmosphere on the set became so congenial that director Walsh even had time to pull a prank on Gail while filming a scene one day. The scene called for Gail's character, Barbara Brooks, to open the front door and welcome Alan's character, Salty O'Rourke, into the house. However, when Gail opened the door this time, she was met by actor Errol Flynn, who was carrying a bunch of roses, and politely inquired of Gail if she would like to sail with him on his yacht! Flynn was a close friend of Walsh from his days at Warner Brothers Studios, and was notorious for entertaining young ladies on his boat, who were sometimes underage. Needless to say, Gail was completely surprised and embarrassed as the whole set erupted into laughter. It proved a great way to relieve Gail's tension on the set, and was a major reason why filming continued without any further serious setbacks.[2]

It was also while filming "Salty O'Rourke" that Gail was to meet another surprise visitor on the set who had also previously worked with Raoul Walsh. One day between takes, Walsh called Gail over to introduce her to actor John Wayne, also a close friend, who had worked with him at Republic Studios while filming "The Dark Command" in 1940. Gail was much impressed with the handsome, tall, six foot four inch actor who towered over her much smaller five foot four and a half inch frame. She also admired his open, friendly manner, and the confidence that seemed to emanate from him. Wayne would later come into Gail's life again in getting her one of her most memorable film roles of her career, as well as being instrumental in Gail's movie "comeback" in 1956.

In the midst of filming "Salty O'Rourke," Gail finally discovered the identity of one of her benefactors who had hitch-hiked a ride with Paramount executive William Meiklejohn, and launched her career into the movies. It seems Gail received a fan letter from Charlie Cates, who was in the Navy serving the war effort. He had seen Gail's film, "Our Hearts Were Young and Gay," aboard ship and had recognized her name and face from their days at Santa Monica Tech. He recalled the incident with Meiklejohn when he told him of their classmate who was "more beautiful than Hedy Lamarr." "From what I have just seen on the screen, he wrote, "we sure called the turn on that one." Gail later wrote back, and thanked him, telling Charlie to come visit her at Paramount as a guest, and take a tour of the studios. She also asked him for the identity of his hitch-hiking buddy so she could also thank him in the same manner.[3]

Gail renewed her love for horses in this latest film about the race track and its colorful society of characters. She purchased another horse, and promptly named him "Salty O'Rourke" after Ladd's character in the movie. Gail would keep him at a riding academy stable in the San Fernando Valley, and would visit him two or three times a week, and go for long rides on weekends.

The film "Salty O'Rourke" also starred, in addition to Gail and Alan Ladd, Bruce Cabot, William Demarest, Spring Byington, and Stanley Clements, who as renegade Jockey Johnny Cate, "steals" the picture with his performance. The film concerns Gail, as Barbara Brooks, who winds up tutoring jockey Johnny Cate who rides for owner Salty O'Rourke. She is courted by Cate, but eventually falls for O'Rourke. This is an above average comedy-drama involving a love triangle, crooked race track gamblers, and other people who inhabit the race track and its colorful society of characters. It was a typical Alan Ladd film with the customary action and eventual gun play. The film was another success at the box office, and critics generally were kind to the actors. Even Bosley Crowther of the New York Times had a kind word to say. He wrote, "Paramount has a sure thing in their monstrously mischievous tale of a 'fixers' titanic tribulations with a cocky jockey on whom he must depend. Indeed, it has a fictional winner which Damon Runyon at his best might have penned... Although Paramount put its money on Alan Ladd, it is a kid named Stanley Clements who, as the jockey, runs away with the show... Mr. Ladd manages to give a nice performance as a plainly soft-hearted tough guy... Gail Russell doesn't quite play the teacher for all of its farce overtones, but that is because the director Raoul Walsh hasn't pitched the farce too well."[5] Gail never seemed to be bothered by her film reviews, for she never really read them, whether they were good or bad.

Gail turned twenty-one on September 21, 1945. She celebrated with her parents and her brother, who had recently returned safely from the Aleutian Islands, with an evening at Ciro's Nightclub in Hollywood. Life couldn't be better for Gail with a growing movie career with the likes of Joel McCrea and Alan Ladd, plus more fan mail was arriving at Paramount asking for her autograph and picture.

It was also around this time that an incident happened that would later prove to have a lasting influence on Gail. She was entering Paramount Studios at the Bronson Avenue gate with film actor Billy De Wolfe, when they were met by voice coach Lester Luther. With him was a young man who had just been released by the Navy, and was taking acting classes at Paramount. His name was Guy Madison. He was introduced to Gail, but just made a casual impression. Little did Gail realize that they were soon to become one of the most celebrated movie couples in Hollywood history.

Gail's first official portrait from "Henry Aldrich Gets Glamour," 1942. Gail was 18.

An early glamour shot of Gail from 1942 by A.L. "Whitey" Schafer.

Glamour shot of Gail, 1943 by A.L. "Whitey" Schafer.
Gail was called Hollywood's "Cinderella Girl"
by the Paramount publicity department.

Glamour shot by "Whitey" Schafer, 1943.

Gail in a 1944 "Whitey" Schafer pose. Hugh Bennett said
Gail had that "Come hither look," that helped make her famous.

"Whitey" Schafer portrait, 1945.

A 1945 A.L. "Whitey" Shafer portrait.

A pensive portrait of Gail from 1945. "Whitey" Schafer.

Portrait of Gail by William "Bud" Fraker, 1947.

Portrait by "Bud" Fraker, 1947. Gail's face,
even in repose, always had a haunting sadness.

Glamour shot of Gail by "Bud" Fraker, 1947.

Publicity shot for "Night has a Thousand Eyes"
by "Bud" Fraker, 1947.

Portrait by "Bud" Fraker, 1947.

Classic glamour portrait by "Bud Fraker," 1947.

Portrait by "Bud" Fraker. 1947.

Gail at the beach in 1948. Gail seldom posed for
"pinup" photos due to her extremely shy nature.

Photo by "Bud" Fraker, 1949.

Galmour portrait by William "Bud" Fraker, 1949.

Portrait from "The Great Dan Patch," 1949.

Gail and Guy announce their impending
marriage to the press, July 1949.

Publicity portrait from "Captain China," 1950.

Publicity photo from "The Lawless," 1950.

Promotional photo from "Air Cadet" 1951.

A publicity shot from "Seven Men From Now," 1956.

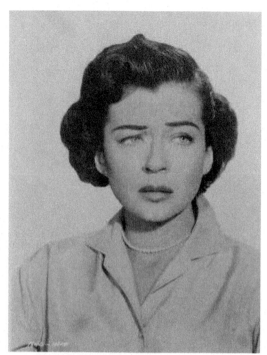
From "The Tattered Dress," 1957.

Gail in her last official portrait, March 1960.
It is evident in this photo that her alcoholism
had nearly destroyed her once famouse beauty.

Chapter 11
Our Hearts Were Growing Up

Gail's next film assignment was in the new Paramount musical comedy extravaganza, "Duffy's Tavern." It was touted as an all-star review based on the popular radio show of the same name. It was to include 32 of the top stars of Paramount, including Bing Crosby, Alan Ladd, Dorothy Lamour, Paulette Goddard, Betty Hutton, and Veronica Lake. Diana Lynn also had a minor role. However, Gail's role was merely a cameo appearance in a musical number involving Bing Crosby, who sang his famous song, "Swinging on a Star," accompanied by young actresses Jean Heather, Helen Walker, and Gail. It was a small part for Gail, yet it must have been a thrill to work with Crosby, whom she greatly admired.

In the movie sequence, you could tell Gail was extremely nervous, since she knew she didn't possess a great singing voice. In the last scene at the end of the movie, where all the stars are gathered for a rousing finale, you could spot Gail hiding timidly in the background, trying to hide from the camera's lens. Gail must have been emotionally overwhelmed to be among so many stars more famous than she. Her shy, insecure nature was in stark contrast to the more mature, confident, and talented stars she was performing with. The film was not a big career boost for Gail since she didn't receive any movie billing on the screen. Even the official Paramount Pressbook didn't list her name on the cast list.

The film's plot involved the manager of Duffy's Tavern, played by Ed Gardner, who tried to help ex-servicemen who work in a record factory next door. The comedy misadventures include trying to juggle the tavern's expense accounts, and salvage the phonograph factory by staging a charity benefit involving several movie stars. It proved to be a hit at the box office due to its all-star cast. The review by the New York Times' Bosley Crowther was typical of most of the film critics. He wrote, "Every so often Paramount throws a great big studio jamboree, and gets every actor on the payroll to pitch in and do a turn... This year's party is "Duffy's Tavern"... all of which makes for low and languid comedy that is straight down an old familiar groove... Bing Crosby and a chorus of assistants, including a likely assortment of studio 'names,' do a very amusing parody of 'Swinging on a Star'... Take it for what it is, a hodge-podge of spare-time clowning by the gang... and you'll find "Duffy's Tavern" fair enough."[1]

Gail by now was getting quite a reputation as a rising young star as numerous movie fan magazines were filled with stories of her amazing rise to fame, her biography, and her personal lifestyle. In addition, there were numerous photos of Gail and her nightlife as she was seen dancing and partying with numerous actors such as Peter Lawford, Billy De Wolfe, Guy Madison, and singer Andy Russell. Gail would be photographed many times in such famous nightclubs as Ciro's, the Mocambo, the Trocadero, and Chasen's.

However, it was not all fun and games for Gail in her movie career. Earlier in the year she had visited, at the suggestion of Paramount executives, and her good friend Diana Lynn, several Army hospitals in the South to comfort and entertain wounded soldiers. It was a kind and patriotic effort on Gail's part, but it was also therapeutic on her behalf because it helped her to overcome her personal shyness by learning to mix with people, and cope with life. Gail was accompanied on the trip by actress/singer Nancy Gates.[2]

1946 was to be for Gail a better year, career-wise, as she was scheduled to appear with good friend Diana Lynn in a so-called sequel to "Our Hearts Were Young and Gay" titled "Our Hearts Were Growing Up." It was also to be directed by her personal drama coach and mentor, Bill Russell. So you can imagine Gail's joy and relief to know she would be making her next film with familiar and friendly faces. Also in the cast were Billy De Wolfe, Brian Donlevy, William Demarest, and young actors James Brown and Bill Edwards whom had also starred with Gail in the prequel.

Director Bill Russell knew Gail and her extremely shy nature, and being her drama coach at Paramount could understand her anxiety and fear when performing before the movie camera. He felt very protective toward Gail, and like a surrogate father, tried to keep her from the tremendous stress of being a Hollywood star. Russell always disagreed with the other Paramount executives who thought that Gail had enough training to be a great star. He also knew that it was due to studio head Buddy De Sylva that Gail had made three films in only six months. He always believed that Paramount was pushing her too fast, and that they were not giving her enough time to become a successful actress. Russell recalled that first meeting with Gail in Milton Lewis' office, "Gail was the most painfully shy person I ever encountered. But you couldn't help liking the kid. There was something appealing in her desperation as she sat across from me, hands clenched, fear in her eyes. She never once opened her mouth. Whenever I asked her anything, she'd nod a reply. All that is over now, but she had to fight. We both had to, in fact. Gail is a wonderful friend once she realizes you want to be friendly." If it had not been for Bill Russell, I seriously doubt if Gail Russell would have been a major star at Paramount Studios, nor would her career have lasted as long as it did. He was to be one of the very few Paramount executives, as well as friends, who would attend Gail's funeral in 1961.

Director Russell finished shooting "Our Hearts Were Growing Up" on schedule, and within its budget. He knew how to handle Gail's shyness and was very sympathetic and patient with her expected retakes. This was his first try at directing, and like Lewis Allen, would later gain even greater fame as a director of numerous television series. The plot of the movie involved Gail, as Cornelia Otis Skinner, and Diana Lynn, as Emily Kimbrough, trying to attend the Harvard-Princeton football game unchaperoned in order to visit their respective boyfriends.

Through many comedy adventures, including a trip to New York city's Greenwich Village section, and a notorious bootlegger's celebration party, they eventually wind up reconciled with their estranged boyfriends. Despite the good cast and the able direction of Bill Russell, the film proved to be a minor disappointment with the public, as well as the movie critics. Sequels are seldom as popular as their predecessors, and the fictional story was not nearly as entertaining as the truthful one. The review of the New York Times newspaper was typical of the film's response, "Another film axiom was tested and proved beyond argument over the weekend with the opening of "Our Hearts Were Growing Up"… It was inevitable that, being a sequel, it could not quite measure up to the often charming "Our Hearts Were Young and Gay" of 1944. The story, a little too involved for light comedy… the frequent hilarities of Donlevy, Demarest, et al. there is much to command the film. But uneven direction, and the super-saccharinity of Gail Russell and Diana Lynn, leave more than a little to be desired."[3]

Despite its less than critical success, Gail enjoyed making the film, and working with her good friend Diana Lynn. It cemented their friendship even further. They were frequently seen out on the town on weekends, double dating, Gail with Guy Madison, and Diana with agent Henry Willson.

By now Gail was making $300 a week, when not working on a film, under her Paramount contract, with the usual bonus options, guaranteed a minimum of 40 weeks of employment. Gail could now afford to move with her family to a larger apartment in Beverly Hills at 138 North Hamilton Drive. They were all still saving for a new home, but this was but a further rise in the Russell family fortunes. Gail's next step in her movie career was to be strange one, due to the fact that she was to be loaned out to another studio for the first time in her life.

Chapter 12
The Bachelor's Daughters

In early 1946, Gail auditioned for the female lead in Paramount's Technicolor production of "A Connecticut Yankee in King Arthur's Court" starring Bing Crosby. She wore a blonde wig for the screen test, but lost the part partly because her singing voice wasn't strong enough. The part went to red-headed Rhonda Fleming. It would have been interesting to see how beautifully Gail would have photographed in the Technicolor process with her lovely blue eyes and raven black hair. Gail was also scheduled to star in a remake of "The Virginian" with James Brown. However, when that Western oater went before the camera, Joel McCrea and Barbara Britton were chosen to play the leads.

Paramount now decided to loan out Gail to producer/director Andrew Stone at United Artists Studios to star in his new film, "The Bachelor's Daughters." It was customary then for major studios to loan out stars to other studios for large sums of money, sometimes for financial reasons, and other times to punish stars for refusing roles they didn't like. In Gail's case, it was strictly financial. The loaned out star usually received almost 10% of the loan out fee. In a letter to the payroll department at Paramount dated March 11, 1946, William Meiklejohn agreed that Gail was to be paid $3,750 a week for eight weeks while "The Bachelor's Daughters" was being filmed.

Gail was not fond of leaving her home studio to do another picture, but she did as she was asked to do. Considering her shy nature and polite manner, it was exactly what one would expect her to do. In a statement to her new star status, Gail was given top billing over her better known co-stars Claire Trevor, Ann Dvorak, Jane Wyatt, and Adolphe Menjou. In addition, she was given more modern, fashionable dresses to wear in the film, rather than the normal, period costumes she wore in "Our Hearts Were Growing Up."

Director Andrew Stone had asked Paramount for Gail personally, having seen her films, and was enchanted with her beauty and gentle manner. In addition to producing and directing the film, he also wrote the original screenplay. His father, A. L. Stone, helped build the Western Pacific Railroad, and he had inherited quite a bit of money. Producer Stone built lavish and extravagant sets for the production, using the grand ballroom of the late Cornelius Vanderbuilt II's fantastic Fifth Avenue mansion on Long Island. It had been in storage since the house was dismantled in 1927. Stone bought the ballroom nearly a year previous from the Vanderbuilt heirs. Made in 1880 in Europe, it cost a sizable fortune. Many of the decorations were in solid gold. The solid silver and glass doors alone cost approximately $50,000. The exquisite wood paneling, marble and crystal fixtures made it a magnificent movie set.[1]

It was a joy for Gail to work on the film, and director Stone handled her stage fright with tact and understanding. Gail made friends on the set, especially actress Jane Wyatt, who taught Gail how to knit socks. The film plot involved salesgirls of the Royal Department Store, Eileen (Gail Russell), Cynthia (Claire Trevor), Terry (Ann Dvorak), and Marta (Jane Wyatt), who pool their money to rent a house on Long Island in order to attract rich men to marry. They are joined by Billie Burke and Adolphe Menjou in their scheme, and the film has many humorous adventures as the girls wind up eventually with the happy ending. It is an above average comedy/drama, reminiscent of the later 1954 20th Century Fox comedy, "How To Marry A Millionaire," starring Marilyn Monroe, Betty Grable, and Lauren Bacall. It did fairly well at the box office, and was further proof of the movie fan appeal of rising star Gail Russell.

The film critics, however, had a less than enthusiastic opinion of "The Bachelor's Daughters." The New York Times was typical of the film's reception. It wrote, "There has been a great deal of speaking of minds, pro and con, about writer's rights in the production of movies they have had a hand in writing... But "The Bachelor's Daughters" hardly makes a concerning argument... For Andrew Stone, who not only wrote, but produced and directed this comedy/drama about four department store salesgirls who unite into a spurious family, apparently had all the authority and brought forth only a passing fair entertainment... Gail Russell, Claire Trevor, Ann Dvorak, and Jane Wyatt are competent in prosaically written roles... In short, Mr. Stone's cast is playing Cinderella again. They haven't improved the story, but they haven't hurt it either."[2]

By now Gail was being seen regularly in the company of rising new star Guy Madison. They were photographed regularly in movie fan magazines dining and dancing at fashionable nightclubs such as Ciro's, the Mocambo, or the Trocadero along the Sunset Strip in Hollywood. Guy, like Gail, had become a movie star quite by accident. A smart agent, Helen Ainsworth, had spotted his photograph in a Navy magazine in 1944.[3] She soon brought him to the attention of famous movie producer David O. Selznick, who was then making his epic film about the American Home Front, "Since You Went Away." Selznick was so impressed with Madison's all-American good looks that he specifically wrote in a small scene to give him a screen debut. Soon the mailroom of Selznick Studios was flooded with letters from man hungry adolescent girls demanding to see more of the handsome young sailor. Guy, like Gail Russell, had come into the movies with no acting experience, and had been chosen primarily for his good looks. Also, like Gail, Guy had decided to try acting to help his family out financially.

Guy Madison first met Gail when he and voice coach Lester Luther ran into her and actor Billy De Wolfe as they were leaving Paramount Studios.[4] Guy had wanted to meet Gail for some time ever since he saw "Our Hearts Were Young and Gay" abroad ship during the war. He distinctly remembered that scene of Gail as she stood on a balcony, her eyes following a flight of pigeons all about her. That scene of her beautiful face had remained with him in his memory for quiet some time.

That first meeting was quite uneventful. Gail was rather casual in her conversation as she and Guy were introduced. He was at first disappointed in her seemingly indifferent attitude. Guy was unaware that it was her natural shyness that prevented Gail from being friendlier. As a natural defense, Guy tried to act as casual as Gail to shield his male ego. When asked about that first meeting with Guy Madison, Gail was asked if it was a case of "love at first sight." She recalled, "No. I thought he was conceited when I first met him. He didn't act conceited, exactly, but I thought any fellow that good looking, and with such assurance must think he's pretty wonderful. I found out otherwise."[5] When Guy was asked the same question about their first meeting, he stated, "No. I thought she had a warm personality, and was different from most girls, but I didn't fall right away. I soon did, though."[6] Then they were asked what they first noticed about each other. Gail's reply, "His hair, which I later made him cut! He'd been life-guarding at the beach, and his hair was long and bleached out." Guy's reply was more to the point, "Her eyes. I thought they were the most beautiful I'd ever seen."[7]

The next time Gail and Guy ran into one another was also quite by accident. Gail was partying with Diana Lynn and Loren Tindall at Ciro's Nightclub in Hollywood when her service man escort had to leave at midnight when his furlough expired. As he was leaving the room, in walks agent Henry Willson and Guy Madison, who was on a weekend pass. Henry and Diana were good friends, and frequently dated, and Diane asked him to join her table. After the evening was over, Diane asked Gail what she thought of the handsome Guy Madison. "That Madison. How was he?" "Humm?" "You danced with him five times. The sailor. How was he?" "Sensational." "He didn't look that good to me. On the floor, I mean." "Oh," said Gail, coming to. "He can't dance."[8]

Gail and Guy's fabled Hollywood romance seemed to continue on a rocky start. At a party the following week, Guy ran into Gail again, and decided to ask her out on their first formal date. However, while shooting a bathtub scene in "Till the End of Time," Guy both sprained and gashed his ankle, ultimately having to cancel his date with Gail. Later, a group of Guy's friends brought Gail over to visit him while he recuperated from his injuries.[9]

When Guy was well enough to walk again, he and good friend Henry Willson would frequently double date with Gail and Diana Lynn. They were seen so frequently together at the local nightclubs that Gail referred to them as the "Gold Dust Foursome". Gail was always kidding Guy about his lack of skill on the dance floor, for Gail loved to dance. She would say the shortest distance on the dance floor for Guy was on her toes![10] One evening, Gail and Guy were watching Henry and Diana tear into a mean samba. Finally, in exasperation, Gail told Guy, "If you don't learn to rumba and samba, I'll kill you!" Guy replied, "Dancing means that much to you?" "It does," said

Gail.[11]   After that episode, Guy took dancing lessons secretly, and a week later surprised Gail by performing a mean rumba while a surprised Henry and Diana looked on.

From then on, Gail and Guy became extremely close to one another. It was to be Gail's second and greatest romance of her life. Whenever their busy movie schedules permitted, they would see each other constantly. Guy was an expert swimmer, so he taught Gail how to do more than dogpaddle in the water. Gail was an expert dancer and horseback rider, so she taught Guy how to do both. They went on picnics together, parties, fishing off Santa Monica Pier, or lobster hunting off Laguna Beach. They would have guest dinners together at Guy's apartment or at Gail's home. They spent hours listening to Gail's music collection, and reading poetry together. Little by little, they grew in intimacy, sharing thoughts and personal beliefs.

Guy Madison was a huge hit with Gail's parents, as Gail recalled to Photoplay Magazine. "I must tell you that the way my folks, particularly my dad, went for Guy at their first meeting was nothing short of atomic. Now both mother and dad move about in a daze over him. He is but their dreamboat. They definitely like him better than any date I've ever had. But that's okay. I do too."[12]

During this time, the mid and late 1940's, the movie fan magazines were filled with photographs and articles on the romance of Gail Russell and Guy Madison. They were an extremely attractive movie couple, and along with Robert Taylor and Barbara Stanwyck, Tyrone Power and Lana Turner, Ann Sothern and Robert Sterling, John Payne and Gloria De Haven, they were among the most famous movie couples of their time.

Gossip columns were filled with stories that they were already married or were soon to be. Some had to be seen to be believed. One report had them eloping to Las Vegas. Another, that they were married in Mexico in some small village consisting of three whole huts and a cantina, wed by a local mustachioed justice. Or they slipped away to Guy's home town of Bakersfield, California, where with the aid of local cooperative officials, they were recently married. Gail later admitted that if they ever decided to get married, it would be the greatest anti-climax in Hollywood history. There was also the time Gail and Guy were sitting in their car eating hamburgers and malted milks when they suddenly heard in the car radio that Gail Russell and Guy Madison had just eloped, and were married.[13] They both laughed out loud with amusement. They had just spent the entire day at Laguna sailing on a boat in short sleeves and shorts, and were not exactly dressed for a wedding.

The following night they were at their favorite Russian restaurant on the Sunset Strip in Hollywood, Bublichki. As they entered the dining room, the orchestra began playing the wedding march. Guy's tanned face turned a beet red, and Gail was blushing to her hair roots. Somehow, they managed to survive that evening.

By 1946, Gail Russell and Guy Madison were definitely a steady couple. Gail was later asked what her first impression of Guy was, when at first she wasn't very interested in him at their first meeting at Paramount with Lester Luther. "We said hello, and that was that. Of course it was rather dark, and I didn't really see him." As to the second meeting at the party at Henry Willson's house, "I thought he was conceited, and a little fresh, the way he made remarks that were either sarcastic or blunt, I couldn't tell which. Then I learned that he was just 'covering up' a little of the shyness I knew so well."[14] Gail was then asked if it was Guy's looks that were his main appeal. "But with me it's not his looks so much – not that I'd change them. It's that he's so sincere. When he says something, you can believe it. And he has a sense of humor – corny, just like mine. And poise, which I don't have. He's never dull, of course, and he's so understanding, and competent, and reliable…"[15]

Gail's romantic life was now apparently set, and her next film was to see her reunited with Paramount's top male star – Alan Ladd.

Chapter 13
Calcutta

Gail was glad to return to the Paramount lot with her next film, "Calcutta," where she was reunited with her good friend, Alan Ladd. The movie public seemed to like the chemistry between the two stars, with Ladd's blonde, good looks, contrasting with Gail's dark, brunette beauty. There was also plenty of action in a Ladd film which always proved successful at the box office. John Farrow was assigned to direct the picture, and he had worked previously with Ladd in "The Glass Key," the "Blue Dahlia," "China," and "Two Years Before the Mast." Gail was a different story. He had never worked with her, and had heard of her shy temperament, her stage fright, along with numerous delays in shooting her scenes. In addition, Farrow had to talk Gail into accepting the role of Virginia Moore, which required her to play the role of a cold-hearted, ruthless villainess in the story. Gail felt she couldn't do the part, but Farrow was insistent. He felt Gail's shy, gentle demeanor was a perfect cover for the character's true nature in the story, allowing Ladd's character to be convincingly fooled in the film. Gail was finally convinced to play the part, for she was very fond of Alan Ladd.

Yet with their new film assignment came a small setback for Gail. Her old drama coach and friend, William Russell, informed Gail that he would no longer train her to act in her films. He thought he had taught her all she had to know about acting, and that she should begin to rely on her own acting talent and instinct. Gail at first was terrified at the prospect of acting without the assistance of Bill Russell. He had been a necessary crutch for her self-confidence ever since her first film at Paramount, "Henry Aldrich Gets Glamour" in 1943. As Gail later recalled in a newspaper article in 1947, "He (Bill Russell) practically held my hand through every picture I made until "Calcutta." Then he told me that he taught me all he could, and I was on my own. Believe me, my next two films were the worst twelve weeks I ever spent in my life. I was finally around making mistakes, behaving like a young bird that had been shoved out of the nest and had to fly – or else. But I'll be forever grateful that Bill was wise enough to turn me loose at the proper time. It wasn't until I worked with those two fine actors, Edward G. Robinson, and John Lund in "Night Has a Thousand Eyes," that I began to have the real self-confidence so necessary in the movie business."

However, Gail found out that she could stand on her own two feet, and that she really had more talent than she had realized. As Gail later recalled on that first day of filming "Calcutta," it was perhaps one of the proudest moments of her life. Without one flaw Gail and Alan Ladd completed an eight minute scene on the first take. "I could see the look of dawning wonder and respect on Alan's face when we were three quarters through. He couldn't believe it, for the betting among the crew was ten to one against our finishing the scene in three days."[1]

That first day of filming was a lark for Gail, yet her discomfort at performing before a film crew still continued to plague her. Farrow noticed that she had a serious habit of clenching and unclenching her hands during an emotional scene. Many times he had to shout "Cut," and stop the filming due to this bad habit of hers. Later during rehearsals he would tell Gail "Hands" to remind her to stop wringing her hands. Farrow later came up with a possible solution to the problem by asking Gail's costume designer, Edith Head, to add pockets to her dresses so she would have a place to put her hands during a scene. This seemed to help, although Gail often had the nickname of "Retake Russell" among the film crew at Paramount. Gail also had a rather bad habit of walking with her head forward, which her good friend Diana Lynn likened to a moo cow on a rampage. Gail was correcting this flaw of hers through daily exercises at the studio. Producer Joe Sistron bribed Gail into faster mastery of that awkward stride by promising her a doll for her collection. It arrived one day on the set of "Calcutta," a tiny Indian doll, well beaded.[2]

The cast in the film, in addition to Gail and Alan Ladd, included William Bendix and June Duprez. Duprez, as the exotic cabaret singer, was quite alluring and equal to Gail in her camera appeal. The plot involved Alan Ladd and William Bendix as commercial airline pilots who fly cargo over the "hump" between India and Chunking, China. They set out to solve the murder of their friend and became involved with jewel smugglers, mysterious women, and desperate killers. Gail, as Virginia Moore, was the "femme fatale" who almost kills Alan Ladd at the climax. It was a typical Ladd film vehicle with fistfights and gunplay. It was successful with the movie going public. However, the critics were another story. The New York Times was typical of the response. "There is just so much that an actor can do on his own to make a character interesting, and then he must depend upon the scenarist to provide him with dialogue and situations which will keep the spectator on edge... The story by Seton Miller... is a sorry mess indeed... Fists fly and guns bark now and then to generate a little excitement... Mr. Ladd saves his Sunday punch till near the end when he slaps Gail Russell across the face four or five times, without as much as leaving a finger mark on her pretty pan... "Calcutta" is the kind of adventure melodrama which... causes audiences to mutter, 'We've seen this before, and it seemed much better then'."[3]

Most critics agreed that Gail was miscast as the villainess. Her shy, quiet manner on screen didn't seem to convince critics that she could possess the cruel, calculating, evil persona of a murderess woman. Perhaps if Gail and June Duprez had switched roles, the result would have been more convincing.

Gail was getting more popular with the movie going public, and she was kept busy answering an increasing number of fan letters. She still answered fan letters herself, and she found it easier to communicate with strangers through the informal form of letter writing. Her movies were very successful at the box office, and she was making bigger and better films with more famous stars.

It was in 1947 that the Motion Picture Exhibitors of America named Gail Russell as a "Star of Tomorrow". Gail was now making enough money with her daily salary and bonus cash options, as stated in her contract with Paramount, to buy the new home she always dreamed of for her family. The family purchased, mostly with Gail's money, a large, three bedroom home at 10526 Wellworth Avenue in Westwood, California. It was the first home the Russell family completely owned in their lives. It was a very proud moment for Gail. For the Russell family to be financially secure was the primary reason Gail decided to become a Hollywood star, and sign with Paramount in the first place. It took so much out of Gail, physically, as well as emotionally, to perform before the movie cameras, that she could never enjoy making movies. She always felt as inadequate as an actress with all the miscues and retakes during scene rehearsals. Also there was that constant fear of the camera, that ever present "all seeing eye" that inexplicably seemed to make her "freeze" before its lens, and make her forget her lines of dialogue.

Gail could be really good at acting, yet the tremendous strain on her nerves and fragile psyche, at times, always proved more than she could bear. She loved making films, yet she feared it at the same time. It was a paradox for Gail, and a problem she never fully solved. Tragically, that fear of film making would prove to be ultimately fatal for Gail. Her need for substance to endure film making convinced Gail she needed a cure to ease her frazzled nerves and endless anxiety. That cure came in the form of alcohol. First it was just one drink occasionally. Then one drink before filming. Then a drink during lunch break, and there was always the drinking while she was partying and dancing with friends at the local nightclubs on weekends. Gail always thought she could handle the liquor consumption. She never realized that she would soon not go a day without drinking alcohol. Paramount executives and movie directors would look the other way, always giving the attitude that it was just the normal excess of youthful exuberance and good natured fun. As of now, however, Gail could handle her liquor intake. She was never late for work, and it was not yet interfering with her career.

Gail was still going steady with Guy Madison, yet his contract with producer David O. Selznick required him to go out of town frequently on East coast tours to promote films, and appear in stage plays. This required Gail to date other men in order to attend movie premiers, and Paramount Studio functions. She was seen on occasion with new male stars Jack Sasoon, John Dall, and Johnny Meyers.

The movie fan magazines were promoting the rumor that Gail and Guy Madison were already secretly married. It was fueled by the fact that Guy and Gail had matching plain, gold wedding rings that Guy wore in public, but Gail did not. Inscribed in the ring was a carved motto which read, "From

This Day Forward." Guy also wore a gold cross around his neck, a gift from Gail that was a match for the one she wore that was a present from actress Carole Landis.[4] Gail's next film was to be a loan-out to another studio. However, this time, Gail was to be co-starring with one of the greatest action heroes the movies had ever seen, and one of the greatest stars Hollywood would ever produce.

Chapter 14
Angel and the Badman

In April, 1946, John Wayne was in the process of producing his first film, "Angel and the Badman," for Republic Pictures, and he was looking for an actor to portray the lead role of outlaw Quirt Evans. After Gary Cooper and Joel McCrea both turned down the part, Wayne decided to play the role himself. Since he was now the leading man in the movie, he wanted to pick his own leading lady. He went through the list of young starlets on the Republic Studios roster, and after rejecting fifty candidates, Wayne decided to look elsewhere.[1] He suddenly remembered meeting Gail Russell on the Paramount lot when he was visiting his good friend Raoul Walsh on the set of "Salty O'Rourke" in 1945. Wayne recalled how enchanted he was by Gail's beauty, grace, and charm. He felt these qualities fit the character of Penelope Worth in the script, and knew Gail was right for the role. Wayne also knew that Gail definitely had box office appeal with the public.

However, Gail was on the roster of Paramount Studios, and Wayne had to agree to a loan-out contract to get her participation in the film project. A memo dated April 29, 1946, went out from the office of William Meiklejohn, head of talent and casting at Paramount, agreeing to loan-out Gail to Republic Studios for $3,750 a week for eight weeks. In addition, Wayne's production company was charged $125,000 for Gail's loan-out services.[2]

Interior scenes were shot at Republic Studios, but exterior scenes were shot on location in Sedona, Arizona. The whole cast and crew were flown to Arizona where art director Ernest Fegté had supervised the building of an entire town, as well as a ranch by the desert.[3]

Gail loved going on location, especially where she could enjoy the great outdoors of the scenic Arizona countryside, and work around horses. In fact, Paramount's official biography on Gail stated specifically that "the only period pictures she really wants to do are those of the Old West. That's because she prefers the styles of that day – small waist, flowing skirts, high neckline. And she wore such outfits off-screen before they once again became the fashion."[4] Gail was provided her own trailer for comfort where she could rest and relax between scenes. A huge tent was provided as a mess hall for cast and crew while they enjoyed their meals during the production of the film. Gail got a kick out of eating off of paper plates on occasion and "roughing it".

Gail and Wayne liked each other from the very start. Wayne, like all the other actors who ever worked with Gail, were enchanted by her gentle, ladylike manner, and stunning beauty. Gail was always so attractive to the male ego, never aggressive in manner or speech, quiet, soft spoken, and a good listener. A man never felt he had to "knock himself out" to impress her. Likewise, Gail was impressed with Wayne and his charm and rugged looks. He was in the mold of the Ideal Man she wanted to marry some day. In a 1944 newspaper article, Gail described the man she hoped to marry one day as "dark haired, blue eyed, not too good looking, who can kid her out of her moods. One who is reliable, self-confident, and able to cope with the world." Wayne seemed to fit the bill with his dark hair, blue eyes, and handsome six foot, four inch frame. In her eyes, Wayne was the ideal cowboy hero – tall, rugged, and very masculine. Gail also appreciated the way Wayne went out of his way to be kind, considerate, and willing to help her with the script. Like Ginger Rogers and Ray Milland, Wayne realized how uncomfortable Gail was in front of the movie lens, as well as her reluctance to perform before the ever present camera crew and technicians. Gail felt she could lean on Wayne for guidance and support to help her with her shyness and stage fright. He was exactly what she needed at the time, now that Bill Russell was no longer there to coach her through her films. A strong man to make her feel she wasn't alone in the world, that there was someone there to help her in time of need. This was one of the great reasons Gail was so appealing on film. She always brought out the protective nature in men, the feeling that here was a woman who needed to be rescued from all the danger and cruelty there was in the world.

Gail soon developed a serious crush on Wayne, which wasn't very surprising. In a 1950 interview, Gail was asked if she ever falls in love with the person she plays with in pictures. She replied, "Yes – a little bit. I think you have to if you're going to give a good performance. But at 6 O'clock I forget it."[5] Gail later paid Wayne the ultimate compliment, considering how much she was in love with her husband, Guy Madison. Asked if she thought her husband was the handsomest man in Hollywood as a writer quoted her as saying, Gail replied, "I never said that. Guy's personality is more important to me than his looks. I think the handsomest actor is John Wayne, as a matter of fact."[6]

In interviews on the set, Wayne would go out of his way to praise Gail to the press, and compliment her on her performance. They spent more time with each other on breaks, and during lunch. Gail saw in Wayne what she admired most in men – honesty, ruggedness, so self-assured, so positive in his approach to life, confident in his talent and his knowledge of the movie making business.

The on screen chemistry between Gail and John Wayne was very evident during filming. The scenes together, especially the love scenes, were poignant, touching, and very tender. I believe this role of Penelope Worth was Gail Russell's finest performance. Perhaps it was because the character of Penelope was so like Gail in real life. Penelope was shy, quiet in temperament, tender in affection, and yet so naïve in regards to the world in general. She was honest, and yet so surprised as to why her open pursuit of the outlaw Quirt Evans so embarrassed him. It was a role tailor made for Gail Russell.

During the filming of "Angel and the Badman," Wayne could sense that Gail was beginning to fall in love with him. However, being more mature than her, and just being recently married to former Mexican actress Esperanza "Chata" Bauer, Wayne knew that he had to be careful how he handled the situation. He told his secretary, Mary St. John, to let Gail know in no uncertain terms, and with tact, that he was just willing to be good friends. "Let her up easy," as Wayne would put it.[7] It was not a romance, as some have suggested. Gail was always romantically linked with her leading men, according to the gossip magazines, and the newspaper columnists. Yet that was just rumor and movie trade fodder. Gail was too honest, too principled, and yes, too naïve, to carry on an affair with a married man. I have to say, however, that if John Wayne had been unmarried at the time, he probably would have married Gail if he had the chance. She was just his type. Shy and reserved, gentle and kind, a lady in manner and bearing, great beauty, coupled with a quiet virtue and grace. Gail was also a brunette, which all Wayne's wives had in common.

Gail got along famously with her director, James Edward Grant, who also wrote the screenplay. He experienced the usual delays in filming in regards to Gail's stage fright and awkwardness while performing before the movie camera. He was patient and understanding, as was Wayne. Gail became friendly with co-stars Bruce Cabot and especially with veteran actor Harry Carey and his wife, Olive.

It was during filming the movie that Wayne became aware of how little Paramount Studios was paying Gail to be in his movie. He thought they were taking advantage of her good nature, so he persuaded director Grant to join him and contribute $500 each to compensate Gail for what she should be making. They suggested the money as a down payment on a new car for Gail, as she had told them that her present car was giving her trouble when driving to Republic Studios to film interior scenes.

"Angel and the Badman" finished shooting on schedule, and as was customary, the cast and crew were given a post production party to celebrate. The party was held at Eaton's Restaurant, and it was well past midnight when the celebration ended. Wayne offered to drive Gail home, and when they arrived at her house, it was early in the morning. Gail asked Wayne to come inside and meet her family, even at that late hour. He was introduced to her mother, father, and brother. By the time more refreshments were offered, Wayne had become quite intoxicated. He excused himself after a while, and phoned for a taxi to drive him home. He apologized to Gail's parents for his condition, and was assisted into a taxi by Gail's brother. The next morning, Wayne sent a dozen roses, together with a note, to Gail's mother, apologizing for his behavior. This incident was later blown way out of proportion by Chata Bauer in her divorce case against Wayne in October, 1953.

When "Angel and the Badman" was released to the theaters, it was well received by the public. Even the film critics gave a tip of the hat to John Wayne's latest western. The New York Times stated, "It is a safe bet that the Society of Friends will appreciate "Angel and the Badman." For the adventure, which has to do with the regeneration of an outlaw by a pretty

Quaker maid, is as much concerned with romance and the Pacifist policies of the Friends as it is with such standbys as rustlers and six shooters. In short, Mr. Wayne and company have sacrificed the usual roaring action to fashion a leisurely Western, which is different from, and a notch or two superior to the normal sagebrush saga. John Wayne makes a grim and laconic renegade... Gail Russell, a stranger to Westerns, is convincing as the lady who makes him see the light."[8]

"Angel and the Badman" is a much underrated film today, and it was, and still is, one of the best Westerns ever made. It was unusual for a Western, particularly a John Wayne Western, in its message – "Thou Shall Not Kill" and "Love Thy Neighbor". Its simple tale of kindness and brotherly love seemed to sit well with the movie going public.

The plot involved a wounded outlaw, Quirt Evans, played by John Wayne, who is rescued and befriended by Quaker family and their daughter, Penelope Worth, played by Gail. Evans is embarrassed by the honest, but naïve Penelope as she openly pursues him. Wayne and Gail's love scenes are charming and poignant. I consider it her best performance in a movie, and my favorite Gail Russell film. Wayne's character is reformed in the end, and gives up his outlaw ways for his Quaker sweetheart. The script was excellent, and the movie had everything a Western could possibly need – action, drama, romance, comedy, and beautiful scenery.

By July 2, 1947, Gail was now making $500 a week, guaranteed for 40 weeks. She was also scheduled for a bonus option of $5,000 by August 13, 1947, according to memo by William Meiklejohn to the payroll department at Paramount.

Gail's next assignment was in the all-star comedy/musical for Paramount, "Variety Girl." It boasted a cast of 40 stars, practically everyone on the Paramount lot. They included Bob Hope, Bing Crosby, Ray Milland, Alan Ladd, Barbara Stanwyck, Paulette Goddard, Dorothy Lamour, William Holden, Lizabeth Scott, Burt Lancaster, Veronica Lake, and others. Gail had two minor scenes, one scene as herself with a lost dog, and another small musical number with Diana Lynn as Indian maidens in a war dance. You could plainly tell in the musical dance number that Gail was very nervous and awkward in her performance. She was very aware of her lack of a singing voice, and she was always very self-conscious while dancing before the movie camera. The film had nothing to further her career as an actress, nevertheless, it was far more elaborate than Gail's cameo appearance in the earlier all-star epic, "Duffy's Tavern," in 1945. This time Gail received star billing in the opening credits, as well as in the movie posters and official Paramount Pressbook.

The movie plot involved screen newcomer Mary Hatcher as she tries to become a Hollywood star by invading the lot at Paramount Studios along with her roommate, played by Olga San Juan. They get into numerous comedy situations as they encounter various Paramount stars on their movie sets. The movie ends with a Variety Club Show involving all the stars in the circus show finale. The film was directed by George Marshall, and due to its all star cast, did well at the box office. The critics also gave film positive reviews, with Variety Film Review saying, "How can it miss with Crosby, Hope, Cooper, Milland, Ladd, Stanwyck, Goddard, Lamour, and the rest of the glittering Paramount stable of personalities. To the credit of all concerned it comes out even better."[9] Special praise was given to young newcomer Olga San Juan, as well as to Mary Hatcher, who had just made her film debut after coming off a successful run on Broadway as the feminine lead in "Oklahoma."

Paramount Studios was in the habit of booking their stars on radio programs to further publicize their films. They now asked Gail to appear on a radio show to promote her new film "Calcutta," allowing her two weeks to prepare for her appearance. It was a huge mistake. Her mother recalled the incident to Modern Screen Magazine, "The studios made the mistake of calling up and telling Gail two weeks in advance that they had booked her into a radio program. Well, that child worried, and fretted, and worked up such an anxiety in her mind that at the last moment she was a wreck, and unable to go through with the show. Her daddy is the same sort of nervous worrier, walks the floor until he's all worn down until the big moment arrives."[10]

Even at this stage in her career, Gail was still unable to perform before strangers or large crowds. That failure to perform that four line speech during the Thanksgiving Play at grammar school, so long ago in Chicago, was still to haunt Gail even as an adult. It was a fear she would never fully conquer.

Chapter 15
Gail and Guy

The movie fan magazines were now filled with stories on the latest romance rumors concerning Gail Russell and Guy Madison. Some stated they were already recently married, or that they were formally engaged, and soon to be married. Other stories had them quarreling, and now officially not seeing each other any more. Gail was seen at nightclubs and restaurants with other actors other than Guy. Little did they realize that Madison was out of town on other movie assignments, or that he had been sent across country to attend movie premiers and appear in stage plays to fulfill his contract with Selznick Studios. Even though Gail and Guy had known each other since 1945, between their respective movie schedules, they had actually spent little time together as a couple.

However, when Guy was in town between movie assignments, he and Gail spent as much time together as they could. Guy Madison was definitely Gail's first choice as a steady date, and Gail was certainly Guy's favorite lady. As he explained to magazine writer Sara Hamilton, "I love her because she has a heart. She cares about people, and she's generous, sentimental, and kind, and I love it. She's not like some of these girls around here who think only of themselves."[1] Guy reminded Sara of the time she admired Gail's purse, and before she knew it, Gail had emptied its contents, and gave it to her as a gift. When Sara tried to protest, Guy remarked, "Don't stop her. It's all a part of why I love her."[2]

Gail also appreciated Guy's honesty and simple sincerity. While he was expected by his studio to date a different girl every night for the sake of publicity, he never even looked at another girl while Gail was around. As Guy would often say, "She knows doggone well I'm a one-woman man."[3]

Gail had lately developed the habit of going on hunting expeditions with Guy. Madison had become quite expert with the bow and arrow. He had been taught by the legendary Howard Hill, who had coached Errol Flynn during the production of "The Adventures of Robin Hood" back in 1938. Guy even knew how to make his own arrows, and construct a bow. He taught Gail to shoot accurately, and she insisted on using a man size bow with a 46 lb. pull instead of a woman's bow with a 28 lb. pull. They were often photographed in the hills above Chatsworth, California, hunting for wild rabbit. Guy would later use them to make a rabbit stew that would last him for a week. He later made a leather quiver for Gail with her initials on it as a gift. As a further token of his affection for Gail, he gave her a gift of a small, gold Oscar, an exact replica of the coveted Academy Awards Oscar. On its base were the words, "Because You Have a Heart".[4]

Yet, for all his love for Gail, Guy couldn't help but notice some disturbing personal traits of hers that troubled him. For instance, her sudden moods of melancholy and brooding silence, those so-called "black moods" that Gail so often complained about. In those instances, Gail would often retreat into her room and paint or draw until the sad feelings would pass. Then she would emerge from those sullen periods and chatter away as if nothing was wrong. Then there was her annoying habit of avoiding large parties if she didn't know most of the people who were attending. Guy noticed that if he told her of the party well in advance, Gail would always come up with an excuse not to go. He later solved the problem by not telling her where they were going, and not telling Gail of the event until that day. This way Gail would spend all her nervous energy deciding what to wear, and how to fix her hair, rather than worrying about the coming affair.[5]

This was always a strange fear that Gail had most of her life. An unnatural fear of large crowds of people that she didn't know, whether at a party or at a movie premiere. It was as if she thought they would try to harm her for some reason. It could have been just a simple manifestation of her stage fright, or just a normal shyness at meeting people for the first time. Whatever the cause, it was very often the cause of Gail being accused of being unfriendly, when the opposite was the case.

There was also Gail's strange habit of always going to the movies alone, even as a young girl. Her mother recalled the time one of her boyfriends called her at home, and when informed by her mother that she had gone to the movie alone, the boyfriend was startled. "'Alone? What a strange girl. She should have told me. I'd have loved to take her.' He just didn't understand she wouldn't have gone with him. She just wants to put all her concentration on the movie. Even when she goes with me, she sits alone."[6]

Gail's parents were very proud of their daughter's accomplishments, and what she had done to help buy their new home. Gail's mother still provided for her two children, and always did their laundry, and made sure they always had a hot meal on the stove when they were hungry. Gail's brother, George, Jr., was a successful musician, and worked nights in a band in a local nightclub. Gail's mother still kept those scrapbooks on Gail and her career, cutting out and saving every newspaper article and magazine story she could find on Gail or her movies. There was even the eventual disagreement with Gail on how she should dress on special occasions. She hoped that now that Gail was a famous movie star, she would love to dress up more and be more glamorous. All she got in response to her request was, "Oh, Mother," delivered with a downward infliction. As Gladys recalled to Modern Screen Magazine in 1948, "After she got the Paramount contract and the studios would call her in for a conference about a script, with a director or a producer, I'd beg her to dress up: 'Look like a movie star for a change,' I'd say. 'You're the one who needs to grow up, Mother,' she'd say. 'This is the way I looked when Paramount sent for me in the first place. I never tried to wow them with wardrobe, why start now.'"[7] Yet, that was Gail Russell. She didn't even own a formal evening gown until a couple of years ago. She went to parties and movie premiers, and looked the movie star, yet that was only because the studio insisted that she look the part. Gail much preferred to wear simple slacks or blue jeans with a blouse at home, or when she went hunting or sailing with Guy Madison on weekends. Even most of her movie star portraits and candids have her wearing usually a simple dress or sports clothes. Seldom is she photographed wearing an elaborate evening gown with jewels and furs that Ava Gardner or Lana Turner would wear.

Gail was so unlike your typical glamorous movie star. Yet, in natural beauty, Gail Russell was second to no one. There have been many actresses as lovely as Gail in the history of Hollywood. However, there was not one actress more beautiful than she was. Gail was devastatingly lovely. If you ever saw her in person, you would be startled at her beautiful, sapphire blue eyes. That luxurious, raven black hair, and that low whisper-like voice so soothing to the ear. Gail was just too beautiful to last. Whenever I think of Gail now, I am reminded of that famous verse by the English poet Percy Bysshe Shelley, "For she was beautiful, her beauty made the bright world dim, and everything beside seemed like the fleeting image of a shade."

One of Gail's earliest portraits from 1943.

Gail with director Lewis Allen on the set of
"Our Hearts Were Young and Gay," 1944.

Gail seated at Chasen's Restaurant with Peter Lawford, 1945.

Gail in an Easter holiday pose by
"Whitey" Schafer, 1945.

Gail poses with her Maltese Terrier "Corny," 1946.

George and Gladys help their daughter answer fan mail at their Westwood,
California home, 1947.

Gail in a shot at the Paramount Ranch in
Agoura Hills 1947. Photo by Malcom Bulloch.

Gail examines her archery skills at a target range,
1947. Gail was an excellent archer having been
taught by world champion archer Howard Hill.

Gail in a publicity shot for "Night has a Thousand Eyes," 1947.

Gail with her Cocker Spaniel, "Kelly," 1947

Gail plays with a young colt on the Paramount
Ranch. 1947. Gail was a devout lover of animals.

Gail in a casual portrait by "Bud" Fraker, 1947.

Gail in a costume for "Night has a Thousand Eyes," 1947.

Gail at the Paramount Ranch, 1947.

Gail at the Paramount Ranch, 1947.

Gail with co-star John Wayne on the outdoor set of
"Angel and the Badman," 1947.

Gail and her mother Gladys, 1948. Gladys was instrumental in getting Gail to sign a contract with Paramount in 1942.

Candid portrait of Gail taken at her apartment in Westwood, California,1948.

Gail and Guy at a yacht party in 1948.

Gail spends some quiet time reading a book with her beloved Cocker Spaniel "Kelly," 1949.

Gail with co-star John Payne. From the movie "El Paso," 1949.

Gail in a costume portrait from the movie
"The Great Dan Patch," 1949.

Chapter 16
Night Has A Thousand Eyes

Gail's next film assignment came to her quite by accident. Paramount had scheduled Joan Caulfield to portray Jean Courtland in "Night Has A Thousand Eyes" with Edward G. Robinson and John Lund. However, Caulfield became ill, and was unable to start filming. Paramount then asked Gail to star in the project, and she accepted. That bonus of $5,000 she was given on August 13, 1947 was specifically for her role in "Night Has A Thousand Eyes." This in addition to the $500 a week Gail was making in the minimum wage clause of her Paramount contract.

The film was to be directed by John Farrow, who had worked with Gail previously in "Calcutta," and knew how to handle her shyness and stage fright. It was Gail's first and only "glamour" role at Paramount, with fashionable costumes designed by Edith Head, and make-up supervision by talented Wally Westmore. Gail was painstakingly photographed by noted cinematographer John Seitz. Director Farrow would use more of the traditional "close-up" shots of Gail to showcase her unusual beauty, yet he was aware of her unnatural fear of the camera's lens while she was performing. It was always a tragic irony that Gail should always be afraid of the motion picture camera, despite the fact that it was her greatest asset at displaying her great beauty. It was also a great mistake not to photograph Gail in color for this role, as she was at the prime of her beauty at twenty-four. It would have been interesting to see what "Night Has A Thousand Eyes" would have done for Gail's career if it had been photographed in glorious technicolor. Then the movie public would have seen how lovely Gail Russell truly was. Even the great movie still photographers at Paramount, such as Whitey Schaffer, Bud Fraker, and Malcolm Bulloch, failed to capture Gail's great beauty. From the glamour black and white portraits to the gorgeous color transparencies, the photographers always failed to capture Gail's inner beauty. In all her films, Gail's exquisite loveliness never fully registered on the silver screen. Perhaps it was due to her unnatural fear of the movie camera due to her stage fright. Or perhaps it was due to the fact, as her mother thought, that Gail had never been in love.[1]

This was to be Gail's second Paramount picture without the assistance of good friend and drama coach, Bill Russell. As in "Calcutta," Gail was uncertain whether she could perform successfully without her former coach and mentor. Again, she struggled at first, but director Farrow was patient and understanding, and was very cautious to warn Gail of her usual bad habit of wringing her hands during an emotional or dramatic scene. Gail was also fortunate to have two very talented and professional stage actors as co-stars in the likes of Edward G. Robinson and John Lund. Robinson was especially helpful to Gail as he worked with her off camera during rehearsals, and went over the dialogue with her during the many script changes. It had to help with her confidence to see how a true professional actor polishes his acting performance before he goes before the movie camera.

Despite fellow actor Robinson's help, and the patient understanding of director Farrow, Gail still was extremely nervous before the lens of the movie camera. She just couldn't completely relax while performing, and all her nervous energy was extended in trying to calm her extreme anxiety while making movies. It had now become a habit with Gail to visit Lucy's Restaurant on Melrose Avenue, across the street from Paramount Studios, during lunchtime, to have a cocktail to calm her nerves, and to relax. There was also the nearby Cock and Bull Restaurant to serve the same purpose. She convinced herself that it was just a temporary remedy to help her get through a day's work while filming. Gail didn't realize it was becoming an uncontrollable addiction to alcohol. She would soon develop the habit of smuggling a bottle of vodka in her dressing room so as to avoid the necessity of leaving the lot to get her needed drink. It was the beginning of a sad, downward trend in her movie career that was ultimately to lead to a tragic end.

There was also a brief moment of unexpected joy during the filming of "Night Has A Thousand Eyes." Gail was visited on the set by actress Jane Russell, who was filming her newest movie with Bob Hope on the soundstage next door, "The Paleface." She and Gail were former classmates at Van Nuys High School back in 1940. Gail recalled how Jane tried to get her to overcome her shyness at school. How she would phone her at the last minute to join her and her brothers to go to a party, not giving Gail time to think of an excuse not to go. Guy Madison would use the same method in the present to cure Gail of her shyness and timidity. Gail laughed at the memory of Jane wearing the sweater of her boyfriend, famous athlete Bob Waterfield, to class that stretched all the way down to her knees. It was a happy reunion.[2]

The filming of "Night Has A Thousand Eyes" was finished within the six weeks timeframe. The film was an above average "film noir" that also dealt with the paranormal or supernatural phenomena. Gail portrayed Jean Courtland, who is told by clairvoyant John Triton, played b Edward G. Robinson, that she is to die "beneath the stars" by an unknown assailant despite the help of her fiancé, Elliot Carson, played by John Lund. The story reveals Triton's part in Jean's life, and at the climax of the film, results in his death while saving her from an untimely end. The film had an interesting twist in describing the paranormal, and ones ability to predict the future. It was a minor disappointment at the box office, but it did attempt to display Gail's rare beauty on the screen. Gail, for one of the few times in her film career, was not in a "period" film, and could wear modern, fashionable clothes to display her charming, feminine beauty. Photoplay Magazine even had a multiple page photo spread of Gail in her Edith Head wardrobe in their October issue of 1948.[3]

The movie critics were not so kind in the reviews of the film, however, and the usually cynical critic of the New York Times, Bosley Crowther, was especially harsh in his review when he stated, "'Night Has A Thousand Eyes'... is such unadulterated hokum that it almost ingratiates itself... But it doesn't... because it tries to put over the pretense that it is serious and solemn stuff. If somewhere along in the beginning of this patently fanciful tale about a man who can foresee the future, the audience were taken aside and told it was just so much nonsense, it might be acceptable. But no... we are asked to believe that a fellow might really have a supernatural sight...

Now, this sort of thing could be charming, or funny, at least, if done in a spirit of thinly veiled fooling or out-and-out fantasy. But here it is done in somber fashion, with Edward G. Robinson playing the gent as a figure of topic proportions... and Gail Russell plays the young lady whom he vainly forewarns against peril in a mood of distinct melancholia, with a face all the way down to here."[4] Ouch! Needless to say, it is a safe bet that Gail's mother didn't save that newspaper clipping to past in her daughter's movie scrapbooks.

Gail's next movie project was to be loaned out by Paramount Studios once again, and to be reunited with John Wayne at Republic Studios.

Chapter 17
Wake Of The Red Witch

In a memo to payroll department dated May 28, 1948, William Meiklejohn authorized the final option to Gail's original contract with paramount for $750. This was the maximum amount she would earn, guaranteed for 40 weeks a year, in addition to her salary each picture. Gail was by now one of the most popular actresses at Paramount, and was getting bigger and better roles to play. This was due in part to the efforts by her personal agents, Barbara Eddington and Jerry Cloutman whom Gail had signed with after leaving her former agent, Myron Selznick, in 1946.

Republic Studios had purchased Garland Roark's famous sea story, "Wake of the Red Witch," in 1948, and had signed its biggest star, John Wayne, to star in the film. Wayne had asked the studio to again borrow Gail Russell from Paramount, as he had enjoyed working with her in "Angel and the Badman" previously. Wayne thought they worked well together, their on screen chemistry was so evident on screen, and that Western had done so well at the box office. In that same memo from William Meiklejohn dated May 28, 1948, Paramount agreed to have Gail paid $3,125 a week for eight weeks while "Wake of the Red Witch" was being filmed. Paramount was also paid $125,000 to loan Gail out to Republic for her services. Wayne and Republic Studios thought Gail was well worth the price.

Although Gail was never too fond of Paramount loaning her out to other studios, Gail was happy that at least she got to work with John Wayne once again. Republic Studios production company went into high gear to bring Garland Roark's sea faring story to the silver screen. Their Special Effects Department constructed three full size replicas of a 19th Century three-masted sailing vessel, one replica over 200 feet long. In addition, they constructed a huge tank for the underwater sequences that measured 55 feet in diameter at the top, and 16 feet deep at the bottom. Producer Edmund Grainger also hired 100 Polynesian extras from Hawaii, including former Olympic champion and world famous surfer Duke Kahanamoku. Many of the exterior scenes were shot on location at Rancho Santa Anita in Arcadia, home of the late "Lucky" Baldwin who spent millions of dollars planting tropical plants and trees on the property. It was the scene of many Hollywood movie and television films, including "Tarzan" and "Fantasy Island."[1] It is now known as the Los Angeles County Aboretum.

Gail had a fun time making the picture with its elaborate South Sea Island scenery. One scene included an elaborate Luau sequence where two tons of bananas and fruit were purchased, along with hundreds of extras dressed in Polynesian costumes. It was while filming "Wake of the Red Witch" that Gail developed a desire to visit the Hawaiian Islands for a vacation, and had hoped that Guy Madison could accompany her there if and when their movie schedules permitted.

In the movie, Gail portrays Angelique Desaix, the young niece of a French Commissioner on the island of Tahuata in the South Pacific. She becomes the love interest between Captain Ralls, played by John Wayne, and Mayrant Sidney, played by Luther Adler. The plot includes a scuttled ship, a search for fabulous pearls, a duel with a giant sea clam and an octopus, a love triangle, and a surprise finale including the dead Angelique and Ralls as they sail away into the sunset aboard the ghostly "Red Witch." Although Gail received top billing along with Wayne, she was only in about one-third of the film involving the flashback sequences. While she was on screen, however, Gail was radiant in her scenes with Wayne. Their love scenes together were especially tender and heartwarming. Although Gail had gotten over her "crush" over Wayne during the filming of "Angel and the Badman," the year previously, you could still tell by her performance that she was till very fond of him, and that emotion carried over well in her love scenes with him. This was to be one of the few films that hero Wayne would perish in, and the only film in which Gail's character would die. It was an average John Wayne film, with a little less action than usual. Wayne's character, Captain Ralls, was a little on the dark side, and more grim than usual. It wasn't as good as "Angel and the Badman," but it did well at the box office. In fact, it was the top money maker for Republic Studios up to that time. In addition to Gail and Wayne, the cast included Luther Adler, Gig Young, Adele Mara, and Paul Fix, who was a constant regular in many of John Wayne's films.

While "Wake of the Red Witch" was popular with the movie going public, it was not as popular with the critics. The New York Times Review, in the person of perennial cynic Bosley Crowther was particularly harsh. He wrote, "No one can say that Republic has exercised caution or restraint in making a motion picture of Garland Roark's popular "Wake of the Red Witch"... everything in it... bespeaks a magnificent indifference to the demands of illusion or good sense... Right from the start of this fable... the ballast of reason and continuity is casually tossed overboard. Harry Brown's and Kenneth Gamet's rambling script will be a distinct determent to the accumulation of interest or suspense. The eye of the beholder will have to be wholly naïve not to spot the conspicuous fakery of the special effects and even the sets. John Wayne is lusty and swaggering... Luther Adler is elaborately tricky... Gail Russell is provokingly flaccid as the lady for whose love they contend."[2]

Despite what the critics had to say about "Wake of the Red Witch," Gail had a wonderful time making the film. There were numerous candid shots on the set with Gail joking and laughing with Wayne on the set. She was truly very fond of him, and even did an oil paint portrait of Wayne which she kept in her home. Gail was thankful that Wayne, like Alan Ladd, Ray Milland, and Edward G. Robinson, went out of their way to help Gail with her scenes. Wayne was, for the rest of her life, her personal hero.

After completing "Wake of the Red Witch," Gail had hoped to spend a much needed vacation with Guy Madison in Hawaii, but he was unable to get out of a commitment to perform back East in a play, and Gail was assigned by Paramount to star in another film. They had planned to sail to Hawaii on a luxury cruise with a couple of their married friends, but had to cancel when they day of departure arrived. It was to be a bitter disappointment for Gail and Guy, refusing to joke about it later, and it remained a touchy subject between them.[3]

However, Gail continued to see Guy Madison on a regular basis whenever their movie schedules allowed it. Gail was getting used to one of Guy Madison's favorite foods – milk. He would drink it at all hours of the day or night. In fact, his meals consisted mainly of hamburgers or steaks, with salads loaded with mayonnaise, all washed down with a quart of milk. There was the time Gail and Guy were driving home at two o'clock in the morning after a night of dining and dancing with Diana Lynn and Henry Willson. Suddenly Guy had a desire to drink some milk. There wasn't a place open that late at night between Hollywood and the beach. Gail had informed Guy that there wasn't any milk at her house, but she knew a girlfriend of hers lived close by, and when they saw her lights on, they asked if they could come in a raid her ice box in search of some milk. Guy found a pint of the white liquid and drank it. Guy was very grateful to Gail's friend, although he had never met her in his life before that unexpected visit.[4]

Guy Madison also liked to tease Gail on occasion. There was the time he sent for a surprise package on the set of "Our Hearts Were Growing Up." Guy knew she was under doctor's orders to take pills to relax her, and to avoid cigarettes and coffee in her daily routine. A messenger delivered box arrived on the movie set with no identifying card. Inside was a large bottle labeled H_2O, together with three matching colored boxes with the labels "Before Breakfast," "Before Luncheon," and "Before Dinner." Inside the boxes were mothballs. Also in the box was a canvas bag filled with coffee beans, along with a label that read "Ixnay." There were also packages of chocolate cigarettes with the warning label of "Verboten." By now, Gail knew who the gig gift was from, but she couldn't figure a way to pay Guy back.[5]

Guy still liked to tease Gail about the time a magazine asked her to pose for a few photographs while pretending to shoot a bow and arrow. When the magazine went to press, letters came pouring into their editorial office from irate archery experts who pointed out that Gail was photographed holding the bow upside down. Gail was upset that Guy, the bow and arrow expert, had not warned her of her big mistake. Guy replied, "Poor child. Any cluck should know enough not to hold the bow upside down." To which Gail replied, "I figured if a bone head like you could manage..."[6] Gail would always get back at Guy by kidding him about his lack of expertise whenever they went dancing or horseback riding.

Gail was dating Guy almost exclusively now, and they were a regular item in all the Hollywood gossip columns. When asked by a reporter which character trait Gail most admired in Guy, she replied it was his honesty. "I let other people swoon over his tall and terrific looks. What I go for is the way Guy gives you a straight answer. He'll level with you even though he knows his answer may hurt… That's personal integrity, a wonderful quality anywhere, a practically unique quality in Hollywood. Maybe it's even a stern quality, but I like it because you know where you stand with Guy."[7]

Chapter 18
Moonrise

Gail was to return to Republic Studios in 1948 for her next motion picture. She was again loaned out by Paramount to that studio to star in "Moonrise," a somber, backwoods drama starring Dane Clark, also to be directed by veteran Frank Borzage. In a memo by Meiklejohn, Gail was to be paid $3,125 a week for eight weeks.[1] She had never worked with Borzage before, so the director had to become accustomed to Gail's "difficulties" while performing before the movie camera. The word had gone out long ago among producers and directors concerning her shyness and constant stage fright.

Borzage learned to have the set closed during Gail's scenes, and not allow any unnecessary onlookers to view the action. This helped tremendously, yet she would tend to stiffen whenever the camera zoomed in for a close-up shot. This would necessitate a "retake" and delay shooting a scene. It was a constant heartache for Gail, and would sometimes drive her to tears. It was also a constant annoyance for directors. Gail's bad habit of constantly wringing her hands during an emotional scene was particularly bothersome for Bozage. As an example of his annoyance at Gail for this bad habit of hers, the final cut of the church scene in "Moonrise" had a close-up of Gail's hands as she nervously clutched a handkerchief while singing a hymn.

Despite the minor setbacks in production, Gail managed to finish the film on time. There was even one amusing incident that befell her during filming. While shooting an idyllic love scene, the canoe in which Gail was riding suddenly tipped over and dumped her into muddy waters. As everyone rushed to her rescue, Gail stood up in the three foot deep pond, and raised a restraining hand to announce, "This moment I want to live all by myself." She walked ashore toward respectful crew members who knew from experience that few stars would react so humorously to the situation.[2]

In addition to Gail and Dane Clark, "Moonrise" also starred Ethel Barrymore, Allyn Joslyn, and Rex Ingram. The story involved Gilly Johnson, played by Gail, a young school teacher in a small, Southern town, whose boyfriend, Danny Hawkins, played by Dane Clark, accidentally kills his childhood bully in a fist fight. Gilly tries to change Danny's attitude toward the local townspeople, and life in general. She eventually discovers his guilt in the killing of his childhood bully, and after a police chase through a dark and muddy swamp, Danny eventually agrees to turn himself in and face his judgment. It was only a fair melodrama, and didn't do nearly as well at the box office as had "Wake of the Red Witch." Critics were likewise lukewarm to the release of "Moonrise." The New York Times review was typical of the film's response when it stated, "The ancient argument as to which medium tells a story best, written words or pictorial images, is again brought into focus by "Moonrise." And, using this adaptation of Theodore Strauss' movie... the book towers above the picture... But the terrible weight of persecution, guilt and loneliness felt by Danny Hawkins, the haunted hero, is indicated obliquely in the film… Except for an occasional bit of forced story acting, Dane Clark, Danny Hawkins is a restrained but haunted youth plagued by memories and desperately striving for latent manhood… Gail Russell makes a convincingly compassionate heroine…[3]

Gail's unusual positive film review by critics was not surprising. Her character, Gilly Johnson, was involved with her boyfriend, Danny Hawkins, who was tormented by his guilty conscience and surrounded by an antagonistic society that never let him forget that his father was hanged for murder. Danny was constantly at war with his environment, and sought desperately for a way out. Gail could identify with that struggle. She was constantly struggling to endure in a movie career she found increasingly hard to love, or even enjoy.

Guy Madison had been a constant visitor at Republic Studios while Gail was filming "Moonrise," and provided a much needed time of relaxation for her while enduring the constant stress and anxiety of filmmaking. He noticed that Gail was losing weight, and that her nervousness seemed to be increasing. Guy recommended Gail see a doctor, who later set down a severe set of rules for her. She must not smoke. She must not drink, even coffee. She should be in bed and asleep every night by nine o'clock. Gail was supposed to drink an average of at least a gallon of water daily, and after each meal she was ordered to swallow a relaxing pill.[4] This was nearly impossible for Gail to do. She was an avid smoker and coffee drinker, and was a natural "night flower", coming into her most wide awake state when darkness fell. Gail agreed to compromise her lifestyle, smoking less and cutting back on the coffee drinking. However, she soon resorted back to her old habits because the stress to her nervous system proved too much due to the tremendous struggle to overcome her stage fright while performing before the movie camera. Gail needed her cigarettes, her coffee, and especially her daily alcohol to endure her movie lifestyle. Her constant nervous condition was enhanced by her extreme addiction to nicotine through her constant cigarette smoking, as well as her dependence on caffeine with her abundant coffee drinking. Gail was an avid coffee drinker, sometimes consuming a dozen cups of black coffee a day.[5] This was usually her breakfast, and she was never really hungry until the evening hours. This was a bad habit of hers since childhood, and was the main reason she only had one large meal a day to sustain her. Her average body weight would be usually 110 lbs., as opposed to the usual 125 lbs. weight of a woman of her stature of 5 feet, 4 ½ inches. This lack of good eating habit, combined with her smoking and drinking would eventually catch up with Gail. Add also the medication she was taking to "relax" her nervous tension while performing before the camera, and it would all eventually create a "perfect storm" situation that would end Gail's career at Paramount. This, however, was still in the future, and Gail still did her best to hide from family and friends her unhappiness at remaining a movie star.

Gail had hoped that somehow she and Guy Madison could make a movie together, considering how popular they were as a romantic couple in all those movie fan magazines that were at the local newsstands. However, when producer David Selznick loaned out Guy to United Artists in 1948 for his next film, "Texas Brooklyn and Heaven," his co-star was not Gail, but her good friend, Diana Lynn. Gail was merciless in teasing Guy and Diana about their love scenes while pretending to be very jealous. It was her way of paying back Guy for all those practical jokes he had used on Gail during their courtship. However, when asked by a magazine writer, Gail had stated that she hoped she and Guy could do a movie together, preferably a Western.[6]

It was at this time when Gail was back at Paramount waiting for her next film assignment, that the studio wanted to give the press an opportunity to interview her. Gail was notorious for avoiding press interviews, but this time the studio wanted noted Hollywood press reporter Jim Henaghen to interview her. Henaghen had been a cub reporter back in 1945, and had written an unfavorable gossip column that had stated that Gail and a fellow Paramount starlet, probably Helen Walker, had been seen drinking and carousing at a local Hollywood bar. Paramount had wanted to reconcile Gail to Henaghen, who held a position of some prominence then, and the Paramount executives had arranged for a hostess to manage a conciliatory meeting in the director's office. The hostess looked at Gail and Henaghen and said, "Why don't you kids shake hands, and make up?" Gail thought it over, very carefully. She knew that Henaghen had written that unfavorable column not as a concerned citizen, but as a smart alleck young reporter looking for a "scoop" to sell newspapers. She remembered how hurt and upset she had been when called into the office of the studio head, and reprimanded for her behavior. Gail had never forgotten that incident, nor the reporter responsible for turning her in. Never taking her eyes from his face, she calmly told the hostess, "Tell him to go to the devil."[7] Years later, Jim Henaghen would remember that incident when writing about Gail's death in 1961. He remembered Gail quite vividly when he wrote, "I knew Gail Russell from the day she first came to pictures. She was an exquisitely beautiful kid, still in her teens, with eyes as blue as a wood hyacinth, direct and daring in their stare, almost challenging. Her mouth was soft and full, and spoke of warmth within her. Her hair was raven black and long – and there was no ego in her beauty, it was as natural as the unprejudiced loveliness of an animal, unadorned and without conceit. She was, to be sure, a natural for pictures... It is with regret that I must admit that I was one of the first to hurt her..."[8]

By the end of 1948, Gail had been in fifteen films in five years, some of them almost made back to back with little or no time off to recuperate. Paramount was determined to get their money's worth out of her in the determined effort to make a great star out of her. Little did they realize that it was taking a tremendous physical and mental toll, and that it would eventually all come crashing down on her in a tragic way. The following year was to be the greatest one for Gail, career-wise, because she was to star in four films in 1949. In addition, she was to bring a successful conclusion to her fabled romance with Guy Madison.

Chapter 19
Song Of India

Republic Studios in February, 1948, issued a short biography on Gail from the Director of Publicity, Mort Goodman. In their brief studio biography, they stated that Gail Russell was her legal name, her birthplace was in Chicago, Illinois, and that her birth date was September 23rd, rather than the September 21st, as in the Paramount Studios biography. They gave her height as 5 feet, 5 inches, rather than the 5 feet, 4 ½ inches in the Paramount version. Gail's weight was given as 109 pounds, close to the 110 pounds in the Paramount biography. Her eyes were stated as blue, as in the Paramount version, but her hair color was given as auburn, rather than black as in the official Paramount biography.

The Republic biography also expanded on Gail's artistic qualities when it stated, "Away from the cameras, Gail continues her art as a hobby. She works in either oils or with pencil, considering water colors 'too dainty' unless absolutely demanded by the subject. Although she scoffs at critical praise, people who have seen her portraits claim that the world lost a good commercial artist when she left her drawing board in favor of acting. She recently has added clay modeling to her pursuits, and has done some excellent work in this medium."[1]

As to Gail's personal preferences, Republic Studios Publicity Department biography added this anecdote, "She dislikes housework and cooking, and reads a lot of poetry. Edgar Allen Poe being her favorite. The movie stars she most admires are Ginger Rogers and James Stewart. She wears sports clothes, suits and slacks almost exclusively, and abhors anything that's "too dressy." It wasn't until 1947 – after she had been a star for several years – that she bought her first formal!"[2]

By January, 1949, Gail was in the prime of her movie career. She was making $750 a week, the top maximum wage in her contract with Paramount, guaranteed for at least 40 weeks a year.[3] Gail was also in the final year of her original contract which lasted only seven years. Therefore, she would be in a great position to renew her old contract, or sign a new one for more money.

In February, 1949, Gail was in between film assignments, and as luck would have it, so was Guy Madison. It was one of the very rare instances where they could plan a vacation together without their film commitments ruining their vacation plans. They didn't want to repeat the bitter disappointment of not traveling to Hawaii. Gail and Guy had decided to visit Havana, Cuba, for a short two week vacation. However, Gail had wanted to visit her aunt and uncle in Chicago first, and then take a short flight to Miami, Florida, where they would board a steamer to Cuba. There was an amusing incident involving Gail as she waited on deck just before the ship set sail for Cuba. A newlywed couple were going up the gangplank as they were showered with rice and confetti while being serenaded by a small band on the deck. Among all that gayety and laughter, there was Gail Russell with her arms perched on the ship's railing with big, fat tears rolling down her cheeks. She was that sentimental.[4]

When Gail and Guy landed in Cuba, they couldn't wait to go sightseeing, so they hired a local guide by the name of Joe Tour, who drove an old limousine. They drove along the scenic streets of Havana and attended the big fiesta that night. The following morning Gail and Guy were offered a tour of the local countryside for free by their guide, Joe Tour. However, the condition was that he would borrow his brother's old car for the tour rather than the customary sleek black limousine. During the tour, unfortunately, the car broke down while trying to climb a steep hill. Gail remembered with amusement the sight of she and Guy pushing that old car up the hill for forty-five minutes until they could get in the car while it coasted down hill. Eventually they managed to make their way back to their hotel.[5] Despite this minor setback, Gail and Guy enjoyed their vacation tremendously, and returned home loaded with souvenirs and gifts for family and friends.

When Gail returned to Paramount Studios from her vacation, she was surprised to learn that she was loaned out once again to Columbia Pictures for her next film, "Song of India" with Sabu and Turhan Bey. In a memo by Meiklejohn to the payroll department, Gail was to be paid $2,500 a week for six weeks.[6] It proved to be very profitable for Paramount Studios to loan Gail out on film assignments on occasion, but Gail wasn't too fond of the practice. However, she never refused a film assignment, even though at times it seemed like being sold to another film studio like a piece of merchandise. She was always too timid and well mannered to object to her home studio, and was never really interested in becoming a great movie actress. Unlike other stars like Bette Davis, Olivia de Havilland, or Katherine Hepburn, Gail never complained about not having better film roles to play. She feared the movie camera rather than adored it.

Columbia Studios went to an unusual expense to film "Song of India." Producer-director Albert S. Rogell hired a menagerie of wild animals to make his movie more realistic in its India locale. An assortment of tigers, panthers, leopards, bears, elephants, crocodiles, even vultures were added to give realism to the film. In some scenes the actor Sabu had to actually interact with a live Bengal tiger.[7]

Gail loved working with animals, especially younger ones. She was thrilled to work with a bear cub and two tiger cubs in her scenes with Sabu. There was one incident, however, which Gail wasn't too fond of being involved in. During a break in filming a scene on location, Gail sat down on a log to rest and read her script. The log turned out to be a live crocodile. Needless to say, Gail leaped to her feet in a hurry and got well out of harm's way.[8] Despite this incident, Gail was a real trouper, and insisted that she do whatever the script required her to do. Like her co-star Sabu and Turhan Bey, she refused to use double in those scenes with the wild animals in unprotected areas.

While shooting exterior action scenes on location in the mountains of Malibu, California, Gail also gave the movie crew an example of her skill as an archer with bow and arrow. Using her personal man-sized bow with a 46 pound pull, as opposed to a woman's 28 pound pull, Gail startled the company by driving an arrow almost completely through a young sycamore sapling. A feat, incidentally, that no man in the company could equal.[9]

Director Rogell worked well with Gail, and had no serious problems with her customary stage fright. This recurring fear of Gail's while performing in front of a movie camera in an open movie set was only severe when working in a different studio other than at Paramount. She gradually became used to regular crew members while at Paramount. However, while at a different studio, Gail was uncomfortable acting in front of electricians, cameramen, grips, and other movie studio personnel she wasn't used to seeing. That memory of a little grammar school girl who was terrified to speak her lines at the Thanksgiving Play so long ago in Chicago, would occasionally return to haunt her once again. However, this time at Columbia Studios, Gail's camera shyness was less severe, possibly due to the fact that she was also working with animals. This seemed to have a relaxing effect on her, as well as Albert Rogell's patient direction. Whatever the reason, Gail finished the film on time and without any unnecessary delays.

The movie plot involved Princess Tara, played by Gail, who is on a hunting safari with her fiancé, Prince Gopal, played by Turhan Bey. While in the jungle, they encounter a lost prince, Ramdar, played by Sabu, who warns them not to hunt in his jungle domain. There is a jungle safari and a kidnapping plot involving Princess Tara. There follows an exciting climax with a duel to the death in a lost jungle temple with a wounded Bengal tiger. At the end, Sabu winds up with Gail as his bride as they drive off amid cheering subjects. It was an average film considering the meager amount Columbia spent on interior sets. "Song of India" was no blockbuster at the box office, but it did please the younger set.

The movie critics, however, were not as generous in their write up of the movie. The New York Times Film Review was a prime example when they wrote, "The eight act variety bill at the Palace is just about the whole show there this week, for the accompanying movie, "Song of India," is a very poor supplementary attraction. Filmed in sepia on a Columbia Studio back lot jungle, inhabited by Sabu, Gail Russell, Turhan Bey, a ragged assortment of extras and tigers, elephants, crocodiles, etc., "Song of India" runs its commonplace course without causing any excitement...[10]

Gail didn't have to wait long for her next film project, and this time she would be back at her home studio at Paramount in a Western that would be filmed in color. It was to be the only color film that Gail would appear in while she was at the height of her beauty and fame.

Chapter 20
El Paso

Gail was glad to return to Paramount Studios for her next film, "El Paso," a Western with John Payne, Sterling Hayden, Dick Foran, and for comic relief, George "Gabby" Hayes. The movie was to be directed by Louis R. Foster, who also wrote the screenplay. The new production team at Paramount, William H. Pine and William H. Thomas, financed the project. Paramount had also introduced its new color film process, "Cinecolor," which was supposedly to replace the more familiar "Technicolor" standard technology. This new color film process should have shown Gail's unusual beauty, her blue eyes and black hair, to film audiences who were unaware of just how lovely Gail Russell really was.

The director of photography for the film was Ellis W. Carter, but his best efforts failed to bring out Gail's true loveliness. Maybe it was the way the film was shot, or perhaps it was the shortcomings of the new "Cinecolor" film process, or even due to the lackluster script. Whatever the reason, it was a major disappointment with regard to Gail's screen appearance. Even the costumes failed to enhance her beauty. Perhaps if they had been more close-up shots of Gail in her dramatic scenes, the audience would have seen unusual coloring, those soulful, sapphire blue eyes, and that luxurious, raven black hair. Yet most of her directors noticed how Gail would stiffen whenever the camera would zoom in for her close-up shots, as if she were terrified of the camera's lens. This was too noticeable on film, so most of her directors avoided any close shots of Gail in her films. This was a great tragedy where Gail was concerned, for the movie camera was actually her best friend, and would have been the perfect medium to showcase her beauty and talent. It was always that eternal paradox for Gail, this love and fear of the movie camera. It was one of the major reasons she so disliked making movies for a living.

For the role of Susan Jeffers, Gail was to be paid $2,500 a week for eight weeks, according to that memo from William Meiklejohn to the payroll department.[1] Director Foster had never worked with Gail before, but he already knew of her acute shyness before the camera, and was very patient with his direction. Gail loved doing Western movies ever since she worked with John Wayne in "Angel and the Badman" in 1947. She also loved the opportunity to work with horses, and was a very good rider. Gail performed quite well with he new leading man, John Payne, who was acting in his first Western. He was to say later in an interview that Gail Russell was one of his favorite actresses to work with. That was saying a lot, since his co-stars had included the lovely and talented Betty Grable, Alice Faye, and Gene Tierney.

The movie plot involved Gail as Susan Jeffers, a Southern Belle from Charleston, South Carolina, who leaves to go West to the Texas town of El Paso. She left home with her father, played by Henry Hull, who had become an alcoholic while serving as a respected judge in their hometown. (It would be a sad irony that Gail herself would become an alcoholic later on in life, and inherit a tragic ending). Susan Jeffers is later joined by her fiancé, Clayton Fletcher, played by John Payne, who later tries to battle the town's notorious lawlessness. There are the customary fistfights, shootouts, and horse chases to complete the customary Western horse opera. The script by the director, Foster, did the film no favors. It was, and it still is, one of the worst Westerns ever made. Even the comic relief of veteran Western actor Gabby Hayes failed to improve the movie. Despite the great cast, it only did a modest business at the box office. I am sorry to say it was the worst movie of Gail's career, considering her star status at the time. The movie critics were almost unanimous in their disapproval of the film. The New York Times film critic, Bosley Crowther, was typical of the reviews when he stated, "Time was when Pine and Thomas . . . were just the rough and ready producers of low budget films at Paramount . . . But then Paramount decided to give them a little more range – and apparently a good bit more money with which to make a film … It let them use Cinecolor and a comparatively classy cast, including John Payne, Gail Russell, Sterling Hayden, and Henry Hull . . . But "El Paso" is rather a third or fourth rate rehash of a standard Western plot . . ."[2] Even the perennial cynic Bosley Crowther seemed correct in his assessment of "El Paso."

Though "El Paso" was not a critical or commercial success, Gail still had a good time making the movie. There were two pleasant surprises while shooting the production. One was the cast and crew surprising Gail on the set with a large cake on her birthday, September 21st. She was completely surprised and overwhelmed, breaking down into tears. The second surprise came when Kelly, her beloved cocker spaniel, interrupted a take while shooting a scene during "El Paso." Gail had brought him to the set with her on occasion to help relax her during production. On this particular day, Kelly had heard Gail's voice during a scene, and came barking, eager to see her, and give her a warm greeting. Director Foster, rather than use a second take, kept the scene as is, and Kelly remained in the final print.

Guy Madison tried his best to see Gail on her birthday on September 21st, but he was on location in Arizona making a film, "When A Man's A Man," for Allied Artists. He found out by coincidence that he would have one free day off from filming on Gail's birthday, and phoned her to let her knew they would be able to get together for that one day. However, when Gail phoned Allied Artists to confirm the day that Guy would be free to visit her, she was mistakenly told that Guy wasn't free that particular Tuesday, September 21st, but was free the following Tuesday. Thinking Guy wouldn't be able to see her for her birthday, Gail made plans to attend a small dinner party with friends that evening. When Guy arrived at Gail's house from a flight from Arizona, he was told she was away with friends to celebrate her birthday. Guy eventually tracked down Gail and her party, but could only spend a few hours with her before he had to return to Arizona to finish shooting his film.

This was typical of the problems he and Gail had to endure to try and see each other when their busy schedules permitted it. Although Guy and Gail had known each other for three years, they hadn't actually been going together for three years. It was a common misconception by the movie fan magazines and the gossip columnists that while Gail and Guy were a steady couple, they really hardly knew each other for very long.[3]

Despite the hardships of trying to see each other while not working before the movie camera, Gail and Guy knew they were deeply in love with each other, and that eventually they would be married. As Guy later confessed to a magazine writer, "I fell in love with her after the third date."[4]

However, as much as Guy was in love with Gail, he couldn't help noticing some peculiar characteristics in Gail's personality. There was this constant fear of meeting new people at a party or social event. Gail and Guy would get numerous invitations to attend house parties where numerous movie stars and movie executives would be present. Gail would often come up with an excuse not to go, or would cancel a date at the last minute.[5] Even if the party was at a friend's house, such as Alan and Sue Ladd, or a charity function at the Atwater Kents, Gail would agonize over having to meet people she didn't know, and finally decide not to go. It was this unnatural fear of meeting new people that prevented Gail from being the maid of honor at the wedding of her good friend, Diana Lynn, to fiancé John Lindsey in December, 1948. Gail was so nervous and distraught that by the time the wedding date was near, she informed Diana that she couldn't go through with it. Diana, ever so kind and understanding, knew Gail well enough, and asked good friend Jane Withers to substitute for Gail as matron of honor. Needless to say, this extreme fear of meeting new people was strange to those who didn't know Gail, yet not surprising to those who knew her. That extreme shyness as a little girl never really left her, and was an additional manifestation of an inferiority complex that was unusual for an actress who was really very talented in addition to being a gifted artist.

No sooner had Gail finished filming "El Paso" than she was loaned out once more by Paramount Studios to United Artists. This was to be the last time Gail was to be sold to another studio, however, this time she was to be working with the horses she loved so dear.

"Henry Aldrich Gets Glamour," 1943. Clockwise: Jimmy Lydon,
Diana Lynn, Frances Gifford, Gail Russell, Anne Rooney.

"Lady in the Dark," 1944. Gail Russell, Ginger Rogers, Rand Brooks.

"Our Hearts Were Young And Gay," 1944. Gail with Diana Lynn.

"The Uninvited," 1944. Ray Milland, Barbara Everest, Ruth Hussey, and Gail Russell.

Gail with Ray Milland from "The Uninvited," 1944.

"Duffy's Tavern," 1945. Clockwise: Bing Crosby, Jean Heather, Helen
Walker, Gail Russell.

"The Unseen," 1945. Gail with Herbert Marshall and Joel McCrea.

"Salty O'Rourke," 1945. Gail with Alan Ladd.

"The Bachelor's Daughters" 1946, with Jane Wyatt, Ann Dvorak, Adolphe Menjou, Claire Trevor, Billie Burke.

"Our Hearts Were Growing Up," 1946. Gail with Sara Haden, left, and Diana Lynn middle.

Gail with Alan Ladd from the movie "Calcutta," 1947.

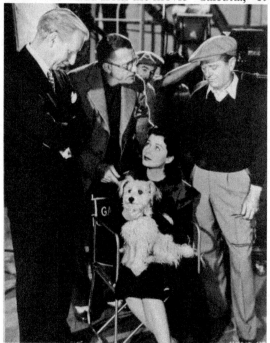

"Variety Girl," 1947. Gail with Frank Ferguson.

Gail and John Wayne from "Angel and the Badman," 1947.

Gail and John Wayne in "Wake of the Red Witch," 1948.

Gail Russell and John Lund from
"Night has a Thousand Eyes," 1948.

Scene from the movie "Moonrise," 1948. Dane Clark and Gail.

John Payne and Gail Russell from the movie "El Paso," 1949.

"The Great Dan Patch," 1949. Henry Hull, John Hoyt and Gail.

"Song of India," 1949. Gail with Turhan Bey, and Sabu.

"Captain China," 1950. Gail, Michael O'Shea, John Payne.

"The Lawless," 1950. Gail with Macdonald Carey.

Gail with co-star Stephen McNally in "Air Cadet," 1951.

A scene from "Seven Men from Now," 1956. With
Randolph Scott and Lee Marvin.

"The Tattered Dress," 1957. Gail with Jeff Chandler.

"No Place to Land," 1958. Gail with John Ireland.

"The Silent Call," 1961. Gail with David McLean,
"Pete" the dog and a young Roger Mobley.

Chapter 21
The Great Dan Patch

When Gail reported for work at Paramount, she was informed that her next film would be another loan out to United Artists for a production entitled "The Great Dan Patch." This would prove to be the last time Gail would be sold to another studio. Another memo by William Meiklejohn to the payroll department stated that Gail would be paid $4,166 a week for six weeks. This would be the most money she ever made while working under her original Paramount contract.[1]

"The Great Dan Patch" was the story of the famous harness racing horse, Dan Patch, who rose to fame at the turn of the Twentieth Century in rural Indiana. The film starred Gail, as well as Dennis O'Keefe, Ruth Warrick, Henry Hull, and Charlotte Greenwood. It was produced by John Taintor Foote, who also wrote the screenplay, and was to be directed by Joe Newman. Gail worked well with director Newman, and enjoyed working with actor Dennis O'Keefe who, like Gail, came from an Irish-American background. They also shared the same sense of humor, as revealed by the many funny candid photos taken of them by the studio's photographer on the set. There was also the added incentive for Gail to be working closely with horses that she loved so well.

Gail portrayed Cissy Lathrop, the tomboy daughter of Ben Lathrop, played by John Hoyt, the trainer of the horses of David Palmer, played by Dennis O'Keefe. The film tells the tale of the raising of the Great Dan Patch, as well as a love triangle involving Cissy, David and his social climbing wife, Ruth Trenbull, played by Ruth Warrick. The story mainly concerns the rise of Dan Patch from young colt to champion harness racer, with the film ending with Cissy and David eventually marrying and selling Dan Patch to continue raising horses. It was an above average country tale filled with drama, humor and harness racing action. It was well received by movie fans – who doesn't love horses? Gail loved making the movie, and it was the most money she made making a film.

The movie critics were not as thrilled with "The Great Dan Patch," as attested by the lukewarm review by The New York Times. The movie critic wrote, "Accorded what the trade calls saturation bookings, 'Black Magic,' and 'The Great Dan Patch,' the story of the famous pacer, opened yesterday in some sixty theatres... 'The Great Dan Patch' is the better of the two, even though the human drama becomes so obtrusive at times that the real hero, Dan Patch, appears to be neglected. Filmed in Sepia tones, the picture has a nice, warm, sentimental quality and manages also to capture the excitement and classical quality of harness racing back in the days when the automobile was a novel and explosively noisy contraption. John Taintor Foote... writes with more feeling when he is dealing with Dan Patch and the people who train and love him than when he is simply concerned with the domestic affairs of Dan's owner and the snobbery and ruthless ambition of his socially climbing wife…" No mention was made of any of the other actors in the film, including Gail.

Movie fan magazine writers and newspaper reporters were always asking Gail why she and Guy Madison were not already married. She told them that even though they had known each other for four years, she wanted to be sure that they were mature enough to start a marriage. Gail explained her hesitation at marriage by stating, "Until now, like Guy, I've been childishly superstitious about happiness. It loomed as such a fragile, elusive mystery. Like Guy, I've had a perfect horror of anything phony, an instinctive shunning of any sham. So I hesitated… Falling in love with Guy was easy. That I accomplished almost at first sight, I'll admit now. I didn't gush about him to interviewers, however. Like Guy, I was terribly afraid of expressing myself to heartbreak in Hollywood. Romances continually crash about you here, and that makes naturally shy persons doubly wary. I was terrified by the notion that something might go wrong as a penalty for daring the love someone as wonderful as Guy…"[3]

Gail was determined not to be rushed into marriage before she was actually ready for it. She wanted to get to know Guy Madison, the person, not Guy Madison, the handsome actor. It was also to be the same for Guy. They wanted to connect as man and woman, to know that they held the same values, and would continue to grow to love one another. "Staying in love was stormy weather sometimes, I confess. Because being so very young, so passionately idealistic and yet so desperately eager to enchant one another, we demanded perfection from one another. Simultaneously, we made much of not wanting to hold the other to any promises. I never wore an engagement ring."[4]

Gail also confessed that she was not an easy person to get along with at times. "I was moody… and so Guy had to learn to just let me come out of my maddening ranges of disposition. I'd sulk. I'd flare up. Or Guy would. Then we'd punish each other by staying away, silent and aloof… I've broken the habit of running away from the effort of making a definite stand when I should, and have ceased to feel crushed beyond repair when criticized. I had a honey of an inferiority complex, you can gather. School had been a trial to me because of the torture of associating with the other children. That's why I took up art – to escape from the necessary adjustments to realities."[5]

Finally, Gail admitted that what she and Guy wanted was what most young people wanted. "We agreed that we wanted true love, a genuine as well as beautiful home, eventually our own children and the joy of sharing their hopes, and the warming affection of a few loyal friends. These unaffected, elementary pleasures were the ones appealing to us. Artificialities of any brand don't…"[6]

1949 would be the toughest year for Gail and Guy to continue seeing each other on a regular basis. The Selznick Company, to which Guy was under contract, had ceased production, and had farmed out all its stars to other studios. Guy was loaned out for a couple of pictures, but the bulk of his assignments were to make personal appearances at lavish movie premiers back East, and to be loaned out to stage producers to star in various plays. So for three quarters of the year, Guy was absent from Hollywood and Gail. It was definitely a long distance romance for the two of them. In the spring Gail grew so lonely with only long distance calls that she took a train to Miami Beach to gaze at him from an audience seat. Most of the time Gail spent worrying whether Guy would develop stage fright, and forget his lines while on stage. This was very reminiscent of the first time she watched Guy's stage debut while appearing in "Dear Ruth" at Laguna Beach, California. Gail recalled, "During the first act I chewed my nails down to the elbow, waiting for his entrance. After the first curtain, I couldn't sit still any longer."[7] Gail retreated to the last row where she could agonize for Guy in private. When the final curtain came down, there was a huge wave of applause for Guy and the cast. There sat Gail in the last row applauding in unison with the audience as she broke down in hysterical tears. She had cried like that only once before, at the end of the first preview of "The Uninvited" back in 1944. This time the tears were for Guy.[8]

1949 would prove to be the most successful year for Gail, both professionally and romantically. She would be at the height of her fame and fortune, and the year would culminate in the successful conclusion of her fabled romance with Guy Madison.

Chapter 22
Captain China

After completing "The Great Dan Patch," Gail returned to her new apartment in Westwood that she had been living in since December, 1948. She had decided to move out of the house she shared with her parents and her brother in order to become more independent. Gail realized that if she intended to marry Guy Madison in the future, she should learn how to manage a household, handle a budget, and to keep lists intelligently. Then one night, as Gail was driving home from the studio with her secretary, Mary Lou Van Ness, she saw a sign advertising an apartment for rent in a white building above U.C.L.A. Even though the building wasn't quite finished, Gail fell in love with the view. She decided to rent it, and taking only her bedroom furniture from her parents' home in Westwood, she moved right in.

It was a modest one room and kitchen apartment. Using only $300 to spend, Gail decorated and furnished the apartment herself. She drew upon her talent as a commercial artist, and repainted the light ceiling and dark green walls. Since her bedroom furniture was blonde, Gail decided to make the décor Chinese Modern. Curtains and cornices were of bamboo, as was the matting that floors the space by the bamboo bar that led to the kitchen. The living room had a Chinese red rug with goatskin rugs lying blonde and thick before the wide couch (actually her bed, stripped of head and foot boards) covered in a unique Chinese print. The goatskin rugs Gail had bought from the Paramount prop department and were used in the films "The Paradise Case" and "Samson and Delilah." The Chinese print of red, green, and black on a white background Gail used on hassocks, draperies, and in a panel set in her radio and record player cabinet. She also sewed a piece of the red, white, and black olio print that papers bathroom and dressing room, and put it under the glass that covered her coffee table. Most of the wallpapering and decorations Gail did herself, as well as painting the kitchen table and four chairs white.[1]

When Guy Madison visited her new apartment, he was so impressed with Gail's decorations that he asked her to find him a similar apartment, which happened to be available upstairs. Guy moved out of the house he was renting, and asked Gail to help him decorate it. Since Guy loved hunting, Gail used a hunting décor. She had Guy's walls painted a light chocolate, chose a yellow, green, and chocolate plaid for his couch bedspread, and hunter's green draperies to match the green in the plaid. Guy insisted on using Gail's oil paintings to decorate the walls of his apartment. Most of the paintings were of animals, and were framed in the same blonde wood as his furniture.[2]

Gail's interest in art came in handy when she decorated her own apartment and Guy's. She had majored in art while attending University High

School in the forenoon, and Santa Monica Technical School in the afternoon. As Gail later recalled, "For me, school was over at noon; the rest was fun. We decorated our classroom, and painted it, in our levis and jeans. I remember we used to go around picking out wallpaper, and working over paints, trying to get the right color. Maybe my interest in decoration stems from that."[3]

Gail found herself back at Paramount for her next film, "Captain China," where she was reunited with actor John Payne and the production team of William Pine, William Thomas, and director Lewis R. Foster. Foster also co-wrote the screenplay. Another memo from William Meiklejohn to the payroll department authorized them to pay Gail $2,500 a week for eight weeks.[4] Also in the cast, along with Gail and John Payne, were Jeffrey Lynn, Michael O'Shea, and Lon Chaney Jr. Gail had worked with director Foster before in "El Paso," so he was familiar with her shyness before the camera, as well as her distaste of unnecessary onlookers while filming her scenes. There were no delays in shooting, although Gail did sprain her wrist while filming one scene that later required a bandage.[5] There was also an unforeseen case of seasickness that involved the whole cast during the first days of filming. The Paramount technical staff had constructed a portion of a tramp steamer inside a water tank to simulate a voyage at sea. The prop boat's movements proved as real that the cast soon became ill. Director Foster then ordered the entire cast to be given two seasick pills to prevent any further delays. From then on it was "smooth sailing."[6]

Gail portrayed Kim Mitchell, a passenger aboard a steamer sailing to Manila in the Philippines Islands. On board is Charles Chinmough, played by John Payne, a former captain trying to reclaim his reputation and rank. The story included a shipwreck, a typhoon, a bloody fistfight, a mutiny, as well as the standard shipboard romance. It was just an average drama at sea, although Gail looked attractive in her Edith Head wardrobe. The film did just average at the box office, and it was Gail's fifth film in a row.

The movie critics were not as generous in their appraisal of the film. The New York Times was typical of their response when it stated, "The good news from the Paramount Theater this morning is not about the new picture called 'Captain China,' which opened there yesterday, but the return of Bob Hope, who was last seen about here in the flesh in 1939, for 'Captain China' is a very ordinary sea adventure, which gets so muscular at times that it becomes unwittingly funny... The producers might just as well called this one 'Slow Boat To China' because there is very little pace to the picture despite the violence of the ocean and the passionate hatreds which lead to mayhem as the freighter Crosswinds plows to the South China Sea to Manila... John Payne as Captain China literally punches his way through the picture... Gail Russell is the passenger who becomes the pivot of amorous contention between the rival skippers..."[7] Although "Captain China" was not a great critical or financial success, Gail was not bothered by what movie critics had to say about her or the films she starred in. She was still very content to be just the pretty girl in the guy's action film.

With the completion of filming "Captain China," Gail was now in the final year of her original seven year contract with Paramount Pictures. Her agents, Barbara Eddington and Jerry Cloutman, had arranged with Paramount executive William Meiklejohn to sign a new contract. The new contract was to begin August 2, 1949 for 2 years at $1,250 a week, guaranteed for at least 40 weeks per year. There were also three possible options to be included. One option at 2 years, $1,500 a week for 40 weeks guaranteed. Second option at 2 years, $1,750 a week with 40 weeks guaranteed. Third option at one year, $2,000 a week, 40 weeks guaranteed. There was in addition of layoff period to begin July 1, 1949 so Gail could enjoy some time off to relax and enjoy a much needed vacation.[8]

This break couldn't have come at a better time for Gail. She was exhausted from filming five pictures in a row, and was lonely for Guy now that he was back East in Connecticut appearing in a play. They were both increasingly frustrated and not being able to see each other on a regular basis due to their individual careers. Then one evening it all came to a head. Guy phoned Gail from Connecticut, and told her that after four years of courtship, they had waited long enough. "This is silly being apart like this!" he exploded. "As soon as this run ends, I'll be on your doorstep, and we're not going to waste any more time getting married!"[9]

Gail happily agreed. She used her time off from filming to take a quick vacation to Balboa Island off Newport Beach, California, with her then best girlfriend Mary Lou Van Ness, the private secretary to the stars at Paramount Studios. However, Gail couldn't enjoy the vacation for long because every lifeguard at the beach reminded her of Guy. She suddenly dragged Mary Lou Van Ness back to Hollywood where she contacted top costume designer Edith Head of Paramount, and asked to borrow the while gabardine suit she'd worn in "Captain China" as her wedding dress.[10]

When Guy's play had closed in Connecticut, he flew in to Hollywood and reserved a bungalow at the Santa Barbara Biltmore Hotel. He filled the living room there with the yellow roses Gail adored. Gail invited just a few close friends, Mr. and Mrs. Howard Hill, who considered Guy as a foster son, and Mr. and Mrs. Jim Davies. Gail had also invited Mary Lou Van Ness, but she was sent on a personal appearance tour with actress Jane Russell, and couldn't make it.[11]

Gail had purposely avoided inviting her parents or Guy's, fearing a large wedding that would attract the movie public, as well as the press. This unnatural fear of strangers and crowds was the determining factor in deciding to elope instead of having the traditional large, church wedding. As Gail told magazine reporter Robin Coons back in 1947, "I don't want a church wedding," she said emphatically. "To me, that would be a little like a premiere, with lights, stars, flowers."[12] Gail didn't even want publicity pictures taken of her wedding, as she told magazine reporter Helen Hover in 1950, "We think marriage is a very personal matter between two people, and we didn't want anything as commercial as publicity photos taken at the ceremony."[13]

Gail's insistence on a small, private wedding without her parents created an estrangement between she and her mother. Gladys, like most mothers, lived for the day she could participate, attend, and enjoy her only daughter's wedding. She dreamed of planning a beautiful, elaborate wedding to honor her famous, movie star daughter. It was to be the wedding she never had, but that she wished for her daughter. Gladys was terribly hurt by her daughter's decision not to include her mother, father, or brother. She also felt sympathy for Guy's mother and father for not being able to attend their son's wedding. This rift between Gail and her mother would never be completely healed, and lasted until the moment of Gail's death in 1961.

When it became time for the wedding ceremony in Santa Barbara, the wedding party consisted of Gail, Guy, Mr. and Mrs. Howard Hill, Mr. and Mrs. Jim Davies, and Judge Robert Quinn. The city of Santa Barbara had been chosen by Guy because his good friend, actor Rory Calhoun, had been married there last summer, and had raved about the beautiful setting of that picturesque, oceanside town. As the judge performed the ceremony, Gail stood in her white, gabardine dress without a hat or the usual bridal decorations of flowers. She was beautiful, but was so nervous that she cried throughout the ceremony.[14] Howard Hill, who was also best man, asked Gail and Guy if he could say a little prayer for them after the ceremony. There were tears in Gail's and Guy's eyes as they knelt for that blessing. They had a small supper afterward before setting out on their honeymoon.[15] Gail Russell and Guy Madison were finally married on July 31, 1949, in a small ceremony presided over by Judge Robert Quinn. Gail was twenty-four, Guy was twenty-seven.

For a honeymoon, Gail and Guy decided to drive to Yosemite National Park in her yellow convertible, accompanied only by her beloved cocker spaniel, Kelly. When they arrived, every hotel and camp was full. Gail, like Guy, hated to make advance reservations. So they retraced their route, but the only hotel they found would not take Kelly. They drove some more miles until they found an old cabin to rent with no windows, screens rapped off, and no bed.[16] Not worrying, they unpacked their sleeping bags in the car trunk, and rested for the night. The first restaurant they ran across had burned down, and was out of commission. They drove on for three more weeks, visiting Lake Tahoe, straight through the Tioga Pass in the High Sierras, hunting and fishing along the way, sleeping outdoors until they reached Yellowstone National Park. Their stay in Yellowstone was unforgettable as they participated in the sporting life they loved so well, wearing sweaters and jeans, hunting and fishing with bow and arrow. Gail had her own personal bow made by champion archer Howard Hill which she called "Little Sister," and Guy had his own bow which he called "Mo" after his real name, Robert Moseley.[17] In the evening, they stood close together while they watched the breath taking ritual at Yosemite – the magnificent fire-fall from the mountains.[18]

Guy and Gail had wanted to be alone on their honeymoon, but Paramount Studios wanted to get in touch with Gail to discuss her next picture, "Outrage." Unable to locate the honeymooners, they asked the forest rangers to locate them. When the other park visitors found out who they really were, they hounded the famous move couple until they forced them to leave the park.[19]

On the way back home, Gail and Guy got lost traveling through the Sierra Nevada Mountains. When they finally arrived, back home in Hollywood, Gail had an additional two months to enjoy her newly married life, and to search for a home to live in. Guy also had some free time between assignments from the Selznick Studios. The eventually found a modern, one story home in Brentwood, California, at 11742 Chenault Avenue, for which they paid $30,000.

So it seemed that by the end of 1949, Gail Russell had finally achieved what most actresses dream of. She was at the height of her movie career at twenty-four years of age, had completed nineteen feature films, signed a generous, new movie contract, and was now married to the man of her dreams, Guy Madison, one of the handsomest actors in Hollywood. It was all so perfect. Yet, tragically, the dark clouds of fear and depression that had for so long followed Gail, would soon overshadow her, and end her successful career at Paramount Studios.

Chapter 23
The Lawless

By October, 1949, Gail and Guy were busy furnishing their new home in Brentwood, California. The house was located on a quiet, residential street and had two bedrooms, den, living room, dining room, and kitchen. It also had a huge front and back yard, patio, and a barbeque in back which Guy had built. Gail was busy making the curtains and the drapes, using a floral design. Guy was busy making bookshelves, built-in closets, and some of the furniture.[1]

Both Gail and Guy were free from studio assignments, and had some time to adjust to married life. It wasn't as easy an adjustment as Gail had thought. As she told Silver Screen Magazine in 1950, "I was such an independent little cuss. I evaded planning, for it was easier to wackily decide on the spur-of-the-second. I'm still a tomboy who delights in going rabbit hunting with Guy, but with my first house to manage, I knew I must keep things like lists – intelligently. Now that I finally have a place where guests can sit down at a table, all the enigmas of married-couple hospitality must be conquered. Cooking, for instance, is a vast blank to me. I've never been interested in food. I never was hungry till evening. Guy always has had an admirable respect for good health, and has been appalled but patient about the thoughtless manner in which I've often ignored a balanced diet. He's a super cook, and he's teaching me how."[2]

Gail and Guy did most of the decorating themselves, preferring not to let their simple life be cluttered by extra help around the house. Guy wallpapered the two bedrooms, one in a horse print, the other in brown plaid. Gail painted her dressing room. The décor was American Modern, and the large living room had a brick lined fireplace in front of which were two sofa chairs nicknamed "Mr." and "Mrs."[3] Above the brick mantelpiece was the picture of a toreador fighting a bull which Gail had painted from a copy of a Mexican print which she had admired. Guy often kept a fire going day and night. One of their favorite rituals was to rise up in the morning when it was still cold and dark, bring in their breakfast on trays, and eat before a roaring fire. It was their way of starting the day, cozy and relaxed, and to bring a little romance into their home that early in the day.[4]

Unfortunately, all honeymoons must come to an end, and in Gail's case, it came quickly. Guy's movie career had come to a standstill. He had made only a few movies since his sensational debut in "Since You Went Away" in 1944. There had been "Till the End of Time" with Dorothy McGuire in 1946, "Honeymoon" with Shirley Temple in 1947, and "Texas, Brooklyn and Heaven" with Diana Lynn in 1948. Most of the time Guy was sent out to act in off Broadway plays, or attend movie premieres and make personal appearances. He was scheduled to appear in a movie in Europe, but refused to go because he didn't want to leave Gail so soon after their marriage. In consequence, the Selznick Studio put him on suspension.

Gail's career also started to unravel. For the first time since she first signed with Paramount Studios, Gail refused a film assignment. A memo signed by William Meiklejohn to the payroll department on August 25, 1949, authorized the suspension of Gail for refusing to appear in a film project titled "Mother for May."[5] She was suspended again on October 7, 1949, in another memo from Meiklejohn for again refusing to appear in another film titled "Outrage" (The Lawless).[6] This may have been Gail's reluctance to work so soon after her recent marriage to Guy. Yet I suspect it was an unconscious effort on her part to finally reject the movie lifestyle she had never fully come to love. Or maybe it was the faint hope that she could retire from film making, and become a full time wife and mother. In any case, Gail was beginning to delay resuming her career.

Gail soon changed her mind, however, for on October 14, 1949, another memo from Meiklejohn lifted the suspension on Gail when she agreed to do "The Lawless." "The Lawless" was Gail's third film for Paramount Studios under the banner of the production team of the Pine Thomas Company. The film was to be directed by Joseph Losey in only his second feature. He has come to prominence in Hollywood while directing his first film at R.K.O. Studios, "The Boy with the Green Hair," in 1948.

Losey had never worked with Gail before, and it was to prove to be a major handicap for him. He wasn't as patient, or as understanding to her extreme stage fright as were his predecessors, Lewis Allen, John Farrow, or Lewis Foster had been. Furthermore, the producers had instructed director Losey to limit production costs, and try and limit the film's shooting schedule to just three weeks. Most of the film was shot on location in the small town of Marysville, a few miles north of Sacramento, California. When it rained, the inside scenes were shot; when it was foggy, the day sequences were changed to night; when the wind howled, it howled on film; and when it was too hot, it was just too bad for anyone who didn't like to perspire.[8] As you can imagine, it was not what Gail was used to at Paramount during her earlier days at the studio.

Then there were the rumors that director Losey had heard about Gail while at Paramount. The occasional cocktail she consumed before and after filming. The various visits to the bar at Lucy's Restaurant across the street from Paramount during lunch break, or to the bar at the nearby Cock and Bull Restaurant. Paramount executives, like director Losey, had finally become aware of Gail's growing alcoholism.

The filming began, but there were difficulties right from the start. Author Michael Ciment quoted Joseph Losey in his book, "Conversations with Losey," – "Gail Russell, who didn't want to be an actress, was picked up by a talent scout when she was a clerk in a department store in Beverly Hills, came from a lower middle class family. She died of alcoholism because she was so deathly frightened of acting, but she had in her the makings of a great star. I had a tragic time with her. I think she had the most beautiful eyes I have ever seen, the most moving eyes. And she was immensely sensitive. She didn't know anything. Paramount had her under contract – like a horse. She got a big salary then, and had absolute instructions from them not to let her have a drink. The very first time I shot with her, I had a long, night tracking shot. It was a half night, we finished at twelve. She couldn't remember a single line, and it was three or four pages of important dialogue. I wasn't trained enough then to say, 'Well, we'll shoot it another way,' and I kept trying to get it by coaching her in her lines, and finally I said, 'What's the matter?' And she grabbed me, her hands were icy cold, she was absolutely rigid, and she said, 'Look, I don't want to be an actress. I'm not an actress. I can't act. I never had a director who gave me a scene this long before. I can't do it.' And I said, 'Oh, yes you can. I'm sure you can, and you are an actress.' 'No, I'm not. I've never kidded myself. I'm not an actress. I hate it, I'm frightened of it. Get me a drink, and I'll be all right.' So I said, 'You know, I've been told not to give you a drink?' She said, 'Get me a drink!' I got her a drink, and she did the scene. By this time, Macdonald Carey couldn't remember his lines. She had absolutely destroyed him. It was a very bad start for me on that quick picture, to spend the whole night on that one set-up. And I just barely got it. If I hadn't, the picture would have never been made, I believe. Anyway, this started her drinking, and she was drunk throughout the rest of the picture. That isn't to say that she was bad. I think that she was very good often, but sometimes I had to shoot scenes in ways to disguise the fact that she was drunk, and sometimes I had to shoot scenes with a stand-in because she was too drunk to stand up."[9]

Tom Milne, in his book on Joseph Losey, "Losey On Losey," also quoted the director on Gail Russell while filming "The Lawless" when he stated, "'The Dividing Line' (The Lawless) is very primitive as a piece of work, with one or two exceptions: the locations were effective, perhaps the kids, and I think poor, desperate, lonely, tragic Gail Russell's eyes counted for a great deal."[10]

Now, reading director Joseph Losey's words, a reasonable person could have to question his actions during the filming of "The Lawless." Knowing that the Paramount executives had warned him of Gail Russell's drinking problems, and specifically telling him not to give her a drink, he nevertheless disregarded their warning, and started her drinking again. Obviously Gail had not developed the habit of drinking while on the set making a movie, but Losey deliberately encouraged her alcoholism in order to finish his film on time, and within budget. Given that Losey was caught between a rock and a hard place, it was still unconscionable what he did to Gail. The consequences of what he did would prove to have disastrous results where her career was concerned.

Regarding his charge that Gail was drunk filming "The Lawless," a review of the film doesn't seem to back up such a statement. Gail seems well under control in most of her scenes, with the sole exception of the courthouse sequence where Gail, as Sunny Garcia, is comforting the parents of Lalo Rios.

She can be seen swaying slightly in the background as she nervously clenches her hands, and later leans heavily on the nearby wooden railing.

As difficult as it was for Gail, she finally finished shooting "The Lawless" within the three weeks of expected production. The film starred Gail as Sunny Garcia, a Mexican-American reporter of the local newspaper who becomes involved with a big city news reporter and former war correspondent Larry Wilder, played by Macdonald Carey. They join forces to defend Mexican-American migrant worker Paul Rodriguez, played by Lalo Rios, as well as fight the bigotry and intolerance displayed by the local townspeople towards migrant workers. It was a social drama well received by the movie critics, if not by the movie going public in general. It would turn out to be one of the best films Gail ever made at Paramount, and an indication of just how good an actress Gail Russell could be.

The New York Times was an example of the film's favorable response by the critics, and even the usually cynical Bosley Crowther had something positive to say about the film, if not about Gail's acting. He wrote, "Let's have a real salute this morning to Paramount's Dollar Bills – William H. Pine and William C. Thomas – who have finally come through with a thing... they have made an exciting picture on a good, solid, social theme – the cruelty of a community when inflamed by prejudice. True enough, no one has bothered to waste too much time or thought on the nature of the bias against 'fruit tramps' in the community under observation here... This is a weakness of the picture. So is a hackneyed romance that develops, amid all the turmoil, between the editor and a working quarter girl. The several slow spots in the picture, which director Joe Losey has allowed, seemed to occur in the vicinity of this couple when vis-à-vis... Macdonald Carey is convincing as the editor, Gail Russell is slightly languid as the girl..."[11] Regardless of the criticism of Bosley Crowther, "The Lawless" is now considered a minor classic of social awareness in cinema, and one of the best films Gail Russell ever made.

As good as "The Lawless" turned out to be, it wasn't the same in Gail's professional or private life. This deeply shy, sensitive woman was now fully aware that her hidden alcoholism was now well known by the Paramount front office, and the personal privacy which she treasured was now gone. Her self control, which allowed her to film movie scenes without the need to consume alcohol, was now gone. Gail was now terrified that she could no longer control her drinking.

This acute alcoholism was now invading her personal life as well. Guy Madison was beginning to become aware of Gail's increasing moods of nervousness, anxiety, and depression. He thought their marriage would have a calming effect on her. Instead, her nervousness and tension seemed to be increasing rather than diminishing. Guy attributed most of Gail's behavior to her former "black moods" that seemed to go away after a solitary walk around the block, or after she went to her room where she painted or drew.

Guy also noticed that Gail was starting to refuse invitations to parties or movie premieres, preferring to stay at home and "relax." Guy was fond of large parties where he could mingle and talk with people. Gail, on the other hand, dreaded large parties where she would have to meet new people and socialize with them. Guy also became aware that they were seeing less of their friends, even when invited to their homes for dinner. He thought it strange that Gail's parents were not invited more often. Guy used to be a regular visitor to their house when Gail was living with them. The rift that existed between Gail and her mother when she wasn't invited to her only daughter's wedding was still evident. The scrapbooks that Gladys kept of her daughter's movie career that included magazine stories, newspaper clippings, film reviews, or magazine portraits of Gail, were blank after the newspaper articles of Gail and Guy's elopement were included.

Guy thought that maybe Gail's troubles were the result of her enduring the emotional strain of handling a movie career, as well as the duties and responsibilities of being a wife, and running a household. He tried to hire servants to help Gail with the housework, but she continually refused to have servants in the house.

It all came to a conclusion on January 12, 1950, when Gail announced to the press that she and Guy had decided to separate, just six months after their marriage. Gail tersely told the press, "We were unable to work things out."[12] Gail also told the reporter for the Los Angeles Times, "I have no further statement to make. Any further information will have to come from my husband."[13]   Guy was on a hunting trip and unavailable for comment. Gail retreated to the Camel Back Inn in Phoenix, Arizona. However, after only ten days, Gail and Guy decided to reconcile, and make a go of their marriage. They flew to Mexico, and stayed at the Riviera Pacifica Hotel in Ensenada. They later called the trip a "second honeymoon."

Gail's mother, Gladys, wrote a thank you letter to movie columnist Hedda Hopper on January 19, 1950, in response to a column she wrote describing the trial separation of Gail and Guy. Gladys wrote:

My Dear Miss Hopper,

Please accept my late note of grateful thanks for your kindly mention of my daughter Gail and Guy in your recent column. I have long been an ardent admirer of your tact in these matters, and wish you to know my personal feelings toward you and your staff. Gail returned home yesterday, and I was so happy to see her looking so well and sunburn from her Arizona rest. Only wish she could have stayed longer, but she was anxious to get back to some radio work, and a play the studio have waiting. She is also interest in taking up piano study, and found a new bright red piano in her home upon her return. She immediately came to the house and had me hunting all over for her Dad's and brother's music books. I am so happy.

Thanks to you Hedda
Truly your friend, Mrs. George H. Russell[14]

When Gail returned home from vacation, and reported for work at Paramount, she was reluctant to resume her career. The tremendous psychological and emotional strain to endure her acting profession had now come to a climax. Unhappy to constantly perform before the movie camera, and to be displayed before movie executives and an unrelenting publicity department, Gail had finally had enough. Gail believed she could now escape behind the façade of a successful marriage, and concentrate on being just a housewife and mother. During all those years at Paramount, even since she signed her first contract at seventeen years of age, Gail had always agreed to film assignments, even though many films were made back to back, with little or no time off. Now Gail believed she had earned the right to say no. She was scheduled to appear in "Flaming Feather," but declined the role, and was replaced by Barbara Rush.[15]   Gail was then scheduled for another Western, "Devil's Canyon," but again refused the role. Paramount executives, knowing that Gail was an alcoholic, and refusing to deal with the problem, quietly decided to terminate her contract. In a memo signed by William Meiklejohn dated November 13, 1950, he cancelled her contract.[16]   After fourteen films with Paramount Studios, Gail's storybook career with that fabled studio was over. No other Hollywood star had ever risen so far from obscurity, reached the height of fame and glamour, and fallen so suddenly, as did Gail Russell in November, 1950.

Chapter 24
Air Cadet

By January, 1951, Gail was struggling to keep her marriage intact. She had thought that just being a housewife, and taking care of her household, was enough to satisfy her inner needs. Gail truly believed she didn't need to be an actress to be a successful human being. However, soon the simple, every day tasks of running a household became drudgeries rather than delights, and she began to neglect them. Gail felt there was still a need in her for something more to give her life meaning. There was that nagging thought in the back of her mind that perhaps, maybe, she had made a mistake in tossing aside her movie career. Then, there was the loneliness without Guy, and the empty home when he was absent making movies.

While Gail's career had come to a halt, Guy's had suddenly been revitalized. Since being dropped by the Selznick Studios two years ago, Guy had made only two films, "Massacre River" in 1949, and "Drums in the Deep South" in 1951. Then came his big break this year when he made the pilot episode for a new Western TV Series, "The Adventures of Wild Bill Hickok."[1] It proved to be a smash hit on television, and soon made Guy Madison a household name with American youth. Guy's sudden rise in popularity and success must have made Gail happy for his sake. Yet it must have also been bittersweet for her to realize what she had lost – the glamour, the fame, the excitement at being a successful movie star.

There was also the added disappointment of not being able to conceive a child. Gail knew Guy loved children, and planned to have "at least a half dozen" to raise and cherish. Gail soon found herself with too much time on her hands during the days when Guy was away on assignment. She inevitably went to the liquor cabinet to get the cocktail that would ease her loneliness, her fear that perhaps she had made a huge mistake in trading a successful movie career for the life of everyday housewife.

Finally, in desperation, Gail decided to resume her movie career. She had not made a film in nearly a year, and was hesitant to renew a career she never really grew to love. Gail was deathly afraid of being a failure at acting. She was always afraid of the movie camera, and yet she couldn't really give up the movie star lifestyle. It was an eternal paradox for Gail. How could she hate something, and yet love it at the same time? It was a dilemma she never solved.

Gail now contacted her agents, Barbara Eddington and Jerry Cloutman, and they arranged a movie deal with Universal Studios to have Gail star in their new action film, "Air Cadet." Universal executives heard rumors of Gail's drinking problem, but they decided to take the risk, and sign her to a movie deal. They believed that Gail Russell's name on a theater marquee could still sell tickets.

"Air Cadet" was to be directed by Joseph Pevney and would star Gail, Stephen McNally, Richard Long, and a very young Rock Hudson in one of his first screen roles. Gail portrayed Janet Page, the wife of Air Force instructor Major Jack Page, played by Stephen McNally. The plot concerns the trials and tribulations of trying to train young Air Force cadets to become fighter pilots. There were the usual comedy hijinks involving young cadets, plus a lukewarm love affair between Janet Page and one of the younger cadets, Russ Coulter, played by Richard Long. It was just an average drama with most of the scenes taking place at Randolph Field in San Antonio, Texas, and at Williams Field, Arizona, where cast and crew went on location.[2]

One could see in the scenes involving Gail that her alcoholism was beginning to affect her looks. She appeared thin and worn, and in her shorter hairstyle, she was not the glamorous, attractive movie star her fans were used to seeing on the big screen. "Air Cadet" proved only to be a moderately successful film at the box office, yet it would prove to be the only film Gail would make for the next five years.

Critics were also lukewarm in their review of "Air Cadet." The New York Times was typical of the film's response when it wrote, "Hollywood, which has flown practically every film course, straight or otherwise, is now proving that the way to the jet pilot's life is not an easy one in 'Air Cadet,' which buzzed into the Palace yesterday. But the basic fact is that the conflicts besetting the student fly boys here are no different from those which plagued their less speedy predecessors... Let it be said that the course of training is stimulating only when the silvery jets are keening through the wild, blue yonder or dazzling the eye in tight formation, barrel rolls or 'lazy eights.' Once on the ground, however, the boys' problems tend to make one airsick."[3] The reviewer didn't even mention Gail.

Gail continued to make a go of her marriage, but she found it increasingly hard to keep up appearances. She would accompany Guy on all his hunting trips, and still go dining and dancing at nightclubs, but the spark in their relationship had apparently vanished. Gail no longer enjoyed all the places they went to.

Guy decided to rekindle their romance when he scheduled a trip to the Catalina Island Guest Ranch, formally known as the Toyon Bay Resort. He loved hunting, and had made reservations to go hunting for wild boar and mountain goats, but only with bow and arrow. Gail and Guy would rise at dawn and go horseback riding on safari with the local guide. Gail was an expert rider, even more so than Guy, yet she was accidentally thrown from her horse while on the hunt. She was unhurt, yet managed to calm her nervous horse.[4] Guy later managed to shoot one wild goat, but the wild boar eluded them. Later in the afternoon, Guy went diving for lobster in the nearby bay, but Gail remained on board the boat. She wasn't a very good swimmer, and the lobsters seemed to frighten her.[5] Later that evening, there was a barbecue and a square dance. Guy wanted to stay on the guest ranch longer, but he had an appointment with his business agent, and returned with Gail to Hollywood.

By now, Gail was turning into a recluse. Not only was she turning down invitations to dinner with friends, she was refusing to travel with Guy on his promotional tours to publicize his movies and TV show. He would make reservations for plane and hotel accommodations, but at the last minute Gail would change her mind, and Guy would travel alone.[6] Even the close companionship of Gail and Guy's best friends, fellow actors Rory Calhoun and wife Lita Baron, as well as John Bromfield and wife Corinne Calvet, were not enough to coax Gail out of her shell of isolation.

When Gail and Guy did go out to parties or movie premiers, it became a rarity. Actress Corinne Calvet, in her autobiography, "Has Corinne Been A Good Girl," recalled one such incident in 1951, "At a reception for 'Modern Screen," the fan magazine, we ran into our friends Guy Madison and his wife Gail Russell. It was one of their rare public appearances. Gail was a delicate little bird, afraid of noises and crowds. She was intelligent and uncomplicated, a person who should never have had a career as an actress. Apart from a pathological stage fright, she was extremely sensitive to the cross motives of the studios, and was unable to overcome deep feelings of loneliness. I feel very sad whenever I think of Gail Russell and the desolate way in which she ended her life some years later just a few houses away from the one we lived in on Beverly Glen. Close to twenty empty bottles of liquor surrounded her in her small bedroom. She had not been seen for a week, and had not answered her phone. She had lain there drinking herself to death. How could all of us who knew this incredibly talented and beautiful woman have failed her so drastically? Guy's arm was guiding Gail toward us. Gail habitually kept her eyes down, and it was always a shock when she lifted her glance, her childlike expression filled with innocent vulnerability. Hers was the beauty of a Madonna, and it threw everyone off balance. She did not understand the effect she had on people, and in fear she would drop her eyes again, as if someone else's interest in her was more than she could bear. She later solved this dilemma by wearing dark glasses constantly."[7]

By 1952, Gail was finding it harder to find work as a film actress. The reputation for being a hard drinker had followed Gail whenever her agents tried to find film roles. Guy Madison tried his best to help Gail, and was unable to find the real reason behind her troubles. He could plainly see Gail was very unhappy, and tried valiantly to ease her feelings of loneliness and fear of not succeeding as an actress, or as a good housewife. Guy noticed that Gail was increasingly more nervous and distraught at home and tried again, unsuccessfully, to convince her to have servants at home to help with the housework, and ease her responsibilities. He felt he was failing in his responsibilities as a husband, and it soon began to affect his health and wellbeing. Guy's closets friends became seriously concerned about his health. He looked tired, drawn, pale and several years older than his age.[8]

Then John Wayne, and Republic Studios, wanted Gail to have the role of Kim-Kim, the Balinese slave girl, in "Fair Wind to Java."[9] However, director John Ford also wanted Wayne to star in his upcoming film, "The Quiet Man," and the actor had to bow out of the film project. When "Fair Wind to Java" began filming in 1952, Gail and John Wayne were out, and Fred MacMurray and Vera Ralston were in. Then in the spring of 1952, Gail was chosen to star in Lippert Pictures independent production of "Loan Shark" starring George Raft. Gail looked over the script, learned every line, stood on the set the very first day, and fell apart emotionally. It was a complete nervous breakdown.[10] She was later replaced at the eleventh hour by actress Dorothy Hart.

All of Gail's doubts and fears about her talent and self-worth had finally come to the surface, and she finally gave in to hysterical tears. It was very reminiscent of Gail's first nervous breakdown after she finished filming "The Uninvited" in 1944.

When Gail returned home, she tried to resume her normal household duties, but was terrified by the fact that she could not return to her acting career. By now, Guy was really worried over Gail's mental health, and urged her, along with her friends, to finally seek psychiatric help.[11] She had consulted doctors previously, but had been too shy, and ashamed to admit that she needed a full-time psychiatrist. What the doctor found out that what had been previously diagnosed as "melancholia" was a little more severe than that. He believed Gail "had for years been subject to such recurrent depressions of such morbid intensity that she had become increasingly unable to work, unable to cope with any of the responsibilities of life." These periodic "black moods" or "blues," phases of dark, brooding melancholy in which Gail cut herself off from friends and family, were characteristic of Gail long before she met Guy Madison.[12]

Gail was also seeing a regular doctor who prescribed she stay at home and seek no more movie work. He also suggested she refrain from smoking, drinking alcohol or coffee, and eat a healthy, balanced diet. Guy made her obey the rules when he was at home, but when he was away on film and TV assignments, Gail was alone to revert back to her old habits. Gail by now was skating on thin ice, psychologically, and her marriage was again in jeopardy.

By January, 1953, Guy Madison's career began to pick up. He made "Red Snow" in 1952, and his TV series, "Wild Bill Hickok," was a huge hit. Then Warner Brothers Studios were looking for an actor to play the lead in their first 3-D Western, "The Charge at Feather River." One of their top executives had an eleven year old daughter who was a fan of the "Wild Bill Hickok" TV series, and suggested her father use Guy Madison to star in their new Western. Guy was chosen for the role, and "The Charge at Feather River" became a huge success. For the next two months, Guy Madison was the most popular movie star in Hollywood.[13]

Then on February 19, 1953, Guy Madison announced to the press that he and Gail had decided to separate again in order to solve their marital difficulties.[14] They also stated that the separation was strictly temporary, and that neither was contemplating divorce. Guy said, "We have some problems to iron out, and we both feel we can get a better perspective on the situation if we live apart for a while."[15]   Gail had become increasingly unhappy and disenchanted with her marriage to Guy. She was happy for his new found success, but felt alone and unwanted as his "tag along wife." Gail couldn't socialize with his new hunting friends and business associates. She felt more like an outsider, a wife who couldn't contribute anything to his success.

Guy moved out of their Brentwood home and into a local motel. He later rented an apartment in Westwood, and transferred some of the furniture from their home in Brentwood. Gail after a few months, also moved out of their home in Brentwood, and rented a home on Beverly Glen. She was also seeing a psychiatrist, and had hired a trained nurse.[16]   Guy continued to visit Gail at least once a month to check on her health and wellbeing. She was hoping to return to acting, and find better days ahead. Then disaster struck suddenly, out of nowhere, in the person of Chata Bauer, the estranged wife of John Wayne, whose accusations in their divorce trial sent Gail into a mental tailspin from which she would never fully recover.

Chapter 25
Dark Days

It was in October, 1953, when John Wayne's estranged wife, Esperanza "Chata" Bauer, stunned a hushed courtroom with her surprising charge that Wayne had committed adultery with his co-star, Gail Russell, after a post production party in 1947. Chata testified, under oath, that Wayne had come home late one night after the post production party, had broken a sliding glass door, and had drunkenly boasted that he had spent the night with Gail Russell. Chata testified that the day Wayne had finished the picture, "Angel and the Badman," she asked him if he were taking her to the party, and Wayne said no. She usually went to those post production parties, but he said it was just for the picture crew.[1]

Chata Wayne further testified that Wayne never called or returned from the party, and that she had dinner waiting for him. She became worried after a few hours, and called the restaurant where the party had been. She was told everyone had left by 6 p.m. Chata waited until late that night and finally went to bed. She was awaked early in the morning by the sound of breaking glass, and thinking it was a burglar, grabbed her gun and went downstairs. She saw someone lying on the couch, and was about to shoot him, when her mother grabbed her arm and told her it was her husband.[2] Chata asked Wayne if he had broken the window. "He just mumbled," she said. "He was very intoxicated."[3] She said Wayne told her he had spent the night at Gail Russell's home, left the studio party with Miss Russell, just the two of them, and went to her home."[4] A few days later, a friend informed Chata that Wayne had given Gail an automobile, and asked him about this. She said Wayne gave Miss Russell the down payment on a car. Chata asked him why anyone would give a person a down payment on a car unless there was some sort of relationship between them. Wayne said there was nothing wrong with that, and that he was not running around with Gail Russell.[5] Chata further alleged that Wayne's car had been parked in front of Gail's house for several hours, and that when she called the restaurant to find out where her husband was, she was given the phone number where he was supposed to be. It turned out to be the phone number of a motel.[6]

John Wayne was fit to be tied. He angrily denied the charges to the waiting press. "Why did she have to drag that poor kid's name into this?" he repeated. "I never had anything to do with Miss Russell except to make a couple of movies with her. True, we had a party at the end of the picture. Every studio and company does. Everybody was there from technician to star."[7] Wayne testified he came home around 2 a.m., and broke in the front door, "not because I was drunk, but because I had no key and my wife refused to open the door. I'm no saint, but this is ridiculous."[8] As to the down payment on a car for Gail, Wayne said, "The poor kid went to work for us on a loan-out from Paramount. She was getting practically nothing.

She did such a good job in our picture that we tried to get her some of the loan-out money, but Paramount said no. So Jimmy Grant, who directed the picture, and I chipped in $500 a piece and gave it to her. Chata knew all about it. Jimmy and I had discussed it half a dozen times."[9]

Needless to say, Gail was angry and distraught when she heard of Chata Wayne's charges in court, and splashed across newspaper headlines and movie fan magazines. These accusations could not have come at a worse time. Struggling to save her troubled marriage, trying to maintain her psychological stability, and fighting to overcome her alcoholism, Gail was being pushed to the limit. Incredibly, Gail managed to bring herself to court to defend her honor and reputation, as well as Wayne's, and testified under oath to refute Chata Wayne's accusations. One could imagine what courage it took for this shy, insecure, emotionally fragile woman to come to Superior Court in Los Angeles, and testify before a packed courthouse. Memories of that shy little girl, who was terrified to speak those few lines in that grammar school Thanksgiving Play so long ago in Chicago, surely must have entered her mind.

Gail's testimony completely contradicted Chata Wayne's charges of misconduct and adultery. As to events surrounding the party, she said, "John took me home after the party. He had celebrated too much, and apologized to my mother for his condition. He called a taxi. My brother helped him into it and he left about 1 a.m. The next morning he sent my mother a box of flowers with a note of apology for any inconvenience he might have caused her. I was contemplating marriage to Guy Madison at the time, and was living with my family. It is upsetting to me that an appearance of impropriety has been placed by some upon the events of that day."[10]

As to Chata's other charge of Wayne giving Gail an automobile as a gift in appreciation of an alleged romantic affair, Gail had this to say, "There was a studio party at Eaton's following completion of "Angel and the Badman." Earlier in the day, James Grant, director and writer, and John Wayne, producer and star of the picture, had surprised me by telling me they were presenting me with approximately $500 because they believed my salary had not been in keeping with the caliber of my work as a feminine lead. Nothing was ever said about an automobile." Gail was also very upset at being accused of aiding and abetting adultery, "I have instructed my attorney to demand a full and complete retraction under penalty of suit for defamation of character."[11] Gail had retained attorney James W. Z. Taylor to investigate possible causes of action. However, Chata Wayne's testimony was given in court, and could not be legally prosecuted for slander.

The trial was a tremendous ordeal for Gail personally, with her shy manner and extreme stage fright. Especially in front of a very public arena with all the press, jury, and viewing public to hear her testimony. After the trial testimony, the case was suddenly settled out of court when Chata Bauer was given $500,000 to settle her divorce suit. Wayne knew what the ordeal of testifying in his behalf had cost Gail emotionally, and when the divorce trial was finally over, he took Gail aside, and thanked her for exonerating him on the adultery charge. He had always admired her, and felt protectively towards her, ever since they made "Angel and the Badman." Wayne told Gail, "If ever there is anything I can do, you let me. Do you get that?"[12]

Guy Madison was hunting in Idaho when the John Wayne divorce trial began, and he returned home to see Gail. Gail was a nervous wreck, emotionally, and through tear swollen eyes finally asked Guy to help her seek psychiatric help. Gail told him she could no longer deceive herself that she could handle her problems alone. Guy arranged for Gail to stay at the prestigious Pinel Sanitarium in Seattle, Washington, the renowned Center for Drug and Alcohol Rehabiliation.[13] Gail agreed on condition that Guy accompany her, so he drove her there himself.

For a while, the treatment at the Pinel Sanitarium seemed to help Gail. However, Guy was unable to stay with Gail due to radio recording dates, television shooting schedules, and pre-production conferences for his next film. Gail could endure the rehabilitation treatment as long as Guy was with her, but refused to stay without him. "Don't leave me," she begged him. "Take me home."[14] So Guy brought Gail back home to Hollywood where they were living in separate homes. "I couldn't force the issue," he said on their return. "No treatment in the world does any good if you're fighting it. Gail has to make up her own mind."[15]

While Gail struggled to work things out in her life, Guy continued to work and maintain his new found career. He didn't want to force Gail into giving him a divorce while she was till in a mental flux. There would be no brutal slamming of doors. However, Guy had made up his mind to eventually seek a divorce. If Gail would not instigate divorce proceedings, then Guy would have no choice but to file suit himself. A property settlement had already been drawn up.

Divorce did not mean that there were other men in Gail's life, or that there were other women in Guy's. As Guy told reporters, "Gail has always known that I am a one-woman man."[16] "I loved Gail," he went on. Their early time together gave him "the greatest emotional experience of my life… There were happy times at the beginning… and don't think I'm laying all the blame on Gail. I know I'm not the easiest man in the world to live with."[17] Gail's decision not to stay at the Pinel Sanitarium in Seattle to cure her acute alcoholism, and to find the cause of her periodic moods of depression, would prove to have disastrous consequences later on in her life.

It was shortly before midnight, on November 24, 1953, when Santa Monica Police Officers Edward Sweeney and Bert Dillinger had stopped for a red light at the intersection of Cloverfield and Santa Monica Boulevard. A 1949 convertible suddenly pulled up behind them, and the driver began sounding her horn impetuously and impatently.[18] Both officers got out of their patrol car, and walked over to the convertible to have a talk with the driver. It turned out to be Gail Russell. The officers got a whiff of her breath, and asked the blue eyed actress to take a sobriety test.[19] She thought they were joking. The officers said Gail was "very drunk," and when she took the test, walking in a straight line while holding her nose, she flunked. Police Officer Dillinger later said when he questioned Miss Russell he noticed a "strong odor of alcohol" on her breath as she asked directions.[20]

Gail was then hauled off to Santa Monica City Jail where she was booked on suspicions of drunk driving. As she was being booked and fingerprinted, she began to realize what was happening to her, and began to sob hysterically. Gail was informally clad in a short sleeved checkered shirt, a vest and dungarees. Police impounded her convertible coupe.[21]

Gail gave her name as Betty Gail Russell, and listed her address as 11746 Chenault Street, West Los Angeles. She listed her occupation as "entertainer."[22] Gail had been given a second sobriety test before being booked, but she failed that test also.

Gail tried calling some friends to post her bail bond, but her pleas were not answered. The bail bondman told her they couldn't get her out of jail before 6 a.m.[23] Gail finally contacted Guy's business manager, Charles Trezona, Jr., who posted the $250 bail bond.[24] As Gail was being released at the front desk with Trezona, Jr., she was nervous and trembling as a swarm of news reporters took her picture. As the flashbulbs popped, she wistfully commented to photographers, "I haven't had my picture taken for some time."[25] This seemed to touch the hearts of the usually stone-hearted jailhouse reporters as they shook their heads while gazing at the once beautiful, brunette actress. Gail looked worn and tired, far older than her twenty-nine years. She had spent over five hours in jail before she was finally allowed to leave the Santa Monica Police Station.[26] Guy waited patiently in his car, parked unobserved down the block to avoid courthouse reporters. He later drove Gail home where she could recover before appearing in court for her hearing on the charges of drunk driving.

Gail appeared with her attorney, Harvey Silbert, at 9:30 a.m. on November 26th, before Municipal Judge Thurlow Taft, Jr., and was granted a weeks delay before making her plea. Her lawyer wanted more time to prepare her case.[27] The following week Gail stood before Judge Taft and pleaded not guilty to the charge of drunk driving. She was smartly dressed, but was nervous as she willingly posed for newspaper photographers.

Finally, on January 18, 1954, after numerous legal delays, Gail pleaded guilty to a plain drunk charge, but not guilty to the charge of felony drunk driving. She was fined $150 and placed on two years probation by Judge Thurlow Taft, Jr.[30] The probation stated Gail was not to drink alcohol, and must seek psychiatric help. Her attorney, Harvey Silbert, explained to the judge that Gail had been in "a highly emotional state" due to her estrangement from her husband, Guy Madison, and testimony following the John Wayne divorce trial. She still had to face trial on March 17th on the charge of felony drunk driving.[31] Gail did not testify herself, but her attorney, Harvey Silbert, blamed her erratic behavior on "severe emotional strain,"[32] that she left her mother's house in Santa Monica after having "several drinks." Silbert stated Gail had stopped voluntarily behind the police car while the two officers were giving a ticket to another motorist.[33] After Judge Taft imposed his sentence, Gail sobbed uncontrollably, and fled the courtroom accompanied by her brother, George.[34]

On May 6, 1954, Gail appeared in court accompanied by her defense attorney, Harvey Silbert, as well as her divorce attorney, Guy Ward, and asked that her trial be delayed until October 21st. Her request was granted.

Then on May 27, 1954, Gail, through her attorney, Guy Ward, filed suit for divorce from Guy Madison, charging extreme cruelty. Under a property settlement signed May 10th, Gail would receive $12,194 in cash, two automobiles, and alimony for 10 years ranging from $2,400 to $6,000 a year, depending on Guy's income. The agreement also provided for the alimony to be scaled down to $250 a month while Gail was working.[35] The agreement also proposed payment by Guy of $3,000 to cover the cost of Gail's attorney, Guy Ward. The suit by Gail accused Guy Madison of "grievous mental suffering," a charge which one suspects was her attorney's idea, and not Gail's.[36]

However, Gail soon had a change of heart, and claiming to be "quite emotionally upset," asked attorney Guy Ward to drop her divorce suit.[37] Gail, true to her good nature, was probably upset at Guy being unfairly portrayed as the villain in her divorce suit. Gail knew she was equally to blame for their failed marriage. Perhaps, deep in her heart, she still believed there was a slim chance to salvage her deteriorating marriage. Unfortunately, Guy Madison thought otherwise. He finally had endured enough. He brought his own divorce suit in Santa Monica Superior Court, and on October 6, 1954, testified before Judge Allan Lynch that he had to keep house and prepare meals because Gail wasn't interested. He said, "It was a terrific personal problem. I tried to hire servants 100 or 200 times during our marriage, but Gail always cancelled arrangements. She wouldn't have servants in the house. In the three years we lived together, she permitted not more than four couples to visit our home. When I invited friends, she became emotional or morose, and demonstrated how she felt sometimes physically, and sometimes by sulking."[38] Guy, in his divorce suit, never mentioned Gail's drinking problem. He was too much of a gentleman to further blacken her reputation. Guy's divorce suit was granted. Gail was given $12,194 in cash, jewelry, two cars, and a minimum of $2,400 a year until August of 1964, or until she remarried.[39] Gail did not appear in court, being too emotionally distraught, and wishing not to have her personal problems aired in public. There was also the added emotional strain of fighting her drunk driving charges in court.

After the divorce proceeding was over, Guy Madison talked to reporters. He was still protective of Gail when he said, "I'm heartsick about our separation. I'm still devoted to Gail. I had the chance to experience a strong, honest emotion. I still believe we'll be back together."[40]   Some reporters then tried to get Guy to criticize Gail, to reveal her shortcomings as a wife, but he replied, "Her basic qualities are as fine, and as sound as anyone's I've ever met… she has that 'spark,' that 'artistic touch'… she has more talent in her little finger than I'll ever have…"[41]

This was the unhappy ending to the famous Hollywood romance between Guy Madison and Gail Russell. Gail was to shed many a tear over the loss of Guy and all her happy memories of their life together. Guy was the greatest love of her life, and tragically, her only love. Gail never remarried, and never became emotionally involved with anyone ever again. Guy, on the other hand, soon married actress Sheila Connolly on October 25, 1954, in Juarez, Mexico, after a courtship of only six months, and barely three weeks after his divorce from Gail.

Gail was to appear in court on October 21, 1954, but had her case delayed.[42]   Her attorney, Harvey Silbert, said Gail was still too upset about her divorce from Guy Madison, and was overwhelmed by her personal problems. Referring to her arrest last November in Santa Monica, Gail was quoted as saying, "I'm just a hard luck girl."[43]   Judge Thurlow Taft continued her case to November 8th.[44]   On November 8th, Gail was again a no show, her attorney telling the judge she was in a hospital, and unable to physically appear.[45]   By December 4, 1954, Judge Thurlow Taft was informed by attorney Harvey Silbert that Gail was critically ill in a hospital, and unable to appear in court.[46]   Three days later, Judge Taft was informed by Gail's physician, Dr. John Howard Payne, that the actress was in a coma, and at the point of death, confined at Good Samaritan Hospital since October.[47]   She was diagnosed with acute hepatitis. It seems that all the years that Gail had endured alcohol abuse, her unhealthy eating habits, and the constant mental strain of making motion pictures, had finally taken its toll. Gail was preparing for a role that was to be the most difficult of her career – that of survivor!

Chapter 26
Out Of The Shadows

Gail Russell had been admitted to Good Samaritan Hospital in Los Angeles shortly before her divorce from Guy Madison. No one, not Guy, not her family, not her friends, knew how deathly ill Gail had become. For three of the five months, Gail was confined in an oxygen tent, hovering between life and death. Hepatitis, along with her prolonged use of alcohol, had severely damaged her liver. Even with a healthy nervous system, it would have been difficult for Gail to recover from a hepatitis attack. However, Gail hadn't possessed a healthy nervous system in years. The constant tension and pressure to perform before the movie camera proved a major stumbling block to her recovery. It would be a long, slow recovery.

The first month in an oxygen tent was the roughest for Gail. She could only have a few visitors at a time at first. Her family, her agents Barbara Eddington and Jerry Cloutman, and good friends Rory Calhoun and his wife Lita Baron. Gail now had plenty of time on her hands to do a lot of soul searching, to go over her life, and near death experience. During the many lonely hours when she had no visitors, and no one to talk to, Gail could begin to realize just what the causes were of her many moods of depression, and which resulted in her nervous breakdowns. She also gave credit to the reasons for her eventual recovery.

As Gail recalled to a magazine reporter in 1956, "I thank my Faith, and the fans who put me on the path toward finding it, for overcoming my illness and depression. Looking back today, it's really hard to remember what really set me off. I think it was overwork and not having enough time to catch up with myself. Before, everything happened so fast, there was no time. One morning I was going to Santa Monica High School, the next day I was talking to a Paramount talent scout and being groomed for a picture. For the next ten years there was a terrific mountain of work, always a sense of pressure, no time to think, to relax, to take stock. I tried to be a good scout, and took on too many things. I didn't take care of my health. I never even had time to appreciate my marriage to Guy because my career was like an avalanche which swept me along. I was moving at such speed, everything was blurred. Then I hit bottom."[1]

Gail, at times, under that oxygen tent, clinging to life, with little or no visitors, seemed almost suicidal, and willing to just give up. "I was lonely," Gail remarked. "Now I had plenty of time to catch up, but I didn't have the will. Barbara Eddington and Jerry Cloutman have been my agents for ten years, but they're much more than that. They're my friends. They used to visit me and say, 'If you were just a little bit better, there's a picture coming up!' Lying in bed, each time I would listen, but there was always two big IF's in my mind. 'Can I do it?' I would ask myself. And always, 'Do I want to do it?' I'd made such a mess of things, I wasn't sure I ever wanted to live.

Nothing seemed worth the effort any more. The turning point was not a sudden thing, but slow and gradual over a period of months. It started with my doctor, and was followed up with the best friends a girl ever had – the fans themselves."[2]

This doctor, who was so instrumental in Gail's recovery, was Nicholas Corey, a young intern from Boston. He was not only responsible for Gail's recovery from the hepatitis attack, but helped to restore her mental outlook on life. Gail refused to reveal his name then, but went on, "The doctor shall remain anonymous, but I'll always remember what he did for me. He was rough, bless him, and made me learn to sweat things out. When I couldn't sleep, he wouldn't let me pamper myself with pills. Instead, he would take time to sit and talk to me by the hour until time to go to sleep. Then if another doctor happened to look in and ask, 'Don't you think maybe you ought to give her a sedative?' he would say, 'She doesn't want anything, do you?' and look at me."[3] Young doctor Corey reminded Gail so much of William Russell, her old drama coach at Paramount, who always looked after her like a mother hen, and was hugely responsible for making Gail Russell a major movie star. It was quite possible that Gail soon developed a minor crush over him.

Soon the second major factor in Gail's recovery materialized. Fan letters began arriving at the hospital where she was recovering. Newspaper stories had revealed that Gail was staying at the Good Samaritan Hospital in Los Angeles, and their written words were beginning to help her find her Faith and self confidence.

"Dozens of letters began arriving," Gail remembered, "at a time when I though no one remembered me or cared. One woman sent a card every day. Many wrote and said they were praying for me to get well, and some enclosed religious pamphlets. One day I began reading them – and thinking. I've always had my Bible, but I guess I didn't understand it. Now, I realized that in reading it before, what I had been doing was one thing, while putting it into practice was quite another. I began feeling better with so many remedies that there is Somebody Upstairs who is bigger than we are."[4] Good Samaritan Hospital was operated by a religious denomination and had regular services for the doctors, nurses, and patients. Gail had now discovered the third factor in improving her health and outlook on life – a returning Faith. Then, one Sunday, Gail had an overwhelming urge to attend services.

"I was still weak and not allowed to walk, so I called for a wheelchair and rolled myself down the long corridor to the chapel. After that, I didn't miss a Sunday while I was a patient, and I began to attend midweek services, too. I'm not a member of any denomination, but in that hospital chapel, surrounded by other sick and disturbed people, I found a Faith which gave me an awareness of life and an incentive to come back."[5] Gail became aware of a Higher Power that was bringing her back from the brink of death. As she told another reporter after her recovery, "Everyone has been very kind to me, but it's the 'Man Upstairs' who pulled me through"… I had always been close to Him before, but my eyes had to be opened."[6]

Slowly, but surely, Gail began to recover her health and her strength. She was up to 125 lbs. now, the same weight she had filming "The Uninvited" back in 1943, and began her meteoric rise to movie stardom. Gail was mentally ready to leave the hospital by January, 1955, but she still wasn't physically able to walk for long periods of time. She grew restless just lying in bed, so got in the habit of walking up to the hospital roof where they had a sun deck, and soon developed a nice tan. Shortly before Gail was to be discharged from the hospital, she would take short excursions around the city, and later travel to Westwood to do some shopping, and look for a new place to live. Gail dreamed of a nice little home on a hilltop with a small pool, but finally decided on a small apartment in Westwood with one bedroom, a living room, and a kitchen.[7] The day she left the hospital, Gail stopped over at her brother's home to retrieve her black, toy poodle, "Peanuts," who had been staying with him while she was hospitalized.[8]

The first week from the hospital was hectic for Gail. Her good friend and agent, Barbara Eddington, dropped by her new apartment, followed by Gail's family, and later by Rory and Lita Calhoun. At first Gail didn't want to see anyone, even family or friends, not knowing how she would react. Then there was her old fear of meeting people which always proved to be a nerve shattering experience. Later Gail went to the home of Rory and Lita Calhoun for dinner and a swim. She also accepted an invitation to visit their ranch in Ojai to relax and ride horses.[9]

Gail soon became used to her new found freedom. She would take long walks at the beach, and shop around Westwood. She soon lost most of her excess pounds while in the hospital, but soon found it hard to sleep at night. Not wanting to take a sedative, Gail would use the late hours to resume her hobby of painting until she would eventually go to sleep. She eventually painted over thirty pictures that were used to cover much of the empty wall space in her apartment.

Gail seemed to be getting her life back in order when trouble once again returned to plague her. On the afternoon of February 11, 1955, a car driven by Leonard Deutsch, along with his wife and young daughter, were stopped at the intersection of Whitsett Avenue and Otsego Street in Van Nuys, California. Suddenly, they were rear ended by a rust colored, 1954, Chevrolet convertible, driven by a brunette they described as in her late 20's, wearing a multicolored scarf on her head, and a red or orange jacket. There was a black poodle dog with her. Leonard Deutsch later told police the woman backed off and sped away. He managed to jot down the license plate if the car, which police later found out was registered to Gail Russell.[10] A warrant was later issued for Gail's arrest for felony hit-and-run charge.

Gail later showed up at the Van Nuys Police Station with her attorney, David Heyler, Jr., to tell her version of the incident. She said she waited a "reasonable time" after the collision Friday night, and when the other driver didn't show up, Gail drove to a nearby service station to check her radiator before going home.[11]   Leonard Deutsch's version was a little different. He stated that he walked back to the brunette driver in her late 20's and asked her to pull over to the curb. Instead she backed up and drove off.

The charge against Gail was later reduced to misdemeanor hit-and-run because none of the victims in the accident required hospitalization.[13] Nevertheless, she was later given a citation to appear in Municipal Court of Van Nuys on the charge of misdemeanor hit-and-run on February 23, 1955.[14]

Then on February 21, 1955, Gail received a stroke of good fortune when the drunken driving charges were dismissed against her for the early morning arrest back in November 24, 1953. The Santa Monica City Prosecutor decided to dismiss the charges against Gail "in the interests of justice." She was too ill to appear in court but was represented by her attorney Guy Ward.[15]

Leonard Deutsch later filed a civil suit against Gail for $30,000, claiming physical injuries as well as medical costs. The irony in all this was that their nine month old daughter, Gail, was named after their favorite actress, Gail Russell![16]   The suit was later settled out of court on a settlement that was "satisfying" to both sides.[17]   Gail later paid a $50 fine on the misdemeanor hit-and-run charge without appearing in court.[18]

Then, with all her legal troubles behind her, Gail finally decided to try and resurrect her lost film career, and to retrieve a promise from an old friend – John Wayne.

Chapter 27
Seven Men From Now

It was now June, 1955, and Gail was willing to try and take the next giant step in her life – a return to acting. She called her good friend and agent, Barbara Eddington, and asked her to contact John Wayne. "Could you call John Wayne?" she asked. "Would you tell him I'd like that help he promised me once?"[1]   Barbara Eddington later called Wayne who readily agreed to help Gail, who in her heart, knew that Duke Wayne always kept his word. The honesty that Gail so cherished in her own life also was paramount in Wayne's.

John Wayne's company, Batjac Productions, was now making a Western with Randolph Scott called "Seven Men From Now." Wayne advised Gail to see Andrew McLaglen, who with Robert Morrison, were co-producing the movie. McLaglen had agreed with Wayne that Gail would be good for the role of Annie Greer, but he hadn't seen her since 1948. He knew that the executives at Warner Brothers Studios, who were helping to finance the film, had to be convinced that Gail Russell could be trusted to finish a motion picture. Had Gail fully recovered from her hepatitis attack? Was she really cured of her alcoholism? After so many years off screen, how much value did her name have on a movie marquee? These questions Andrew McLaglen also asked himself. McLaglen had to see if Gail was up to the task of resuming her career. He invited her to a party at the home of actor Robert Stack.[2]

Gail was a little hesitant at attending such a huge party with so many people she didn't know. Her old fear of meeting new people threatened to end her try at a movie comeback. McLaglen later recalled that movie industry party. He said, "It was the first party Gail had attended in nearly four years, and at first she seemed a little nervous about meeting so many important people in the industry again. But she was popular with everyone there, and within minutes her composure was beautiful. I made up my mind that night that she was the girl for the part, but I didn't tell Gail. First, I had to sell her to the other members of Batjac and Warner Brothers.[3]

After the party, Gail knew she was being considered for the part. However, some weeks had passed, and still no final word on whether she would be given that rare commodity in Hollywood – a second chance. Gail recalled, "Once the suspense would have put me in a sanitarium, but I left all that behind me at the hospital. If the Man Upstairs gave me a second chance, I told myself, maybe Hollywood would too."[4]   Then one day, while Gail was in Pismo Beach digging for clams with her agent Barbara Eddington and a couple of girlfriends, they stopped at a café to eat lunch. Gail was asked by her friends on the status of her health, and whether she had taken her vitamin pills. Sensing that something was up, Barbara Eddington finally blurted out "Well, Gail, you test Monday." Gail remembered, "The blood left my face.

Then I realized it was true, there was a terrible moment of doubt when I thought, 'Maybe I can't remember lines. Can I really get the rust out of the wheels?' I not only wanted to – now, I had to. Everything depended on me alone."[5]

Warner Brothers Studios had decided to gamble on the chance that Gail could finish a picture without the assistance of alcohol. They also trusted the confidence of producers John Wayne, Andrew McLaglen, and Robert Fellows. Budd Boetticher was assigned to direct the film, and he would go on to direct many more fine Westerns with Randolph Scott. The entire cast and crew were sent on location to Lone Pine, California, among the Alabama foothills, where many famous action and Western movies had been shot.

However, Gail was at first a little apprehensive at starting her movie career once again after a five year absence. Would she have the same fear of the movie camera once again? Could that paralyzing stage fright, which for so long had plagued her during those many years at Paramount Studios, still haunt her? Did she really want to continue to be an actress? All those things Gail pondered in her heart, but she was determined not to fail again at being an actress.

That first day of filming was the worst. Gail could feel that all eyes were upon her, that the cast and crew were waiting to see how the "notorious" Gail Russell would react to her first day of shooting. She reached into the pocket of her costume and found a note which read, "We're praying for you."[6] Gail later dissolved into tears when she received a telegram from a set worker who had known her from the early days at Paramount Studios. For a moment, Gail didn't think she would be able to go on. She said as much to director Budd Boetticher. He realized that Gail needed the shock treatment, so Boetticher suddenly seized her arms and said, "Look here – you're not going to louse this thing up!"[7] His tough talk seemed to do the trick, and after that first scene was shot, that first day of filming was finished without further delays.

Gail was relieved that the tremendous anxiety of that first day of filming was finally over. She was overwhelmed by the congratulating telegrams that arrived from old friends and acquaintances. Diana Lynn sent a telegram which read, "Make it a smasher, Gail, and be sure and make friends with the horses." Paramount Producer William Dozier also sent a telegram which said, "Get well, come on, we're with you." The village of Lone Pine had also constructed a huge banner at either end of town which read, "Gail Russell is Back and Lone Pine Has Got Her." However, the cast and crew came in from the wrong direction and Gail was unable to see it that first day. The one person Gail was happiest for was her father. "The one who is happiest about it is my dad. He has had three heart attacks and been very unhappy. When I phoned him to tell him I was working again, he said, 'you'd better talk to your mother now!' He couldn't talk because he was crying."[8]

"Seven Men From Now" began on location work at Lone Pine, and it lasted about two and a half weeks. Gail would rise up at 4:00 a.m. to arrive on the set for make-up and costume fitting. Work would start at 5 a.m., and shooting would usually finish by 5:00 p.m. Gail would arrive very tired at the Portal Motel, where she was staying, usually eat her dinner in her pajamas in her room. She would often be handed revisions of the movie script on the next day's filming, and was usually off to bed by 8:00 p.m. Gail was no longer bothered by sleeplessness due to the good mountain air, and the long day's schedule.[9]

Gail was now confident she could finish a picture without the assistance of alcohol. She even welcomed the interviews with reporters that she had always avoided in the past. Gail told INS' Emily Belser, "It's great to be back at work and to know that I'm being accepted as an actress instead of a notorious character."[10] Gail also told AP's Bob Thomas, "Everyone has been very kind to me, but it's the Man Upstairs who pulled me through. I'd always been chose to Him before, but my eyes had to be opened. I was helped by having so many people pull for me. I'd reach in a pocket (while at work) and pull out a note from someone saying, 'We're praying for you'."[11] Gail's director, Budd Boetticher, also told Bob Thomas, "She's doing a fine job. She's not as pretty as she once was, but she's better looking. Her face has more character and she's bound to be a better actress after all she's gone through."[12]

Director Boetticher was immediately impressed with Gail's professionalism and stamina, especially during the second day of filming. The scene called for Gail to fall into a cold pool of water, covered in mud. However, Boetticher wasn't satisfied with the make-up people using the artificial mud to make her look like she really fell into the water. Then Gail, on her own initiative, called the crew aside and deliberately fell face first into the mud. This she tried for take after take until Boetticher was satisified.[13]

Needless to say, director Boetticher's respect and admiration for Gail grew tremendously, and all his initial misgivings were now gone.

Even veteran Western star Randolph Scott was impressed. He said, "All day Monday she was knee deep in mud, covered with it from head to foot and blue and cold, and yet she stayed with it for six hours and never said a word... I've never seen a girl covered with mud look so beautiful. Tuesday was even worse. She was in the river the whole day, and that water coming from those mountain peaks nearly 14,000 feet up is ice cold. She was soaked the whole time and shivering from morning till 4 in the afternoon, and yet what a great job she turned in."[14]

Gail even rode to the location set in the Alabama Foothills on horseback, along with co-star Randolph Scott and director Budd Boetticher. Everyone was impressed with Gail's attitude, on and off the set. John Wayne called her personally from the Warner Brothers Studio, and congratulated Gail on her performance after viewing the daily rushes from the set.[15]

Gail finished the film on schedule, and later celebrated with the cast and the crew. However, she only drank ginger ale on the rocks. Warner Brothers' executives still kept a wary eye on Gail, but she gave them no reason to be worried about her struggle with alcoholism.

"Seven Men From Now" concerned an ex-marshal Ben Stride, played by Randolph Scott, who is on the trail of seven men who robbed a Wells Fargo office, and in the process, killed his wife. He comes across John Greer, played by Walter Reed, and his wife, Annie, played by Gail. They are soon joined by Bill Masters, played by Lee Marvin, where they are soon involved in chasing the fugitive bank robbers. The film is a good Western, and the first one involving Randolph Scott and director Budd Boetticher. It did good business at the movie theaters, but it was best known as Gail Russell's "comeback" film.

The critics were almost unanimous in their praise of "Seven Men From Now." The review from Variety was typical when it said, "Revenge is the driving force cueing the action in *Seven Men From Now* and it stacks up as one of Randolph Scott's better Western entries. The fans will like it and it should have a good ride through the outdoor market... Scott delivers a first rate performance as an ex-sheriff out to get seven men who killed his wife during the holdup of a Wells Fargo office. Gail Russell, off screen for some time, has not lost her appeal and is good as a woman who becomes interested in Scott, even though she is married to Walter Reed, tenderfoot not implicated in the holdup but being used to transport the loot."[16]

A sneak preview was held for "Seven Men From Now" back in Hollywood on July 5, 1956. Gail was in attendance along with her father and good friend, Diana Lynn. Gail recalled that night, "Sitting in the darkness and watching myself up there on the screen, it seemed as though I had never been away. I was in a daze four days later, and I still can't believe that I have made another picture. In the old days, after a preview I had an uncontrollable urge to slip out a side door before anyone saw me. I usually did, too. This night, though, I walked out in the lobby afterward and talked to everybody around, with no effort at all. But for me it was a momentous night for another reason. My wonderful doctor from Good Samaritan Hospital was there, counting the house for me. 'You're taken three years off my life,' he fumed, tongue-in-cheek. But when I looked in his face, I knew he was happy, not only because of what I had done, but because of the fact that I was able to do it."[17]

It was a huge moment of success for Gail. It not only bolstered her own self-confidence in her ability as an actress, but it also proved that she could conquer her need for alcohol to endure the emotional strain of making films. Gail looked forward to the future, and truly believed that all those dark days of fear and depression were far behind her. She was now living in a brave, new world of old friends, and a few new ones. One of her best friends and companions was singer Dorothy Shay, billed as the "Park Avenue Hillbilly." Guy Madison continued to pay her medical bills, and Gail still wore his wedding ring, mostly out of sentiment and habit. She still hoped to find romance some day, but not just now.[18] "I may marry again some day, but now I want to get my career going. I'd like to get some security. As to the future, 'It's an open door.' It's what I make of it. But with the help and confidence people have shown they have in me, it's the best go ahead signal I know."[19]

Chapter 28
The Hedda Hopper Interview

On November 22, 1955, Gail arranged an interview with famous Hollywood columnist Hedda Hopper at her home in Beverly Hills, California. Gail was accompanied by her agents Barbara Eddington and Bill Latham. As they sat down to talk, Hedda noticed that Gail came dressed in black and white, full circle black skirt, white jersey blouse, over black and white vest, black shoes, and a large tan purse which didn't match the tan pumps. She also noticed a wedding ring on Gail's left hand, and that she wore small, shaped gold earrings.

HH: Glad to see you.

Gail: It's about time.

HH: What do you think I should do? Interview you in the hospital? I nearly did. How many pictures have you made since recovery?

Gail: Just one. I think that is a big step. Last year I was in the hospital.

HH: Tell me. Did Howard Hughes pay your hospital bills?

Gail: No, Hughes didn't pay for the bills.

HH: Did Guy pay?

Gail: That is being worked out.

HH: Did you know what brought about all this – I mean your illness?

Gail: I don't know. Think a lot of work and not having enough time to catch up with myself.

HH: When you started your film career, didn't you have fear of it, and fear of sound stages?

Gail: Yes, but I love it.

HH: What did you fear?

Gail: The people you see, it takes me time to get sort of acclimated. Once there, then I am all right. You know you get your feet in the door. Meeting new people is always nerve shattering. I think it is to everyone.

HH: Not to everyone. Are you still shy, or have you buried it?

Gail: It still takes a little time.

HH: I hear you used to go on a sound stage and would upchuck because you were so nervous.

Gail: Probably too much coffee.

HH: Are you a coffee fiend?

Gail: I don't want to count how many cups I've had this morning.

HH: How many?

Gail: About 4.

HH: You know it is bad for you, and you still drink it?

Gail: Yes.

HH: So do I. About a year ago I was sick. My doctor took me off coffee and put me on postum.

Gail: You can't give up all your vices at once.

HH: I have so few left.

Gail: Let me have my coffee and cigarettes.

HH: I stayed off coffee for five months. Then it got too dull. I was taking postum and pablum. Are they your only bad habits – coffee and cigarettes?

Gail: Yes, Dammit.

HH: How about men?

Gail: I'm not going with anyone now. I'm available.

HH: Have you any advice to give young girls who might be in the same nerve condition you were in? There are a lot of insecure girls starting out in life and business.

Gail: I think the main thing is I tried to satisfy the demands of too many people. I did so many pictures. One right after another, and tried to be a nice guy, and tried to do too many things (that went against her own inner and higher self). I didn't take care of my health like I should. I think the answer would be to learn to be temperate.

HH: You were just about 18 when you started in pictures, weren't you?

Gail: Yes. I didn't want to be thought of as a bad sport. Result is that you can't satisfy everyone. When you try to do it, this is what happens. All of a sudden it stops. Then you can't satisfy anyone. You can't even satisfy yourself!

HH: Now you are going to take things a little easier?

Gail: Cut down on coffee and cigarettes and lead a dull life.

HH: Weren't you in an oxygen tent for almost three months?

Gail: It is so lonely in there, and no one to talk to, except the Man Upstairs.

HH: And did you converse with the Man Upstairs?

Gail: Oh yes. That is why I'm here.

HH: Did you ever go to A.A. meetings?

Gail: I've talked to several people in it. It has helped a great many people. I know it is good for some people. It depends upon the particular thing that helps that one person. You can't use the same rule for all people, I think. Not even with the same problem.

HH: When you turned to the Man Upstairs, did you read the Bible?

Gail: Of course. I'd always had that – church, Sunday school, and so forth. But it was just something you did on Sunday. When you are really in need and are really scared, then you seek for something bigger, and more.

HH: When there is nothing else to turn to, you turn to it. Then you read the Bible with greater understanding. Religion is something you have to live with daily. There's a book I must send you. Not religious, but another book. I think would be of vast help to you. It has been to me. I started to read it two weeks ago. It makes you know what you are and what you can do. Was there any particular individual, a minister, or someone like that who came to you when you were sick? Or did you work it out for yourself?

Gail: Through people, and thinking. This time I spent in the hospital, I had time to go over a period in my life when I was working so fast, I didn't have a chance to think. I realized I had been selfish. I found that what I was doing for others and always trying to be a nice guy, wasn't being nice at all. It was being selfish. I wasn't giving of myself. I was giving of what they wanted to do. In other words, I wasn't being true to my own design. I was putting on a mask in order to be acceptable to others. Even when it was going against all my own inner feelings and sensibilities.

HH: I know what you mean. When I was a child, my mother told me I had to love the neighbor's brat. But I didn't. I hated her, and one day I tried to hit her over the head with a hammer and bash in her brains. Were you happy in your marriage?

Gail: I didn't appreciate it. I didn't have time to appreciate it.

HH: How old were you when you were married?

Gail: Let's see. It was in August (voice trailed off vaguely, apparently either didn't remember or didn't want to say).

HH: I see you are still wearing a wedding ring.

Gail: Yes.

HH: Is it Guy's?

Gail: No, mine, and it's paid for (with finality, didn't want to discuss).

HH: You were both pretty young when you were married. You were young, 18(?), and Guy was young for his age. I think he just started to grow up in the last two years. Do you still see Guy, or is that a closed chapter?

Gail: Yes.

HH: Don't even see him on the screen anymore?

Gail: No.

HH: When you cut it, you cut if off, like that!

Gail: I remember the time we came to your home. Guy picked me up after I finished work. We were late. You were doing a magazine layout and had the girls line up on the stairs. Pete Lawford was your favorite then. You got perturbed because I was late. The fact was, I was frightened and didn't want to come in. Finally, we gathered up strength and walked in, and you put a hat on me. You know I've hated hats ever since. I've hated them. You acted like a school Maarm – "Get over there in line!" Then you took a turn and took it out on Guy. You had him take off his clothes and get in a bubble bath. He said to me, 'What am I going to do?' I said, 'Do it, and be a good sport. She'll never use it.' Then everyone went home and poor Guy put on his clothes. Your son was sitting there. Then I told you up and down. Next day, I thought I can't do this, and I sent you a pill box by special delivery. That was turning point in my life. That is off my chest. I've said it and I'm glad. You will never know what that did to Guy, and me. I was embarrassed. I though I'd die when you put him in that bubble bath, with that bunch of girls standing around. Little things like that in this business, if you are shy at all, they can be devastating. Next time someone says, "Come on. Let's go. They are making another magazine layout," you think, "Now, how will I dress? Shall I wear a bathing suit underneath in case I get put in a bubble bath?"

HH: I don't even remember. I know I did some of those corny picture layouts.

Gail: I'm sorry you didn't get the pill box. I put a note in it that went something like, "Thank you for the lovely party, From one pill to another." I remember, because it took me such a long time to figure out what to put in the note. We met once after that. I asked if you received the pill box. You didn't remember anything about it. I have a fabulous memory. I wish I could lose it.

HH: I remember the party. Pete Lawford was there.

Gail: Yes, and June Haver. We all had charades to do. June and I went out of the room together. She said, "I'm so embarrassed to do this." I said I couldn't think. The idea of getting up in front of people and Bill Williams, and Barbara Hale were there, and I think Jane Powell.

HH: Isn't that funny. That stuck in your mind all that time, and you still resent it.

Gail: This really hurt because I went down and got a beautiful pill box. I'd seen your collection, and I wasn't making much money.

HH: Guy should have hated me more than you, making him get into a bubble bath.

Gail: Your son was there, and when I said I was mad, he said to tell you.

HH: He'd tell anybody to beat up Mother. Always did.

Gail: Guy said, "Don't say anything," and I said I'm going to tell her.

HH: (Discussion about incident with Wayne). Then "I don't think Guy liked me for a long time."

Gail: You see, that was my trouble. I kept things inside and let them work up.

HH: If you could spit it out. Now can you spit it out? Will you to other people?

Gail: I have been.

HH: Speaking of Guy, two years ago I gave a party, and he was among the first to arrive. A few of us were in the garden, and he gave his order on the way out. When I saw him, I said, "You're drinking orange juice!" He'd look at the waiter and order another. They stayed and stayed. I have a bad back, once in a while my sacroiliac goes out, and it takes about three hitches to get up out of a chair. At 12:30 I said, "If you haven't got sense enough to go home now, I'm going to bed. You can stay as long as you like. There's food and the drinks." Guy said, "I'm going to carry you up," and grabbed me. I said, "Put me down, you fool!" He insisted he was going to carry me up. I finally struggled free and flew up the stairs and locked the door. I didn't want anybody coming up. The next day I said to Bill, "I can't understand why Guy did that. He wasn't drinking anything but orange juice." Bill said,

"Orange juice! Don't be so naïve, he was drinking screwdrivers!" (To Gail) You must remember hundreds of incidents.

Gail: I've got lots of them. One of the first I remember was at Paramount. I was being posed in a red bathing suit. Everyone had just broken for lunch. It was raining. There was a big puddle there, and we were doing publicity shots. It was like pulling teeth for me because I've always been self-conscious about my knees. Here I was in this bathing suit, wearing boots and standing in this puddle. All of a sudden, people started coming past going into the commissary. Mr. Meiklejohn, and then here comes my idol, Alan Ladd, and here I am standing in this cold, drizzling rain. I wished I could pick up the puddle and pull it over me, but it wasn't deep enough. After this, I was a little leery about doing anything.

HH: Is Alan still you ideal? (idol?)

Gail: He and Sue sent me the most beautiful bouquet at the hospital, and I never even thanked them. Then so much time went by, and it was too late.

HH: Alan does lots of sweet things. He sends me fresh eggs every week from his farm.

Gail: Bill Dozier sent me a telegram from New York. When I came back to do the first picture, and was sitting up there on that wagon, and looked down and saw all those people smiling encouragingly, and then after I'd said the first speech and the director called "Cut," I knew it would be clear sailing. From now on, I had such wonderful notes from people. My pockets were filled with little prayers and gook luck wishes. I always have pockets in my dresses, so I'll have some place to put my hands. I think they are too big.

HH: Why your hands and feet are just right for your size.

Gail: Diana Lynn sent me a wire. It said, "Make it a smasher, Gail, and be sure and make friends with the horses." You know how they say animals steal your scenes in picture? I had all these wonderful, wonderful things from people. Up at Lone Pine, they put up a sign at either end of the village that said, "Gail Russell Is Back and Lone Pine Has Got Her." So we came in the other way and I didn't get to see it. Bill Dozier sent a wire – "Get Well, Come On, We're With You."

(Gail turned to Mrs. Eddington and discussed whether or not she should mention her doctor, didn't think he would want publicity of any kind. He's a young, unmarried doctor from Boston, Nicholas Corey at Good Samaritan.) She requested that we do not use his name in print. He wouldn't like it.

Gail: Dr. Corey in the hospital has the most wonderful philosophy about things. He was an intern in the hospital when I went there. He'd give me a boost when I needed it, and a slap when I needed it. Right now he's putting me out on a limb. It's like Bill Russell, drama coach who worked with me on "Dear Ruth" and "Our Hearts." He held my hand during the picture until finally one day he said, "Well, Goodbye." I said, "What do you mean, I'm starting a picture." He said, "I've taught you all I know, you take it from here. You're on your own. You've learned technique and everything I can give you. The only thing you need now is experience. There are people who can only help you so far. Then there comes a point where it has to be broken off. You've got to try you own wings."

HH: Like a mother bird tossing the baby out of the nest.

Gail: Dr. Corey taught me to grow up. He is going to make a simply wonderful doctor. He is one now. He's not a psychiatrist, but he understands people. They had me fat and sassy by the time I got out of the hospital. They were just wonderful to me.

HH: How long were you in the hospital?

Gail: Seemed like ages to me.

HH: Then you never really knew Howard Hughes?

Gail: I met him just once. I stopped in to have my dinner. I still had my make-up on. Howard was at the table. All he wanted was a plain salad and a plain piece of meat. He couldn't make the waiter understand. So he sent it back a couple of times. People at the table started talking. That got my dander up. I told the waiter just what he wanted and said bring it to him right away. He hasn't had dinner. He was leaving as I started out, so I said I'll drop you at the studio. This was my only meeting with Hughes. I dropped him off at the gate and said goodnight.

HH: I understand he got in touch with the hospital and wanted to do something for you. You know he flew in doctors from all over America for Mala Powers. He's interested in medicine, understand he'll leave his money to a cancer foundation in Texas. Were there any stars, or older women, who helped you from the studio?

Gail: Yes, close friends. There was Lindsay Durand of Paramount Publicity. She took me on my first trip to New York, and had an appendicitis attack along with the whole thing. I started out weighing 125 lbs., went through "The Uninvited," a fast picture. Then went to New York for it. After the opening, I returned home weighing just 106 lbs. Lost that weight in just seven or eight weeks. They had me going at such a fast pace, a cup of coffee, hors d'oeuvres, and away we'd go. So if I were to give advice, it would be to space your time. Take time out for a horseback ride in the mountains. Get back to normality and nature. They put you on a merry-go-round here and never let you off. Not even to have a cup of coffee.

HH: Any advice or love to give the young?

Gail: I don't know what to tell you.

HH: You're still shy?

Gail: That I can't help.

HH: You won't believe it, but I was too when I was very young, and even after I married DeWolf Hopper. If anybody noticed my color, and I had lots of color then, I'd go scarlet. Tears would come, and I'd leave the room. But I got that beaten out of me. I guess I've beaten it out of a few people since. I don't realize this. I don't mean it to be unkind. I have so much work to do and so much time to get it done. Are you under contract to anyone now – Batjac?

Gail: No. I'm available. When I went over to Paramount, everyone was very nice to me. Milt Lewis threw his arms around me and had tears in his eyes.

HH: You have lots of friends around this town.

Gail: It was nice being here, and getting everything off my chest.[1]

Chapter 29
The Tattered Dress

After the release of "Seven Men From Now" in July of 1956, Gail received no further film offers from movie producers. Her five year absence from the silver screen, the reluctance to attend the usual Hollywood parties and movie premieres, the reclusive lifestyle, all these had kept Gail away from the necessary social contacts an actress needed to continue to be available to movie industry executives.

Tired of waiting for that phone call from a movie studio, Gail decided to try and find work in television. The old movie studio system was in decline, this coupled with falling movie revenues due to the popularity of the growing television medium. It was no longer a stigma for established actors and actresses to appear in television programs to make a decent living.

Gail was cast in an episode of Studio 57 entitled "Time, Tide, and a Woman." She portrayed Jane Finley, who helps to prevent a shipboard mutiny. It was directed by Herschel Daugherty, and also starred John Baer as the first mate, Mike Brenner. It was a standard TV melodrama, but Gail looked attractive and comfortable in her role as the only lady aboard ship.

It wasn't until February of 1957 that Gail finally found employment in a major motion picture. She was offered the role of Carol Morrow in Universal International's courtroom drama, "The Tattered Dress," starring Jeff Chandler, Jeanne Crain, Jack Carson, and Elaine Stewart. The film was to be directed by Jack Arnold. For the first time in many years, Gail was not to be the female lead, but instead that key role went to Jeanne Crain. The other major female lead went to rising young actress Elaine Stewart, whose role was pivotal to the nature of the plot. It was a small, but subtle testimony to the decline of Gail's star power, and to the fact that she could no longer sell a movie solely on the prestige of her name.

Under Jack Arnold's direction, Gail did a very capable job of acting, particularly in the tense courtroom scenes with Jeff Chandler. In fact, that old habit of Gail's to constantly ring her hands during a scene proved disastrous to the pair of tan kid gloves she was using as a prop. The scene called for Gail to break down emotionally as she was being mercilessly cross-examined by attorney Blane, played by Jeff Chandler, in a long courtroom sequence. As she was being badgered by the pitiless questioning, Gail twisted and pulled at the gloves until at the end of the scene, they were in shreds. Filming of the scene from another angle couldn't be started until the prop department could find a pair of duplicate gloves.[1] It was mute testimony to the fact that Gail still struggled while performing before the unrelenting glare of the movie camera. Nevertheless, Gail put in an above average performance in the movie, and director Arnold was more than satisfied with her work.

"The Tattered Dress" was the story of top New York criminal defense attorney James Gordon Blane, played by Jeff Chandler, who is brought to a small town in California to defend Michael Reston, played by Philip Reed, who has killed a man to defend his wife, Charlene, played by Elaine Stewart. The story involves murder, rape, jury tampering, adultery, a frame-up, and enough melodrama to keep an audience interested. It was an above average courtroom drama with a fine cast. It was a success with movie goers, if not with the movie critics. The New York Times was a prime example of the film's response when it said, "If the Goddess of Justice is not blind, as generally pictured, then she certainly is myopic, to judge by "The Tattered Dress," which was exposed by the Mayfair yesterday. For this workmanlike and sometimes absorbing melodrama is weakened by this basic premise – that its young, famous but cynical criminal lawyer can sway juries by using either a vast knowledge of human failings and legal tricks of the trade or, when his own fate is at state, simple fervent truths. The evidence presented in both cases is nominal… as the beleaguered lawyer, Jeff Chandler does a forthright forceful stint. Jack Carson does a slick job as the smiling but scheming arm of the law. Gail Russell has an effective scene or two as his partner in double dealing."[2]

After this second successful film performance, Gail seemed well on her way to resuming her acting career. However, it would all soon come unexpectedly to an end just a few short months later. On the morning of July 4, 1957, Gail was driving westbound on Beverly Boulevard near La Cienega in West Los Angeles, when she suddenly lost control of her brand new white convertible. She crossed the center divider in the road, and crashed through the front windows of Jan's Coffee Shop at 8424 Beverly Boulevard. Gail had narrowly missed another car traveling eastbound on Beverly Boulevard, but her car had penetrated all the way to the front counter of the restaurant, seriously injuring the night porter.[3] The night porter, Robert Lee Reynolds, was pinned against the counter by Gail's car and suffered a broken leg and hip. He was pulled free by Jerry Reichman, a U.S.C. pre-legal student. Reichman told the two officers who arrived first on the scene, Herb Wharmly and G.L. Williams, that the car Gail was driving "missed me by inches, if I hadn't slammed on my brakes, I would have been hit."[4]

Gail was only slightly injured with only a slight cut on the bridge of her nose. The police officers instantly noticed that Gail seemed to be under the influence of alcohol, and lead officer Sgt. C.H. Specht gave her a preliminary drunk driving test, which she failed. She gave her address as 1526 Veteran Avenue, West Los Angeles, but the car was registered to Gail R. Moseley of 8470 Santa Monica Boulevard. When asked her line of work, Gail allegedly said, "I work for God." The officers also noticed that Miss Russell seemed to be reacting hilariously to the drink test. When Sgt. Specht asked Gail to extend her arm for a balance test, she exclaimed, "I'd rather dance," and seizing the sergeants arm, performed a fast step or two.[5] Specht then asked

Gail to touch her nose from the arm extended position, but instead tapped the sergeant's nose, gurgling, "You're cute!"[6]   Then Gail was asked by the officers how many drinks she had, which she replied, "I had a few drinks." Then later said, "I had two. No. Four. Oh, I don't know how many I had. It's nobody's business anyway."[7]

The officers noticed also that Gail was wearing a pair of white ballet slippers, tan jodhpurs, and a trench coat.   When she noticed that news photographers were taking pictures of her taking the sobriety test, Gail asked to be taken back in the restaurant kitchen where she could be examined in private. "Would you mind, please," she asked the photographers, "This isn't fair, you know. I'm more worried about that boy (Reynolds) than anything else."[8] As Gail took out her wallet to show police officers her driver's license, she remarked, "I'd give all the money in here or anything else I've got it only that boy hadn't been hurt. I'm more worried about that boy than anything else."[9]

When asked where she was headed when the accident happened, Gail replied, "I was on my way to visit my dad on Maple Drive. He's suffered three heart attacks, the most recent three days ago. I've been very upset about him."[10]   When Gail was finally told she was gong to jail to be booked on suspicion of misdemeanor drunk driving, the stark reality of her situation finally dawned on her.[11]   She began to sob uncontrollably. Gail was later taken to Lincoln Heights jail where she spent the next five hours. Police later stated that Gail would be charged with misdemeanor drunk driving.[12]   She was released on a $263 bail on July 5th, accompanied by her attorney Fred Kraft, and Jay Thompson, her press agent. Gail told waiting reporters that she would never again touch a drop of intoxicating liquor.[13]

Gail later faced a second charge of felony drunk driving, released on $1,000 bail, and ordered to appear later at a Municipal Court arraignment on July 19th.[14]   She was also served with a civil suit for $75,000 by the night porter who was injured when her car crashed into the coffee shop on July 4th. Gail again told reporters she was "very sorry it happened," and added "I'm never going to drink again."[15]

It is not hard to imagine Gail Russell's state of mind at this point in her life. The second chance of a movie "comeback" was now gone, and Gail knew in her heart that Hollywood never gives a penitent actor or actress a third chance at redemption. Even worse, this extremely shy and emotionally fragile young woman now had her tragic alcoholic relapse now spread all over the front pages of America's newspapers. In addition, all those loyal friends and movie fans who once stood by her side, and cheered her physical and emotional comeback, were now nowhere to be found. Gail's bright star, which had risen so brilliantly with the release of "The Uninvited" in 1944, had fallen to earth. Gail Russell, who had been voted "A Star of Tomorrow" by the Motion Picture Exhibitors of America in 1947, was now a fallen star. It was such a tragic ending to a once promising movie career.

Municipal Court Judge Gerald C. Kepple set a preliminary hearing for Gail in Los Angeles on the charge of felony drunk driving on July 19, 1957. However, when the day arrived, Gail failed to show up. Then on August 21st, a felony warrant was issued for Gail Russell, where sheriff's deputies were sent to her apartment at 1526 Veteran Avenue, West Los Angeles.[16] When Sgts. H.W. Trail and G.A. Corbett arrived at Gail's door, they were met by her mother, Gladys, who told them, "Gail's on the bathroom floor. Will you help me get her up?"[17] The officers found Gail unconscious on the bathroom floor with a half finished highball nearby. She was barefooted, in green pajamas, and was immediately put in an ambulance where she partly regained consciousness in route to the hospital, but was incoherent. Gail was put in the prison ward of General Hospital where she was treated for an upset stomach. She was later transferred to the County Jail to await hearing on the drunk driving charge.[18]

Gail was now in court on October 15, 1957 before Superior Court Judge Lewis Drucker, where she pleaded not guilty to the charge of felony drunk driving. Bail was set at $2,000, and the thirty-three year old actress was set free to appear on trial at another date. Gail was represented by her new defense attorney, Rexford Eagan.[19]

When Gail was well enough to appear at court, it was February 2, 1958.[20] She appeared before Superior Court Judge Richard C. Fildew, and was convicted of misdemeanor drunk driving. She was fined $420 and given a suspended 30-day jail sentence, placed on three years probation, and had her driver's license suspended for an indefinite period.[21] The charge was reduced to a misdemeanor after Gail's attorney, Rexford Eagan, argued there was evidence a tire on her car blew out shortly before she crashed into Jan's Coffee Shop on July 4, 1957.[22]

Gail was extremely fortunate to escape the felony drunk driving charge, as well as spending time in jail. However, now she was known as a convicted drunk driver, as well as unable to control her alcoholism. It was a reputation Gail was to carry for the rest of her life.

Chapter 30
No Place To Land

It was October, 1958, and Gail Russell had spent nearly a year back in the hospital recovering from her alcoholic relapse. She was determined to try and regain her movie career once again, but was finding it extremely difficult to find movie work. Gail was reduced to living off Guy Madison's alimony payments until she could find employment. However, the word was out – Gail Russell was an alcoholic, and a convicted drunk driver. Movie executives were afraid to give her a third chance at redemption.

Even Gail's good friend and trusted agent, Barbara Eddington, couldn't find her work. In desperation, Gail hired high powered talent agent Glen Shaw to try and find her employment. Yet he almost had to fight with movie producers and directors to give Gail a chance at resuming her career.

Finally, Republic Studios offered Gail a role in their upcoming film, "No Place to Land," starring John Ireland and Mari Blanchard. It was the first "B" movie Gail had ever been involved with. She was cast in a secondary role of Lynn Dillon, the wife of a crop duster, who falls for the pilot friend of her husband, Jonas Bailey, played by John Ireland. The film was produced and directed by Albert C. Gannaway. It was just an average melodrama about the migrant life of crop dusters with a love triangle involving Jonas, Lynn, and the wife of Jona's boss, Iris Lee, played by Mari Blanchard.

Mari Blanchard was the real star of the film, and most of the movie publicity was full of her face and figure to promote the film. It was a typical low budget film usually on the lesser side of the movie bill playing at the local cinema. Director Gannaway did a commendable job working with Gail, although you could tell by her appearance that her movie days were almost over. Gone was the lustrous beauty that had catapulted her to Hollywood fame, and had so captivated as well as enchanted movie audiences. She could no longer depend upon her physical beauty to attract movie goers. The damage that hepatitis had done to her liver and health, as well as the prolonged abuse of alcohol, had almost completely destroyed her beauty. Gail looked old, well beyond her thirty-four years.

"No Place to Land" was not well received by the movie public, neither by the movie critics. Despite this, Gail continued to try and continue in the acting profession. She wanted people to know, especially those in the entertainment industry, that Gail Russell could be trusted to finish a film, and that she could stop drinking. The newspaper interviewers and magazine reporters that she once shunned, Gail now eagerly courted. She no longer avoided frank and personal questions. As Gail told one reporter, "You might as well go ahead and say I'm an alcoholic, because that's what I am. You might also say I hope to God I'm off the stuff for good, because an alcoholic just doesn't drink and live. I have to stay in this business. It's all I know. I never finished high school, you know. I'm going to win this fight. I know I'm going to."[1]

Erskine Johnson, a Los Angeles Mirror Newspaper columnist, was given a rare personal interview by Gail in her apartment at 1527 Veteran Avenue in West Los Angeles. It was considered "on the wrong side of the tracks" by Hollywood social standards. Gail welcomed the columnist wearing spotless white slacks, a pale green sweater, open sandals, a multicolored bandana, and a warm smile.[2] Johnson had known Gail from her early days at Paramount and was very familiar with her troubled past. He was impressed with her modest apartment, especially the many professional-like paintings that covered the walls of her living room. Paintings that Gail had painted herself. Johnson also noticed a frame with these words, "When God is going to do something wonderful, He begins with a difficulty. If it is going to be something very wonderful, He begins with an impossibility." He recognized instantly that it was a famous quote practiced by people who were involved with Alcoholics Anonymous. Gail told him with a sound of hopefulness in her voice, "I start every day reading those words."[3]

Gail talked with Johnson about her recent drunk driving arrest last July 4th, and her determination not to repeat any more automobile accidents or drunken escapades. Gail swore to him, "I'm going to win this war!"[4]

In her conversation with Erskine Johnson, Gail recalled her early years in high school when she was just a shy, naïve little girl at University High School who was studying to become a commercial artist. Then there was her sudden discovery by Paramount Studios, and before Gail knew what was happening, she was a star opposite Ray Milland in "The Uninvited." Studios executives told her she was a star, but all Gail knew was that she was still a frightened high school girl, naturally shy and reserved, with no acting talent. All she had was a beautiful face, haunting eyes, and a low, whisper-like voice that was unforgettable. With no previous acting experience, Gail now had to memorize dialogue, know where to stand, how to look. Directors, producers, and movie directors had to pound performances out of her. They closed her movie sets to visitors while they had to rant and rave over countless rehearsals, countless mistakes.[5]

This is when Gail got into the tragic habit of going across the street from Paramount for that quick drink to give her the courage to endure filmmaking. This started the decent into alcoholism. The more the directors pounded the performances out of Gail, the more often she made the short walk across the street to Lucy's Restaurant on Melrose Avenue. Finally, Erskine Johnson asked Gail if she had any regrets about Hollywood giving her fame and fortune at nineteen years of age. She thought for a minute, and then said, "My only regret will be if I can't make something good out of all this to give comfort to other people."[6]

Another reporter for the Los Angeles Mirror Newspaper, Roby Heard, remembered Gail Russell, the "Girl with the Tragedy Air," whose film colony friends knew was destined for unhappiness. When he interviewed them after

Gail's first arrest for drunk driving in November, 1953, friends told him, "Something like this was bound to happen eventually."[7] They blamed her troubles on Gail's inability to adjust to sophisticated movie circles. "After all, she was just a high school kid in Santa Monica when a talent scout spotted her beauty and signed her to a contract."[8] Her shyness and feelings of insecurity made it impossible for Gail to mingle freely and with ease in movie social circles. "She was brought into the movies so suddenly and in such a spectacular fashion that Hollywood stardom and sophisticated living were too much for her."[9]

Another studio official told Heard that Gail was catapulted to fame "without knowing what it was al about."[10] He also said that on the set and at parties, Gail was shy and distant, and avoided contact with other people in favor of solitude in her dressing room. Lacking the courage to face the mores and morals of Hollywood, Gail became a "Lone drinker." When forced to attend parties, she sat alone, shunning the company of other guests and quietly sipping from a cocktail glass.

It was also in this year of 1958 that Gail had a personal family tragedy. Her father, George, Sr., who had been struggling with health problems for years, died of a heart attack. Gail had been previously close to her mother, Gladys, but it was her father of whom she was particularly fond. He had been her close friend and confidant during her early childhood, and had understood her childlike fear of people while performing in public. Gail could still remember those late night talks with her father after he would come home from work. She fondly recalled that gentle tapping on her bedroom door, and later raiding the refrigerator for a midnight snack. Gail could still see herself perched on the kitchen table, wearing her long, flannel nightgown, solemnly reciting Edgar Allan Poe's "The Raven." It was a devastating loss for Gail, even more devastating than the loss of Guy Madison.

The relationship with her mother, Gladys, was not as close, particularly in the years after her marriage to Guy Madison. Her mother was very hurt and resentful at not being invited to her only daughter's wedding. Gail's father had forgiven her long ago, but not Gladys. It was a rift that Gail had failed to go out of her way to heal, and was one of the main reasons her mother was not involved in her life.

There was also Gladys' reaction to Gail's failure to succeed as a Hollywood star. Gladys couldn't believe that Gail so carelessly "threw her career out the window" at Paramount Studios with her drinking, along with her refusal to do scheduled film projects. How could any young girl not want to be a glamorous movie star, and refuse an opportunity most young girls or women would die for? It was a mother's natural reaction to her daughter's failure to handle success when it was offered.

Gail's mother has come under criticism by some for pushing her daughter to succeed in a career she never truly loved. While it may be true to a certain extent, it was Gail who retrieved that note from Milton Lewis from the school wastebasket back in 1942, asking her to come to Paramount Studios for a screen test. However, it was Gail who later said that "Mother practically dragged me to that test at Paramount" according to actress Yvonne De Carlo in her autobiography.[11]   One of the great tragedies in Gail's life was that there was no support system for her to fall back on when she tried to stop drinking. Her family, her husband, even her so-called close friends, failed to help her to the fullest when she needed it the most. Then again, perhaps, it was Gail's extreme shyness that prevented her from seeking help. Yes, there was blame to go around for everyone with regard to Gail and her problems. Yet, perhaps it was Gail's own nature that was ultimately responsible for her downfall.

Chapter 31
Noblesse Oblige

After Gail completed "No Place to Land" in 1958, no further offers came from movie producers. She was finding it increasingly difficult to supplement her income. If Gail didn't have Guy Madison's monthly alimony check, she would have been in dire financial straits. Even high powered agent Glen Shaw was finding it hard to persuade movie producers to hire Gail. She was using her free time to indulge in her other passion – art. Gail's paintings were primarily in oil, usually landscapes and animals. They were really quite good, and there were a lot of people who thought the world lost a very talented artist when Gail chose to become a movie star.

Gail kept her apartment clean and tidy in case visitors dropped by, but her home, at 1526 Veteran Avenue in West Los Angeles, was considered "on the wrong side of the tracks" by her Hollywood friends. They never dropped by for a visit, and her only visitors were representatives from Alcoholics Anonymous. Gail used to attend meetings at their facility, but her extremely shy nature preferred that their officials come to her home.

It wasn't until December, 1959, when Gail finally found work, but it was only to be on television. She got a phone call from her agent telling her there was an offer to appear in the television series, "The Rebel," produced by Andrew J. Fenady.

Andrew J. Fenady was just a high school senior in Toledo, Ohio, when he first saw Gail Russell on the big screen in "The Uninvited" back in 1947. He took one look at the lovely, dark haired beauty and developed a serious "movie star crush." After Fenady graduated from high school and college, he moved out West to California to seek fame and fortune. By the age of twenty-nine, he had produced a significant television series called "Confidential File," had bootlegged a feature called "Stakeout On Dope Street," and had written and produced a low budget Paramount feature, "The Young Captives." Andrew Fenady had become something of a "Wonder Boy" of network television by 1959.

Fenady, as creator, producer, and writer, had written an episode of "The Rebel" television series called "Noblesse Oblige." He had cast the two male leads, Robert Vaughn and Kenneth Tobey, as well as the every day lead in the series, Nick Adams. Fenady only had to cast the female lead of Cassandra Bannister. He suddenly remembered that haunting brunette beauty of his youth, Gail Russell, and the recent troubles of her life. He called in Bernie Kowalski, who was directing the episode, into his office and said, "Bernie, how would you like Gail Russell for the part of Cassandra?" Kowalski said, "You think she'd do it?" Fenady thought for a moment, then said, "I don't know if she would – I don't know if she could."[1]

Fenady got on the phone to Gail's agent, Glen Shaw, and told him Gail could come over to Paramount Studios where they were filming the series, and read for the part. He told Shaw if Gail got the part, she would have to stay sober for the two days of filming, and get paid $400 a day.[2]

When Gail walked into Fenady's office to read for the part, he could feel the blush come to his cheeks as she extended her hand. Even though he was a happily married man, Fenady could still remember the old school boy crush he had as he beheld Gail Russell in the flesh.

Fenady recalled that first meeting with Gail years later. He said, "She had eyes like a frightened fawn, except they were blue. A little mysterious, a little mischievous, and very large and very vulnerable."[3] Gail finally broke the awkward silence when she said, "You know, Mr. Fenady, this used to be Charlie's office."[4] Fenady looked puzzled for a moment, then said, "Charlie who?" Gail smiled and said, "Charlie Brackett, he produced 'The Uninvited.'"[5] Gail continued with, "I stopped by and saw Edith. Edith has picked out a gown that Margaret Sullivan wore in "So Red The Rose." I visited with Nellie. She said she'd do my hair. And Wally wants to do my make-up."[6] "Edith" was Edith Head, famous costume designer for Paramount Studios. "Nellie" was Nellie Manley, chief of hairdressing at Paramount. "Wally" was Wally Westmore, one of the best make-up men also at Paramount.

Fenady was beginning to regain his composure. He suddenly asked, "Did you read the script? Did you like the part?" Gail nodded her head and said, "Yes, very much."[7] She suddenly pointed to a huge picture of John Wayne on the wall behind Fenady's desk. "Do you know Duke?" Fenady sheepishly grinned and said, "Sort of," and then unconsciously stood in his John Wayne stance. Gail couldn't help but smile as she answered, "So do I. I made a couple of pictures with him." Fenady finally had to admit, "I haven't."[8] Gail decided to save him some embarrassment by saying, "You know, that's the way Duke stands – except with his right leg forward. More like this."[9] Fenady couldn't believe it. Gail suddenly rose from her chair and imitated John Wayne. Right leg forward, right shoulder canted. Furrowed brow. She was John Wayne. Gail went on, "You know, the one word that defines Duke is 'honest.' He's an honest man. He can't be otherwise."

All Fenady could say was, "Yes, Mamm." Gail suddenly shook his hand again. "Well, thank you, Mr. Fenady, I'll be waiting for my call." All he could say was, "Yes, Mamm," and escorted Gail through Charlie Brackett's former office. After Gail left, director Bernie Kowalski laughed and said, "Well, I guess you told her. Did you like the way she read the part?"[10]

The morning they started filming the episode at Paramount's Stage 17, Fenady noticed that Gail was surrounded by all her old friends at Paramount. In addition to Edith Head, Wally Westmore, and Nellie Manley, there were grips, electricians, executives, and others whom had worked with Gail so long ago during her glory days at Paramount Studios. They all came by to wish her well, especially Milton Lewis. He was the Paramount executive who had helped discover Gail back in 1942. There were tears in his eyes as he hugged her and wished her well in filming the shot. He always felt partially responsible for not preparing Gail adequately in becoming a Hollywood star, and in pushing her too hard before she was ready to be an actress.

The first scene was an elaborate one. Gail was to walk down a spiral staircase carrying a bouquet of rhododendrons giving a long speech as to why the South lost the war. Gail muffed the first couple of takes, and she, as well as everyone on the set, laughed. By the ninth take, no one was laughing. Fenady grabbed his director Kowalski and said, "Bernie, we should have started with something simple." Kowalski shot back, "I think you're making her nervous." Whereas Fenady replied, "She's making me nervous."[11]

Fenady then took the assistant director aside, Mike Caffey, and said, "Mike, I'm going to the office. Call me when you get the shot." It was an hour before Caffey called back. Fenady asked him if they got the shot. Caffey replied, "We're on take 26, and it's getting worse. You'd better get down her and make a decision."[12] Fenady told Caffey to make some fast calls to see who else was available to play the part.

After an unsuccessful take 29, Gail came up to Fenady with tears in her eyes, saying, "I'm sorry. Really sorry. I know I can do it. Please, just one more take." Fenady then tried to reassure Gail with a little "white lie." "It's a lousy scene," he said. "I'm going to rewrite it. Bernie, go to something else."[13] Fenady then went back to his office, and wrote a much simpler scene with Robert Vaughn saying most of the lines.

Meanwhile, Gail started to improve her performance. After a couple more scenes, she began to gain more confidence. Then the cast and crew broke for lunch. Fenady and Kowalski invited Gail to join them for lunch at Oblath's Café across the street from Paramount. When they had all sat down at their booth, the waitress came over and asked them if they wanted something to drink. Andrew Fenady and Bernie Kowalski both quickly said no, fast. Gail knowingly smiled and said, "Please, go ahead. It won't bother me. I've won that battle." The men quickly changed the subject and told Gail how well she was doing with the part. Gail then looked Fenady in the eyes and pleaded, "Andy, please don't rewrite that scene. I can do it. Let's shoot it right after lunch."[14]

Fenady still had misgivings about Gail, but looking into her pleading face, with those haunting, lovely eyes, he decided to give her a second chance. He said yes. After lunch, they shot the scene on the first take. Gail never flubbed another line, and the episode of "Noblesse Oblige" was finished on time.

In the "Noblesse Oblige" episode of "The Rebel" television series, Gail played the part of Cassandra Bannister, the Southern Belle sister of brothers Quincy, played by Kenneth Tobey, and Asa, played by Robert Vaughn. Johnny Yuma, played by Nick Adams, visits the home of his former commanding officer in the Civil War, Quincy Bannister, and becomes involved in a murder mystery. Gail did a good job of acting with her Southern accent, but one could not fail to notice that Wally Westmore had to use a considerable amount of make-up to camouflage the effects of Gail's prolonged alcohol abuse, as well as the damage done to her health due to the hepatitis attack. It was a noble attempt on her part to continue to salvage her career, although it produced only two days worth of film work.

When it was time to say goodbye to Andrew Fenady, Gail kissed him softly on the cheek, and told him how much she appreciated that he had given her the chance to finish the role of Cassandra. There must have been a small lump in his throat as Fenady watched Gail walk quietly out the door, still doing the best imitation of the John Wayne walk he had ever seen. Gail was never to know how much in love with her Andrew Fenady was, so long ago in Toledo, Ohio, when he first saw her in "The Uninvited" in 1947.

Chapter 32
The Silent Call

It would not be until June of 1960 that Gail would find work again. She had been rumored to have started in MGM's "The Man Who Grew Younger," and an untitled Joel McCrea Western, but the movie deals never materialized.

Then Gail was signed to do a segment of the television series, "Manhunt," staring Victor Jory, in an episode entitled "Matinee Mobster." She portrayed the role of Mrs. Clark, who is robbed in her apartment by a professional thief. Mrs. Clark is questioned by Lt. Howard Finucane, played by Victor Jory, of the San Diego Police Department, and his partner, reporter Ben Andrews, played by Patrick McVey, of the Chronicle Newspaper. These two men end up tracking down the notorious thief dubbed "The Matinee Mobster." It was a bit part for Gail, testimony to the fact that she was accepting roles no matter how small the part. It was evident, however, that Gail required heavy make-up to disguise her premature aging.

Gail was asked by newspaper and magazine reporters after the filming of the television episode about her current status. Little did she know it was to be her last public interview. She told VIP's Joe Finnegan, "I'll still have to use the word 'alcoholic,' because that's what I am. You don't get over alcoholism, you just don't drink. When I used to go to some offices, producers would ask me if I was drinking any more. They don't do that now, and that's the best thing that could happen to me. I guess there are still a lot of doubts about me, which is one reason I want back in the business, to prove to people that I can do a picture. I'm stronger now. The future looks pretty good."[1]

Another reporter asked Gail why her career took such a bad turn. She recalled, "Everything happened so fast. I was in high school, and the next I knew, I was being groomed for a picture. There was this terrific mountain of work, and no time to catch up with myself. It was that way for ten years, always a sense of pressure, and no time to think, to relax, to take stock. I didn't know how to be temperate. I was afraid people would think I was a bad sport." However, Gail prided herself on the fact that, despite her drinking, "I've never been late to work."[2]

Then one reporter asked if Gail had finally come to terms with her alcoholism. She hesitated, only for a moment, then replied, "There's no known cure for alcoholism. It's a disease – like cancer – a disintegration of the mind and spirit. But alcoholism can be arrested permanently, and I thank the A.A. that I've been able to do it. The thing I never realized was that it was impossible for me to do anything about it unless I had people around me who understood an alcoholic's fears, an alcoholic's nervousness and embarrassment at facing the world. I needed people who understood my very depths, people who would believe in me as a human being. Not just sympathizers. Sick people don't need sympathy nearly as much as they need proper care and help. I'm still not able to work much, no. I'm lonely, yes. But I'm no longer afraid of my loneliness. I live alone in my little apartment, and I spend my time pulling myself together. It's a long process. I know that. But I know it's going to end all right. I want friends around me again. I want to get married again. I don't know to whom, just to a good man. I want a proper life again, and I never want to fail anyone again. Most of all, myself."[3]

Gail was not to find another film assignment until February of 1961. By then she had moved once again, this time to a small apartment at 1436 S. Bentley Avenue in West Los Angeles. It would prove to be her final residence. Gail had reported to Twentieth Century Fox Studios to appear in their production, "The Silent Call," starring David McLean and a young Roger Mobley. Gail portrayed Flore Brancato, the wife of Joe, played by David McLean, and mother of young Guy, played by Roger Mobley. It was a charming tale of Guy, who has to leave his dog behind in Nevada when his father finds a better job in Los Angeles, California. His parents promise Guy they would send for the dog, Pete, when they get settled in Los Angeles. Peter later escapes from a neighbor's care, and the rest of the film is his adventures in trying to reunite with his young master. Although Gail got top billing, the real stars were Roger Mobley and the dog, Pete. The film was ably directed by John Bushelman, and was a low budget film, a "B" movie usually on the under card of a theater program. Gail did a fine performance, although you could tell by her appearance that she looked gaunt and very thin. She didn't look at all well, and it was very evident that alcoholism, in addition to the hepatitis, had done its damage.

There was one interesting incident during the filming of "The Silent Call." During the shooting of one dramatic sequence between Gail and young Roger Mobley, the young star accidentally threw up on Gail, showing the obvious strain and anxiety of the emotional pressure to give a good performance. If there was anyone in the world who could understand the tremendous strain a young actor would find himself in, it would be Gail. It must have brought back many unhappy memories of her early days at Paramount. After the unfortunate incident with Roger, Gail took him into her dressing room where she helped clean him up. After a change of clothes, the scene was re-shot.

The Silent Call was only moderately successful, however, the movie critics generally liked it. Variety Magazine, in its review, was typical of the film's response when it said, "The off-told, but durably disarming tale of the faithful dog that journeyed 1,000 miles is search of its departed and despondent young master is retold in "The Silent Call." As in most boy-and-his-dog films... the production fares better with the dog than it does with the boy... The talented dog truly earns his Ken-L-Ration. Miss Russell and McLean are capable as the parents, and Master Mobley is adequate as the boy."[4] "The

Silent Call" was not to be released into theaters until December, 1961, after Gail's death.

It was on February 8, 1960 that Gail was inducted into the Hollywood Walk of Fame, and given a star on Hollywood Boulevard. She wasn't given a public ceremony like the major stars, and none of the major newspapers even mentioned it. Gail's star is located at 6933 Hollywood Boulevard near Orange Avenue.

Chapter 33
Journey's End

It was in March of 1961 that Gail, for some inexplicable reason, started to drink once again. She had been sober for nearly a year, but the dark clouds of depression and fear returned once again to haunt her. Gail's neighbors near her apartment on 1436 S. Bentley Avenue, Virginia Darrell and Katherine Fappiano, didn't know why the brunette actress suddenly started drinking again, or what her problem was. They later told reporters, "She was always pleasant enough, but she didn't talk much to any of us."[1]

Whatever the reason was, Gail began to drink that day in March. It was vodka again. Virginia Darrell, who lived at 1432 Bentley Avenue, recalled that day when she said, "It was a binge. It lasted about a week. She was away for five weeks after that. We figured she went off to a sanitarium."[2] When Gail returned from the sanitarium, she was glum. She rarely left the apartment. May came, then June and July. Gail became a virtual recluse, always staying indoors. She had her groceries delivered to her apartment, but it was mostly liquor. She started to drink all day. Mrs. Darrell recalled, "I saw her once when the delivery boy came. She stood by the door and she looked terrible, about a hundred years old."[3] Gail would drink all night now, or for as long as she could. Mrs. Darrell remembered, "I guess she fell into the stupor about ten o'clock every night. I looked in her window once and the lights were on, and she was lying on the couch, all dressed, but out. The lights were on. They burned all night. It was eerie. It reminded you of a funeral parlor."[4] Mrs. Darrell later told reporters, "I know she had a sincere desire to stop drinking, but she couldn't. It's a tragic thing. She was a lovely, shy girl with her dark hair, large eyes and husky voice."[5]

Then came that fateful week of August 27, 1961. The weather was hot and sticky, and everyone seemed to slow down. Mrs. Darrell tried to be a good neighbor and look out for Gail, but the sad eyed actress wouldn't come out of her apartment. Mrs. Darrell recalled, "She didn't seem to have any friends except the neighbors who tried to look out for her."[6]

Mrs. Katherine Fappiano, who lived at 11051 Ohio Avenue, also recalled that fateful week in August. "We all felt so sorry for her. Only about three months ago, she went on a binge and had to be hospitalized for three weeks. A man from Alcoholics Anonymous visited her and seemed to help her. But then she started drinking again."[7]

Mrs. Darrell still hoped Gail would stop drinking, but the liquor deliveries kept arriving. "Still, always, every second day, the boy from the liquor store would come, like clock-work, and the lights would be on, and you knew what she was doing in there."[8]

Then came Monday, August 21st, and Gail arrived at the door of the home of Mrs. Darrell and pleaded, in the name of mercy, for a drink. Mrs. Darrell politely refused, and sadly watched as Gail slowly walked back to her apartment and locked the door, never to come out again. Other neighbors became worried and came to her apartment on Thursday, but Gail refused to admit them and only talked to them through the window. It was the last time anyone would see her alive.

Then, on Friday, the lights in Gail's apartment went out. Mrs. Darrell became worried. "We thought maybe she went away." The lights remained out the second night. "I though she was just too drunk to turn them on." The third night arrived, and still no lights. "I got worried. I went to look in the window. I saw her there. She was on the floor. She'd obviously fallen from the couch. She was on the floor, and next to her was a bottle, empty."[9]

Mrs. Darrell called the police, and a few minutes later they arrived along with an ambulance. They broke down the door to Gail's apartment, and found her on the floor, unconscious, dressed in a red print blouse and print pajama bottoms. An empty vodka bottle was near her empty hand. The police carefully lifted her to the couch, and tried to waken her. They tried to talk to her. Gail didn't respond. Mrs. Darrell recalled, "I was standing by the door, watching. She looked so pretty again. She looked like a young girl who'd fallen on the floor and was maybe knocked out for a few minutes. But I knew it wasn't that. I knew, that moment, the truth of the matter... that it was worse than that."[10]

The paramedics on the scene couldn't revive Gail, and she was pronounced dead. When police searched her four rooms, $130 a month apartment, they found more than a dozen empty liquor bottles scattered in the closets, kitchen pantry, and in the waste baskets."[11]

When the Los Angeles newspapers came out the following day, the headlines read that Gail Russell, the once famous movie actress, was found dead in her West Los Angeles apartment on Sunday, August 27, 1961.[12] The story was on the "B" section of the local papers. Stars like Gary Cooper and Jeff Chandler were printed on the front pages or "A" section when they died. It was mute testimony to the forgotten status of Gail Russell.

The police notified Gail's brother, George Jr., who was vacationing in Mexico. Her mother, Gladys, was eventually found in her apartment, in Beverly Hills. Guy Madison was in Italy, where he had been making a movie, but was unavailable for comment. George Russell arranged for Gail's funeral service to be held the following Tuesday at the Westwood Village Mortuary. The funeral service was to be private, and only for the family and a few close friends.[13] Burial was to be at the Valhalla Memorial Park, 10621 Victory Boulevard, in North Hollywood. Gail would be laid to rest beside her father.

Newspaper reports at the time of Gail's death initially listed the reason as "natural causes." However, the official document two weeks later by the Medical Examiner of the Coroner's Office, Dr. Alex Greswold, stated the exact cause of death as "severe fatty liver, due to acute and chronic alcoholism." A secondary condition contributing to the cause of death was listed as "terminal aspiration of stomach contents."[14]

It was a small, but loyal groups of mourners who gathered for Gail's funeral on Tuesday, August 29, 1961. At the memorial service, the minister tried to sum up Gail's life as best he could by saying, "You and I know that Gail Russell had a problem. And we know how desperately hard she tried to solve it."[15]   After the funeral, reporters asked Gail's sister-in-law, Mrs. George Russell, about her thoughts on Gail's death. "I talked to her every day of the week before she died. She was very busy and she seemed happy. She said she was going for an interview for a T.V. role and she was sketching and doing commercial art work."[16] Mrs. Russell also said Gail had a definite drive to regain her fame. Gail told her, "I have to act, I have to!"[17]   Mrs. Russell added, sadly, "I think she wanted to prove to everybody that she could beat her alcoholic problem. She was really, really and truly, trying to stop drinking. It was tragic because she was so talented and suffering so much. If she had enjoyed drinking it would have been something else – but she didn't. But I guess her system demanded it."[18] Then Mrs. Russell added an afterthought, "No matter what they say about Hollywood, the people there were always wonderful to her through the long years she had her problem. She always got through when she made a call, and anybody who ever worked with her always believed in her."[19]

There were a few newspaper reporters covering Gail's funeral, but not near the number that usually reported a major movie star's memorial service, such as for Jean Harlow, Clark Gable, Tyrone Power, Errol Flynn, or even Gary Cooper.[20] Yet that was to be expected. Gail had long been forgotten by the press, her fans, and yes, even her so-called movie star friends.

Following the memorial service, the short funeral procession left the Westwood Mortuary Chapel and made the mournful trip north up the San Diego Freeway, then east along the Ventura Freeway, until finally they arrived at the Valhalla Memorial Cemetery in North Hollywood, in the San Fernando Valley. There, among the tall pine trees, near the feet of the San Gabriel Mountains, Gail was gently laid to rest beside her father, beneath the cool, green grass. Gail would have appreciated the surrounding view, because she so loved the outdoors. In addition to the family members, there were a few, a very few, Hollywood friends whom had remained loyal to the very end.[21] They included Hollywood stars Alan Ladd and his wife, Susan. Ladd had co-starred with Gail in "Sally O'Rourke" and "Calcutta." Also Diana Lynn, her longtime friend who had starred with Gail in "Henry Aldrich Gets Glamour," "Our Hearts Were Young and Gay," and its sequel, "Our Hearts Were Growing Up." Then there was actress Mona Freeman, and Jimmy Lydon, who had starred with Gail in her first film at Paramount, "Henry Aldrich Gets Glamour." There was also Paramount secretary Lindsay Durand, as well as producer Bill Dozier, Paramount executives Milton Lewis and William Russell.

Gail Russell was only thirty-six years of age when she died. Her extraordinary rise to Hollywood stardom is only one of the many legendary tales in move history. The spectacular rollercoaster ride of her life, from the heights of fame and glamour, to the utter depths of despair and degradation, was finally over. That shy, little girl who only wanted to become a commercial artist, and who was so afraid of life, could finally rest in peace. Gail didn't have to be afraid anymore.

Epilogue

Just a few concluding thoughts regarding Gail. If you could choose one word to describe her, it would be "Unforgettable." Her films, movie portraits, even her color photos, could never fully capture her extraordinary beauty. Gail's eyes were the blue of sapphires, and her hair was as black as a raven's wing, which was luxurious, curling softly to her shoulders. Her hair, under certain lighting conditions, would glow a blue shade. Gail always spoke in a low, soft whisper, and you sometimes had to listen very carefully to what she was saying. Yet it was her eyes that first drew your attention. She had the loveliest, the most moving eyes any actress ever had. God must have eyes like hers. If you could have asked any director who ever worked with Gail – Lewis Allen, Raoul Walsh, John Farrow, or Joseph Losey – they would have all told you the same thing, Gail Russell had the most beautiful eyes they had ever seen.

However, Gail was not only lovely on the outside, she was just as beautiful on the inside. Her basic principles, as well as her personal character, were as fine as any human being could possible possess. Loyal to friends, kind to strangers, and a great lover of animals, especially dogs and horses. Gail was a very talented individual. A gifted artist with oil on canvas, a sketch artist who could draw caricatures of anyone she knew. A commercial artist who could draw fashion designs, an interior designer who could decorate homes. Gail was also an avid outdoorswoman, who loved to go camping. She could ride horses, hunt, fish, and was a very good hunter with bow and arrow. Gail had been taught by Howard Hill, the champion archer who had coached Errol Flynn during the filming of "The Adventures of Robin Hood" in 1938. Howard was also Guy Madison's best man at his wedding to Gail on July 31, 1949.

Now, as to the reasons for Gail Russell's downfall, and her descent into alcoholism, there have been many different theories over the years. Some have attributed it to the possibility that Gail was molested as a child, but that hypothesis has never been proved. Others say Gail must have been propositioned by some executive or casting director in exchange for some coveted screen role. The old "Casting Couch" syndrome. That also has never been proved. Still others hold out for the idea that Gail was driven to drink due to her mental instability. One psychiatrist even diagnosed her as "manic depressive." Others thought it was "melancholia," even "bi-polar disorder." Not any of these reasons for Gail's alcoholism has been definitely proven.

I have been a fan, and ardent admirer of Gail Russell for over forty years. During that time, I have researched and studied her life and career. I believe I can say, without any amount of modesty, that I have come to know her quite well. That Gail was a very shy and insecure person, there can be no doubt. Certainly her severe stage fright, whether one wants to call it glossophobia or not, was a major factor in her life long struggle to perform in films. The only person who knows the real cause of her downfall was Gail herself. If you just read her conversation with Hedda Hopper in November of 1955, the ultimate cause was very self-evident. Gail was unhappy with her life. She was unhappy with her career, she was unhappy in her marriage to Guy Madison, and she had inherited a liver DNA that prevented her from becoming aware of when a person has had too much to drink, which in layman's terms led to be addiction to alcohol. It was a "Perfect Storm" scenario. It was amazing that Gail lasted as a movie star for as long as she did. To a certain degree, alcoholism could be named as one of the main causes as to why Gail's career ended so abruptly. However, the ultimate cause, and the great misfortune of Gail Russell's life, was the irony that she possessed the great beauty of a movie star, but tragically, not the temperament.

Gail has been dead for over half a century, yet her timeless beauty and charm still lives on whenever her films are shown on television, or on the Silver Screen in cinema retrospectives around the world. I still miss her very much. Whenever I hear the song "Stella by Starlight," I think of Gail and her performance in "The Uninvited." One can still see the potential making of a great star. Whenever I see yellow roses in bloom, I think of Gail, because she loved them so.

The memory of Gail Russell has faded over the years, and few people remember her, or even know who she was. Gail has become the stardust of the past, the forgotten legend of a Hollywood legacy of beauty and glamour that has long since vanished from the Hollywood scene. Yet, I can still remember Gail and the unforgettable image of her bright, blue eyes, as blue as a wood hyacinth. I can still hear that low, whisper-like voice of hers, as soft as a warm, summer breeze. I can still see her luxurious hair of midnight hue that seemed to shimmer in the moonlight. Gail Russell was a bright and shining star that vanished all too soon from Hollywood history. I am reminded of that famous sonnet by the English poet, John Keats, "The Day is Gone." It is so reminiscent of Gail --

"THE DAY IS GONE AND ALL ITS SWEETS ARE GONE!
SWEET VOICE, SWEET LIPS, SOFT HAND, AND SOFTER BREAST
WARM BREATH, LIGHT WHISPER, TENDER SEMI-TONE,
BRIGHT EYES, ACCOMPLISHED SHAPE AND LANG'ROUS WAIST!
FADED THE FLOWER, AND ALL ITS BUDDED CHARMS,
FADED THE SIGHT OF BEAUTY FROM MY EYES,
FADED THE SHAPE OF BEAUTY FROM MY ARMS,
FADED THE VOICE, WARMTH, WHITENESS, PARADISE,
VANISHED UNSEASONABLY AT SHUT OF EVE..."

This should have been Gail's epitaph.

Postscript

For a movie historian or for the appreciative movie-goer, the Academy of Motion Picture Arts and Sciences (best known for bestowing the "Oscar" at the Academy Awards) is a priceless treasure house. The Margaret Herrick Library, located in the Fairbanks Center of Motion Picture Study in Beverly Hills, contains extensive archives of the many stars who made the small community of Hollywood famous throughout the world. Contained within is the Gail Russell Collection, part of which are the personal scrapbooks of Gail, documenting her life and career. They are old and crumbling, but inside the front cover of one of these scrapbooks, Gail carefully posted the simple item not directly connected with her. But among all the yellowed clippings, it is the one in which she evidently recognized herself most clearly during those last, tragic years. It was a poem entitled "Ex-Star" which read,

THE LIGHTS ARE OUT THAT FLASHED HER MAGIC NAME,
THE PLAYS SHE DID ARE BURIED IN THE PAST,
SHE WORE THE PRICELESS RUBY KNOWN AS FAME,
BUT TIME WORE THIN AND SORROW JOINED THE CAST;
SHE DID NOT KNOW THE MOB WAS QUICK TO COOL,
SHE DID NOT KOW THAT ANY STAR CAN FALL,
THAT EVEN QUEENS CAN LOSE THE POWER TO RULE,
AND FATE STILL TAKES THE FINAL CURTAIN CALL;
SO NOW SHE HAS HER CLIPPINGS AND HER GHOSTS...
THOSE NIGHTS WHEN ALL THE WORLD WAS AT HER FEET,
WHEN THERE WAS GLAMOR IN THE MAGIC TOASTS,
THAT DIED LIKE MUSIC DOWN A LONELY STREET;
THE LIGHTS ARE OUT... THE WINDS ARE STRANGELY COOL,
AND SHE WHO PLAYED THE STAR...
NOW PLAYS THE FOOL!
Don Wahn

Acknowledgements

I sincerely wish to thank the following people and organizations for their great help in aiding me to write this book. Eddie Brandts Saturday Matinee Store in North Hollywood, Larry Edmunds Bookstore in Hollywood, the staff at the Special Collections Department of the Margaret Herrick Library in the Fairbanks Center for Motion Picture Study in Beverly Hills, Paramount Pictures, United Artists, Republic Pictures, Columbia Pictures, Warner Brothers Pictures, Universal Pictures, Twentieth-Century Fox Pictures, United Press International, Associated Press, Los Angeles Times, Los Angeles Herald, Los Angeles Examiner, Los Angeles Mirror, Photoplay Magazine, Screenland Magazine, Movie Stars Parade, Modern Screen Magazine, Motion Picture Magazine, Screen Stars Magazine, Silver Screen Magazine, Movieland Magazine, K.C Motsinger, Ron Stephenson, the greatest Gail Russell fan I ever met, and the numerous Gail Russell fans around the world, especially those on YouTube, who asked me to write a book on Gail. To these, and others too numerous to mention, I give my heartfelt thanks.

The Films of Gail Russell

1. "Henry Aldrich Gets Glamour," Paramount, 1943. Director Hugh Bennett. With Jimmy Lydon, Charles Smith, John Litel, Olive Blakeney, Frances Gifford. 72 minutes.

2. "Lady in the Dark," Paramount, 1944. Director Mitchell Leisen, with Ginger Rogers, Ray Milland, Jon Hall, Warner Baxter, Barry Sullivan, Mischa Auer, Mary Phillips. 100 minutes.

3. "The Uninvited," Paramount, 1944. Director Lewis Allen. With Ray Milland, Ruth Hussey, Donald Crisp, Cornelia Otis Skinner, Dorothy Stickney, Barbara Everest, Alan Napier. 98 minutes.

4. "Our Hearts Were Young and Gay," Paramount, 1944. Director Lewis Allen. With Diana Lynn, Charlie Ruggles, Dorothy Gish, Beulah Bondi, James Brown, Bill Edwards. 81 minutes.

5. "The Unseen," Paramount, 1945. Director Lewis Allen. With Joel McCrea, Herbert Marshall, Phyllis Brooks, Isabel Elsom, Norman Lloyd, Mikhail Rasummy, Elizabeth Risdon. 81 minutes.

6. "Salty O'Rourke," Paramount, 1945. Director Raoul Walsh. With Alan Ladd, William Demerest, Bruce Cabot, Spring Byington, Stanley Clements, Darryl Hickman. 97 minutes.

7. "Duffy's Tavern," Paramount, 1945. Director Hal Walker. With Victor Moore, Marjorie Reynolds, Barry Sullivan, Ed Gardner, Guest stars Bing Crosby, Betty Hutton, Paulette Goddard, Alan Ladd, Dorothy Lamour, Veronica Lake, Diana Lynn, Eddie Bracken, Brian Donlevy, Sonny Tufts, Arturo de Cordova, Barry Fitzgerald, Cass Daley, Robert Benchley, William Demarest, Howard de Silva, Billy De Wolfe. 97 minutes.

8. "Our Hearts Were Growing Up," Paramount, 1946. Director William D. Russell. With Diana Lynn, Brian Donlevy, James Brown, Bill Edwards, William Demarest. 83 minutes.

9. "The Bachelor's Daughters," United Artists, 1946. Director Andrew Stone. With Claire Trevor, Ann Dvorak, Adolphe Manjou, Billie Burke, Jane Wyatt, Eugene List. 89 minutes.

10. "Calcutta," Paramount, 1947. Director John Farrow. With Alan Ladd, William Bendix, June Duprez, Lowell Gilmore, Edith King, Paul Singh, Gavin Muir. 83 minutes.

11. "Angel and the Badman," Republic, 1947. Director James Edward Grant. With John Wayne, Harry Carey, Irene Rich, Bruce Cabot, Paul Hurst, Lee Dixon, Stephen Grant. 100 minutes.

12. "Variety Girl," Paramount, 1947. Director George Marshall. With Mary Hatcher, Olga San Juan, De Forrest Kelley, William Demarest, Guest stars Bing Crosby, Bob Hope, Gary Cooper, Ray Milland, Alan Ladd, Barbara Stanwyck, Paulette Goddard, Dorothy Lamour, Veronica Lake, Sonny Tufts, Joan Caulfield, William Holden, Lizabeth Scott, Burt Lancaster, Diana Lynn, Sterling Hayden, Robert Preston, John Lund, William Bendix, Barry

Fitzgerald, Cass Daley, Howard Da Silva, Billy De Wolfe, Macdonald Carey, Urleen Whelan, Patrick Knowles. 83 minutes.

13. "Night Had A Thousand Eyes," Paramount, 1948. Director John Farrow. With Edward G. Robinson, John Lund, Virginia Bruce, William Demarest, Richard Webb, Jerome Cowan, Onslow Steven, John Alexander, Ramon Bohmen. 80 minutes.

14. "Wake of the Red Witch," Republic, 1948. Director Edward Ludwig. With John Wayne, Luther Adler, Gig Young, Adele Mara, Edward Franz, Grant Withers, Henry Daniell, Paul Fix, Dennis Hoey, Jeff Corey, Erskinse Sanford. 106 minutes.

15. "Moonrise," Republic, 1948. Director Frank Borzage. With Dane Clark, Ethel Barrymore, Allan Joslyn, Henry Morgan, Rex Ingram, David Street, Selena Rogle, Harry Carey Jr., Irving Bacon, Lloyd Bridges. 90 minutes.

16. "Song of India," Columbia, 1949. Director Albert S. Rogell. With Sabu, Turhan Bey, Anthony Caruso, Anita Dyne, Fritz Leiber, Trevor Bardette. 77 minutes.

17. "El Paso," Paramount, 1947. Director Lewis R. Foster. With John Payne, Sterling Hayden, George "Gabby" Hayes, Dick Foran, Henry Hull, Mary Beth Hughes, Edwardo Noriega, H.B. Warner, Catherine Craig, Arthur Space. 92 minutes.

18. "The Great Dan Patch," United Artists, 1949. Director Joe Newman. With Dennis O'Keefe, Ruth Warrick, Charlotte Greenwood, Henry Hull, John Hoyt, Arthur Hunnicutt. 94 minutes.

19. "Captain China," Paramount, 1950. Director Lewis R. Foster. With John Payne, Jeffrey Lynn, Lon Chaney Jr., Edgar Bergen, Michael O'Shea, Ellen Corby, Robert Armstrong. 97 minutes.

20. "The Lawless," Paramount, 1950. Director Joseph Losey. With Macdonald Carey, John Sands, Lee Patrick, John Hoyt, Lalo Rios, Maurice Jara, Walter Reed, Martha Hyer. 83 minutes.

21. "Air Cadet," Universal International, 1951. Director Joseph Pevney. With Stephen McNally, Alex Nichol, Richard Long, Charles Drake, Robert Arthur, Rock Hudson, Peggy Castle. 94 minutes.

22. "Seven Men From Now," Warner Brothers, 1956. Director Budd Boetticher. With Randolph Scott, Lee Marvin, Walter Reed, John Larch, Donald Barry, Stuart Whitman. 78 minutes.

23. "The Tattered Dress," Universal International, 1957. Director Jack Arnold. With Jeff Chandler, Jeanne Crain, Jack Carson, Elaine Stewart, George Tobias, Edward Andrews, Ed Plett. 93 minutes.

24. "No Place to Land," Republic, 1958. Director Albert C. Gannaway. With John Ireland, Mari Blanchard, Douglas Henderson, Jackie Coogan, Robert Middleton. 78 minutes.

25. "The Silent Call," 20th Century-Fox, 1961. Director John Bushelman. With David McLean, Roger Mobley, Joe Basser, Jack Younger, Roscoe Ates, Milton Parsons. 62 minutes.

The Television Appearances of Gail Russell

1. For "Video Theater," 1957, Gail appeared briefly to plug "The Tattered Dress."
2. For "Studio 57," Gail did an episode entitled "Time, Tide, and a Woman." 1956. Director Herschel Daugherty. With John Baer, Arthur Space, Robert Burton.
3. For "The Rebel" TV Series, 1960. "Noblesse Oblige." Director Bernard Kowalski. With Kenneth Tobey, Nick Adams, Robert Vaughn.
4. "Manhunt," TV Series, "Matinee Mobster," 1960. Director Fred Jackman. With Victor Jory, Patrick McVey, Chuck Henderson.

Videos

"Gail Russell." Mysteries and Scandals. E Channel. Television Series, 2000.

"Seven Men From Now." DVD. The John Wayne Stock Company.

"Gail Russell." Paramount Home Video, 2006.

Footnotes

Chapter 1

1. "I Am A Movie Star's Mother," by Mrs. George Russell, Modern Screen Magazine, April, 1948.
2. "Movie Life of Gail Russell," by William Lynch Vallee, Movie Life Magazine, June, 1949.
3. "My Daughter's Miracle," by Mrs. George Russell, as told to Kate Holliday, Screenland Magazine, May, 1944.
4. Ibid.
5. "Dark Angel" by George Benjamin, Modern Screen Magazine, November, 1946.
6. Ibid.
7. Ibid.
8. "Secrets I'll Tell My Daughter," by Gail Russell, Movie Stars Parade Magazine, October, 1950.
9. "Confessions of An Introvert," by Gail Russell, as told to Helen Weller, Motion Picture Magazine, November, 1950.
10. Ibid.
11. "Confessions of A Scared Cat," by Gladys Hall, Screenland Magazine, May, 1945.
12. "Our Gail Is Growing Up," by Sara Hamilton, Photoplay Magazine, March, 1946.

Chapter 2

1. "Confessions Of A Scared Cat, by Gladys Hall, Screenland Magazine, May, 1945.
2. Ibid.
3. "I Am A Movie Star's Mother," by Mrs. George Russell, Modern Screen Magazine, April, 1948.
4. Ibid.
5. Ibid.
6. Ibid.
7. Ibid.
8. Ibid.
9. "Secrets I'll Tell My Daughter," by Gail Russell, Movie Stars Parade Magazine, October, 1950.
10. "Gingham Girl With Sequins," by Harriet Eaton, Photoplay Magazine, June, 1945.

Chapter 3

1. "Confessions Of An Introvert," by Gail Russell, as told to Helen Weller, Motion Picture Magazine, November, 1950.
2. Ibid.
3. "Gingham Girl With Sequins," by Harriet Eaton, Photoplay Magazine, June, 1945.
4. Ibid.
5. Ibid.
6. "I Am A Movie Star's Mother," by Mrs. George Russell, Modern Screen Magazine, April, 1948.
7. "Gingham Girl With Sequins," by Harriet Eaton, Photoplay Magazine, June, 1945.

Chapter 4

1. "Gail Russell's Tragic Secret," by Henry Kramer, QT Magazine, January, 1962.
2. "Dark Angel," by George Benjamin, Modern Screen Magazine, November, 1946.
3. "Lana: The Lady, The Legend, The Truth," by Lana Turner, Pocket Books, 1983.
4. "Ava – My Story," by Ava Gardner, Bantam Books, 1990.
5. "Confessions Of A Scared Cat, by Gladys Hall, Screenland Magazine, May, 1945.
6. "Gail Russell's Tragic Secret," by Henry Kramer, QT Magazine, January, 1962.
7. "Confessions Of A Scared Cat, by Gladys Hall, Screenland Magazine, May, 1945.
8. Ibid.
9. Los Angeles Herald Examiner, July 18, 1942.
10. "Gail Russell: A Woman Re-born," by Ruth Waterbury, Photoplay Magazine, March, 1956.
11. "Gail Russell's Tragic Secret," by Henry Kramer, QT Magazine, January, 1962.

12. "Yvonne, An Autobiography," by Yvonne De Carlo, with Doug Warren, St. Martins Press, 1987.

Chapter 5

1. "Confessions Of A Scared Cat, by Gladys Hall, Screenland Magazine, May, 1945.
2. "Our Hearts Were Young And Gay… and Now They Are So Sad," by Greg James, Movie Digest Magazine, May, 1972.

3. "Mysteries and Scandals – Gail Russell," E Channel Television Series, 2000.
4. "Movie Stars Of The 40's," by David Ragen, Prentice-Hall, Inc., 1985.
5. "Stars Attend Funeral of Gail Russell," Los Angeles Times, August 30, 1961.
6. "Femme Noir, Bad Girls of Film," Gail Russell, Vol. 2, by Karren Burroughs Hansberry, McFarland and Co., Inc., 1998.
7. Variety Film Review, December 30, 1942.

Chapter 6

1. "Confessions Of A Scared Cat, by Gladys Hall, Screenland Magazine, May, 1945.
2. "Hollywood Director," by David Chirichetti, Curtis Books, 1973.
3. New York Times Film Review by Bosley Crowther, February 23, 1944.
4. Archives of the Margaret Herrick Library, Gail Russell Collection, A.M.P.A.S. Fairbanks Center for Motion Picture Study, Beverly Hills, California.
5. Ibid.

Chapter 7

1. "Gail Russell's Tragic Secret," by Henry Kramer, QT Magazine, January, 1962.
2. "Confessions Of A Scared Cat, by Gladys Hall, Screenland Magazine, May, 1945.
3. Ibid.

4. "Gail Russell's Tragic Secret," by Henry Kramer, QT Magazine, January, 1962.
5. "Science Fiction and Fantasy Film Flashbacks," Lewis Allen, by Tom Weaver, McFarland and Co., Inc., Publishers, 1998.
6. "Confessions Of A Scared Cat, by Gladys Hall, Screenland Magazine, May, 1945.
7. Ibid.
8. "Gail Russell (1924-1961), The Short and Pitiful Tale Of A Girl Who Never Wanted To Be An Actress," Modern Screen Magazine, December, 1961.
9. Ibid.
10. Ibid.
11. New York Times Film Review, February 23, 1944.
12. "My Daughter's Miracle," by Mrs. George Russell, as told to Kate Holliday, Screenland Magazine, May, 1944.

13. "Gail Russell's Miracle," by Joe Roberts, Screen Stars Magazine, July, 1956.

14. "The Truth About Guy Madison's Marriage," by Mike Connelly, T.V. Show Magazine, January, 1954.

Chapter 8

1. "Romance and Gail Russell," by Robbin Coons, Screenland Magazine, January 1947.

2. "Confessions Of A Scared Cat, by Gladys Hall, Screenland Magazine, May, 1945.

3. "The Role I Liked Best," by Gail Russell, Saturday Evening Post Magazine, May 27, 1950.

4. "Confessions Of A Scared Cat, by Gladys Hall, Screenland Magazine, May, 1945.

5. Ibid.

6. Ibid.

7. Ibid.

8. "Our Hearts Were Young And Gay… and Now They Are So Sad," by Greg James, Movie Digest Magazine, May, 1972.

9. New York times Film Review, October 12, 1944.

10. "Our Hearts Were Young And Gay… and Now They Are So Sad," by Greg James, Movie Digest Magazine, May, 1972.

Chapter 9

1. "Gingham Girl With Sequins," by Harriet Eaton, Photoplay Magazine, June, 1945.

2. New York Times Film Review, May 14, 1945.

Chapter 10

1. "Our Girl Is Growing Up," by Sara Hamilton, Photoplay Magazine, March, 1946.

2. "Salty O'Rourke," Pressbook, Paramount Pictures, 1945.

3. Ibid.

4. Ibid.

5. New York Times Film Review, April 27, 1945.

Chapter 11

1. New York Times Film Review, September 6, 1945.

2. "Movie Life of Gail Russell," by William Lynch Vallee, Movie Life Magazine, June, 1949.

3. New York Times Film Review, August 12, 1946.

Chapter 12

1. "The Bachelor's Daughters," Pressbook, United Artists, 1946.
2. The New York Times Film Review, October 7, 1946.
3. "Gail Russell: A Woman Reborn," by Ruth Waterbury, Photoplay Magazine, March, 1956.
4. "I'm Not Married," by Guy Madison, Modern Screen Magazine, March 1949.
5. "We're Both As Stubborn As Mules," by Helen Hover, Motion Picture Magazine, June, 1950.
6. Ibid.
7. Ibid.
8. "Dark Angel," George Benjamin, Modern Screen Magazine, November, 1946.
9. "I'm Not Married," by Guy Madison, Modern Screen Magazine, March 1949.
10. "My Kind Of Guy," by Gail Russell, Photoplay Magazine, March, 1946.
11. Ibid.
12. Ibid.
13. "Wife In Fame Only," by Gail Russell, Modern Screen Magazine, September, 1949.
14. "Romance and Gail Russell," by Robbin Coons, Screenland Magazine, January, 1947.
15. Ibid.

Chapter 13

1. "Our Gail Is Growing Up," by Sara Hamilton, Photoplay Magazine, March, 1946.
2. Ibid.
3. New York Times Film Review, April 24, 1947.
4. "Open Letter To Guy And Gail," by Sara Hamilton, Photoplay Magazine, May, 1947.

Chapter 14

1. "The John Wayne Stock Company: Gail Russell," *Seven Men From Now* DVD, Paramount Home Entertainment, 2006.
2. Ibid.
3. "Angel and the Badman," Pressbook, Republic Pictures, 1947.
4. "Gail Russell," Biography, Paramount Pictures, Revised, January, 1950. Archives of Margaret Herrick Library, Fairbanks Center for Motion Picture Study, Beverly Hills, California.

5. "We're Both As Stubborn As Mules," by Helen Hover, Motion Picture Magazine, June, 1950.
6. Ibid.
7. "The John Wayne Stock Company: Gail Russell," "Seven Men From Now" DVD, Paramount Home Entertainment, 2006.
8. New York Times Film Review, March 3, 1947.
9. Variety Film Review, July 16, 1947.
10. "I Am A Movie Star's Mother," by Mrs. George Russell, Modern Screen Magazine, April, 1948.

Chapter 15

1. "Open Letter To Guy and Gail," by Sara Hamilton, Photoplay Magazine, May, 1947.
2. Ibid.
3. Ibid.
4. Ibid.
5. "Confessions Of An Introvert," by Gail Russell, Motion Picture Magazine, November, 1950.
6. "I Am A Movie Star's Mother," by Mrs. George Russell, Modern Screen Magazine, April, 1948.
7. Ibid.

Chapter 16

1. "Our Gail Is Growing Up," by Sara Hamilton, Photoplay Magazine, March, 1946.
2. "Confessions Of An Introvert," by Gail Russell, as told to Helen Weller, Motion Picture Magazine, November, 1950.
3. "Photoplay Fashions," with Gail Russell, Photoplay Magazine, October, 1948.
4. New York Times Films in Review, October 14, 1948.

Chapter 17

1. "Wake Of The Red Witch," Pressbook, Republic Pictures, 1948.
2. New York Times Film Review, January 10, 1949.
3. "I'm Not Married," by Guy Madison, Modern Screen Magazine, March, 1949.
4. "My Kind Of Guy," by Gail Russell, Photoplay Magazine, March, 1946.
5. "Guy Loves Gail," by Marcia Daughtrey, Modern Screen Magazine, May, 1947.
6. "For Sentimental Reasons," by Kaaren Pleck, Modern Screen Magazine, September, 1947.
7. "My Kind Of Guy," by Gail Russell, Photoplay Magazine, March, 1946.

Chapter 18

1. Archives of Margaret Herrick Library, "Gail Russell, Collection, A.M.P.A.S. Fairbanks Center For Motion Picture Study, Beverly Hills, California.
2. "Moonrise," Pressbook, Republic Pictures, 1948.
3. New York Times Film Review, March 7, 1949.
4. "Gail Russell: A Woman Reborn," by Ruth Waterbury, Photoplay Magazine, March, 1956.
5. "Gail Russell's Miracle," by Joe Roberts, Screen Stars Magazine, July, 1956.
6. "We're Both As Stubborn As Mules," by Helen Hover, Motion Picture Magazine, June, 1950.
7. "You Don't Have To Be Afraid Anymore, Gail," by Jim Henaghen, Modern Screen Magazine, December, 1961.
8. Ibid.

Chapter 19

1. "Gail Russell," Biography, Republic Studios, February, 1948, Mort Goodman, Director of Publicity, Archives of Margaret Herrick Library, A.M.P.A.S., Fairbanks Center For Motion Picture Study, Beverly Hills, California.
2. Ibid.
3. Ibid.
4. "Not The Siren She Seems," by Reba and Bonnie Churchill, Screenland Magazine, August, 1949.
5. Ibid.
6. Archives of Margaret Herrick Library, "Gail Russell, Collection, A.M.P.A.S. Fairbanks Center For Motion Picture Study, Beverly Hills, California
7. "Song of India," Pressbook, Columbia Pictures, 1949.
8. Ibid.
9. Ibid.
10. New York Times Film Review, June 10, 1949.

Chapter 20

1. Archives of the Margaret Herrick Library, Gail Russell Collection, A.M.P.A.S., Fairbanks Center for Motion Picture Study, Beverly Hills, California.
2. New York Times Film Review, March 24, 1949.
3. "I'm Not Really Married," by Guy Madison, Modern Screen Magazine, March, 1949.

4. "Gail Russell's Miracle," by Joe Roberts, Screen Stars Magazine, July, 1956.

5. "Confessions Of An Introvert," by Gail Russell, As Told to Helen Weller, Motion Picture Magazine, November, 1950.

Chapter 21

1. Archives of the Margaret Herrick Library, Gail Russell Collection, A.M.P.A.S., Fairbanks Center for Motion Picture Study, Beverly Hills, California

2. New York Times Film Review, November, 9, 1949.

3. "Why I Wanted 4 Years To Marry Guy," by Gail Russell, Silver Screen Magazine, February, 1950.

4. Ibid.

5. Ibid.

6. Ibid.

7. "Romance and Gail Russell," by Robbin Coons, Screenland Magazine, January, 1947.

8. Ibid.

Chapter 22

1. "Gail Lives Alone," by Alice Tildesley, Modern Screen Magazine, March, 1949.

2. Ibid.

3. Ibid.

4. Archives of the Margaret Herrick Library, Gail Russell Collection, A.M.P.A.S., Fairbanks Center for Motion Picture Study, Beverly Hills, California.

5. "Captain China," Pressbook, Paramount Pictures, 1950.

6. Ibid.

7. New York Times Film Review, March 2, 1950.

8. Archives of the Margaret Herrick Library, Gail Russell Collection, A.M.P.A.S., Fairbanks Center for Motion Picture Study, Beverly Hills, California.

9. "Why I Wanted 4 Years To Marry Guy," by Gail Russell, Silver Screen Magazine, February, 1950.

10. Ibid.

11. Ibid.

12. "Romance and Gail Russell," by Robbin Coons, Screenland Magazine, January, 1947.

13. "We're Both As Stubborn As Mules," by Helen Hover, Motion Picture Magazine, June, 1950.

14. "Is Love Enough?" by Helen Hover Weller, Motion Picture Magazine, May, 1950.

15. "Gail Russell Married to Guy Madison," Los Angeles Times, August 1, 1949.

16. "Why I Wanted 4 Years To Marry Guy," by Gail Russell, Silver Screen Magazine, February, 1950.

17. "Gail Lives Alone," by Alice Tildesley, Modern Screen Magazine, March, 1949.

18. "Is Love Enough?" by Helen Hover Weller, Motion Picture Magazine, May, 1950.

19. Ibid.

Chapter 23

1. "The Private Life of Guy and Gail," Movie Stars Parade Magazine, January, 1950.

2. "Why I Wanted 4 Years To Marry Guy," by Gail Russell, Silver Screen Magazine, February, 1950.

3. Is Love Enough?" by Helen Hover Weller, Motion Picture Magazine, May, 1950.

4. Ibid.

5. Archives of the Margaret Herrick Library, Gail Russell Collection, A.M.P.A.S., Fairbanks Center for Motion Picture Study, Beverly Hills, California.

6. Ibid.

7. Ibid.

8. "The Lawless," Pressbook, Paramount Pictures, 1950.

9. "Conversations With Losey," by Michael Ciment, Methuen Inc, New York, 1985.

10. "Losey On Losey," by Tom Milne, Doubleday Press, New York, 1985.

11. New York Times Film Review, June 23, 1050.

12. "The True Story Of Guy Madison's Heartbreak Marriage," by Pauline Swanson, Photo Play Magazine, February, 1954.

13. "Gail Admits Leaving Guy Madison," Los Angeles Times, January 12, 1950.

14. Archives of the Margaret Herrick Library, Gail Russell Collection, A.M.P.A.S., Fairbanks Center for Motion Picture Study, Beverly Hills, California.

15. "Gail Russell," by Jim Meyer, Film Fan Monthly Magazine, May, 1971.

16. Archives of the Margaret Herrick Library, Gail Russell Collection, A.M.P.A.S., Fairbanks Center for Motion Picture Study, Beverly Hills, California

Chapter 24

1. "The Truth About Guy Madison's Marriage," by Mike Connelly, T.V. Show Magazine, March, 1954.
2. "Air Cadet," Pressbook, Universal International, 1951.
3. New York Times Film Review, May 11, 1951.
4. "Safari To Catalina," by Gail Russell, Modern Screen Magazine, October, 1950.
5. Ibid.
6. "The Truth About Guy Madison's Marriage," by Mike Connelly, T.V. Show Magazine, March, 1954.
7. "Has Corinne Been A Good Girl?" by Corinne Calvet, St. Martins Press, New York, 1983.
8. "The Truth About Guy Madison's Marriage," by Mike Connelly, T.V. Show Magazine, March, 1954.
9. "Gail Russell," by Jim Meyer, Film Fan Monthly Magazine, May, 1971.
10. "The Truth About Guy Madison's Marriage," by Mike Connelly, T.V. Show Magazine, March, 1954.
11. "The Story Of Guy Madison's Heartbreak Marriage," by Pauline Swanson, Photo Play Magazine, February, 1954.
12. Ibid.
13. "The Truth About Guy Madison's Marriage," by Mike Connelly, T.V. Show Magazine, March, 1954.
14. "Gail Russell and Guy Madison in Second Separation," Hollywood Citizen News, February 19, 1953.
15. "Gail Russell, Guy Madison Part For While," Los Angeles Times, February 20, 2953.
16. "The Truth About Guy Madison's Marriage," by Mike Connelly, T.V. Show Magazine, March, 1954.

Chapter 25

1. "Ghosts Of The John Wayne Divorce Case," by Louis Reid, Screenland Magazine, April, 1954.
2. Ibid.
3. Ibid.
4. Ibid.
5. Ibid.
6. "Gail Russell's Miracle," by Joe Roberts, Screen Stars Magazine, July, 1956.
7. "Ghosts Of The John Wayne Divorce Case," by Louis Reid, Screenland Magazine, April, 1954.
8. Ibid.
9. Ibid.

10. "Gail Russell Threatens To Sue On Wayne Case Charge," Los Angeles Herald Express, October 21, 1953.

11. "Gail Russell Shocked, Denies Impropriety," by Louella Parsons, Los Angeles Examiner, October 21, 1953.

12. "Gail Russell: A Woman Reborn," by Ruth Waterbury, Photoplay Magazine, March, 1956.

13. "The Story of Guy Madison's Heartbreak Marriage," by Pauline Swanson, Photo Play Magazine, February, 1954.

14. Ibid.

15. Ibid.

16. Ibid.

17. Ibid.

18. "Film Star Gail Russell Jailed As Drunk Driver," Los Angeles Daily News, November 25, 1953.

19. "Gail Russell Goes To Jail As Drunken Driver," Los Angeles Mirror, November 25, 1953.

20. "Gail Russell Granted Delay In Drunk Case," Los Angeles Examiner, November 26, 1953.

21. "Gail Russell Arraigned On Drunk Driving Charge," Los Angeles Times, November 26, 1953.

22. "Film Star Gail Russell Jailed As Drunk Driver," Los Angeles Daily News, November 25, 1953.

23. "Gail Russell Goes To Jail As Drunken Driver," Los Angeles Mirror, November 25, 1953.

24. "Actress Gail Russell Is Jailed As Drunk Driver," Los Angeles Herald Express, November 25, 1953.

25. Ibid.

26. "Arrest Gail Russell," Beverly Hills, November 25, 1953.

27. "Gail Russell Granted Delay In Drunk Case," Los Angeles Examiner, November 26, 1953.

Chapter 26

1. "Gail Russell Tells Her True, Untold Story," by Fred D. Brown, Movieland Magazine, June, 1956.

2. Ibid.

3. Ibid.

4. Ibid.

5. Ibid.

6. "Gail Russell's Miracle," by Joe Roberts, Screen Stars Magazine, July, 1956.

7. "Gail Russell Tells Her True, Untold Story," by Fred D. Brown, Movieland Magazine, June, 1956.

8. Ibid.

9. Ibid.

10. "Gail Russell Sought In Hit-And-Run," by Kandis Rochlen and Carl Weilti, Los Angeles Mirror, February 12, 1955.

11. "Gail Russell Tells Crash," Los Angeles Examiner, February 13, 1955.

12. "Gail Russell Gives Up In Hit-Run Case," Los Angeles Times, February 13, 1955.

13. "Gail Russell Must Face Misdemeanor Complaint," Hollywood Citizen News, February 14, 1955.

14. "Gail Russell Sent Citation," Los Angeles Examiner, February 15, 1955.

15. "Drop Drunk Driving Suit On Gail Russell," Los Angeles Herald Examiner, Febarury 21, 1955.

16. "Gail Russell Faces Fan In Court," Los Angeles Examiner, November 22, 1956.

17. "Gail Russell Settles $30,000 Damage Suit," Los Angeles Times, November 28, 1956.

18. "Gail Russell Pays $50 Fees," Los Angeles Mirror, April 23, 1955.

Chapter 27

1. "Gail Russell: A Woman Reborn," by Ruth Waterbury, Photoplay Magazine, March, 1956.

2. "Gail Russell Tells Her True, Untold Story," by Fred D. Brown, Movieland Magazine, June, 1956

3. Ibid.

4. Ibid.

5. Ibid.

6. "Gail Russell's Miracle," by Joe Roberts, Screen Stars Magazine, July, 1956.

7. Ibid.

8. Ibid.

9. "Gail Russell Tells Her True, Untold Story," by Fred D. Brown, Movieland Magazine, June, 1956.

10. "Gail Russell," by Jim Meyer, Film Fan Monthly Magazine, May, 1971.

11. Ibid.

12. Ibid.

13. "Gail Russell Tells Her True, Untold Story," by Fred D. Brown, Movieland Magazine, June, 1956.

14. "Seven Men From Now," Pressbook, Warner Brothers Pictures, 1956.

15. "Gail Russell Tells Her True, Untold Story," by Fred D. Brown, Movieland Magazine, June, 1956.

16. Variety Film Review, July 11, 1956.

17. "Gail Russell Tells Her True, Untold Story," by Fred D. Brown, Movieland Magazine, June, 1956.

18. Ibid. 19. Ibid

Chapter 28

1. Archives of the Margaret Herrick Library, Gail Russell Collection, A.M.P.A.S., Fairbanks Center for Motion Picture Study, Beverly Hills, California.

Chapter 29

1. "The Tattered Dress," Pressbook, Universal International Pictures, 1957.
2. New York Times Film Review, March 15, 1957.
3. "Gail Russell Crashes Car Into Restaurant," Los Angeles Herald Express, July 6, 1957.
4. Ibid.
5. "Gail Russell Jailed After Auto Hits Café," Los Angeles Examiner, July 5, 1957.
6. Ibid.
7. "Gail Russell Crashes Car Into Restaurant," Los Angeles Herald Express, July 6, 1957.
8. Ibid.
9. Ibid.
10. Ibid.
11. "Gail Russell Jailed As Drunk Driver After Auto Rams Café, Hurts Man," Los Angeles Times, July 7, 1957.
12. "Gail Russell Faces Felony Charge," Hollywood Citizen News, July 8, 1957.
13. "Gail Russell To Quit Drinking," Los Angeles Examiner, July 9, 1957.
14. "Gail Faces Drunk Hearing," Los Angeles Herald Express, July 19, 1957.
15. "Gail Russell Faces Court," Los Angeles Times, July 19, 1957.
16. "Gail Russell Taken To Prison Ward," Los Angeles Examiner, August 21, 1957.
17. "Police Find Gail Russell Unconscious In Home," Los Angeles Times, August 21, 1957.
18. "Gail Russell Moved To Jail," Los Angeles Times, August 23, 1957.
19. "Gail Russell Trial Set For Oct. 15," Los Angeles Times, August 27, 1957.
20. "Gail Russell Convicted In Drunk Case," Los Angeles Mirror, February 3, 1958.
21. "Gail Russell Fined $420 For Drunk Driving," Los Angeles Herald Express, March 14, 1958.
22. "Gail Russell Fined; License Suspended," Hollywood Citizen News, March 14, 1958.

Chapter 30

1. "Gail Russell's Tragic Secret," by Henry Kramer, QT Magazine, January, 1962.
2. "Gail Russell," by Erskine Johnson, Los Angeles Mirror, September 28, 1957.
3. Ibid.
4. Ibid.
5. Ibid.
6. Ibid.
7. "Troubles Shadowed Little Gail," Los Angeles Mirror, November 25, 1953.
8. Ibid.
9. Ibid.
10. Ibid.
11. "An Autobiography, Yvonne," by Yvonne De Carlo and Doug Warren, St. Martins Press, 1987.

Chapter 31

1. "Reverie, Gail Russell By Candlelight," by Andrew J. Fenady, Hollywood Studio Magazine, April, 1983.

Chapter 32

1. "Gail Russell," by Jim Meyer, Film Fan Monthly Magazine, May, 1971.
2. Ibid.
3. "Gail Russell (1924-1961). The Short and Pitiful Annals Of A Girl Who Never Wanted To Be An Actress," Modern Screen Magazine, December, 1961.
4. Variety Film Review, June 15, 1961.

Chapter 33

1. "Gail Russell (1924-1961), The Short And Pitiful Annals Of A Girl Who Never Wanted To Be An Actress," Modern Screen Magazine, December, 1961.
2. Ibid.
3. Ibid.
4. Ibid.
5. "Actress Gail Russell Found Dead At Home," Los Angeles Times, August 28, 1961.
6. Ibid.
7. "Autopsy Ordered In Death Of Actress Gail Russell, 36," Los Angeles Mirror, August 28, 1961.

8. "Gail Russell (1924-1961), The Short And Pitiful Annals Of A Girl Who Never Wanted To Be An Actress," Modern Screen Magazine, December, 1961

9. Ibid.

10. Ibid.

11. "Actress Gail Russell Found Dead At Home," Los Angeles Times, August 28, 1961.

12. "Gail Russell, Hard Luck Beauty, Dies," Los Angeles Examiner, August 28, 1961.

13. "Autopsy Ordered In Death Of Actress Gail Russell, 36," Los Angeles Mirror, August 28, 1961.

14. "Copy, Certificate of Death, Gail Russell Moseley, #69403, State of California, Dept. of Health Services, State File #61-096737, Certificate #7053-17774.

15. "Gail Russell," by Jim Meyer, Film Fan Monthly Magazine, May, 1971.

16. "Our Hearts Were Young And Gay... And Now They Are So Sad," by Greg James, Movie Digest Magazine, May, 1972.

17. Ibid.

18. Ibid.

19. Ibid.

20. "Gail Russell Last Rites Held Today," Los Angeles Mirror, August 29, 1961.

21. "Stars Attend Funeral Of Gail Russell," Los Angeles Times, August 30, 1961.

Bibliography

Calvet, Corinne. "Has Corinne Been A Good Girl?" St. Martins Press, New York, 1983.

Chierichetti, David. "Hollywood Director." Curtis Books, New York, 1973.

Ciment, Michael. "Conversations With Losey." Methuen & Co., London, New York, 1985.

De Carlo, Yvonne with Doug Warren. "Yvonne, An Autobiography." St. Martins Press, New York, 1987.

Gardner, Ava. "Ava, My Story." Bantam Books, New York, 1990.

Hannsberry, Karen Burroughs. "Femme Noir. Bad Girls of Film." McFarland & Co., Jefferson, North Carolina, London, 1998.

Ragan, David. "Movie Stars of the 40's." Prentice-Hall Inc., Englewood Cliffs, New Jersey, 1985.

Turner, Lana. "Lana, The Lady, The Legend, The Truth." Simon & Schuster. New York, 1982.
Weaver, Tom. "Science Fiction and Fantasy Film Flashbacks." McFarland & Co., Inc., Jefferson, North Carolina, London, 1998.

Magazine Articles

1. Benjamin, George. "Dark Angel." Modern Screen Magazine, November, 1946.
2. Churchill, Reba and Bonnie. "Not The Siren She Seems." Screenland, March 1949.
3. Connolly, Mike. "The Truth About Guy Madison's Marriage." T.V. Show, January, 1954.
4. Coons, Robin. "Romance and Gail Russell." Screenland, January, 1947.
5. Daughtrey, Marcia. "Guy Loves Gail." Modern Screen, May, 1947.
6. Eaton, Harriet. "Gingham Girl With Sequins." Photoplay, June, 1945.
7. Feneday, Andrew J. "Gail Russell By Candlelight." Hollywood Studio, April, 1983.
8. Hall, Gladys. "Confessions of A Scared Cat." Screenland, May, 1945.
9. Hamilton, Sara. "Open Letter to Guy and Gail." Photoplay, May, 1947.
10. Hamilton, Sara. "Our Gail Is Growing Up." Photoplay, March, 1946.
11. Henaghan, Jim. "You Don't Have To Be Afraid Anymore, Gail." Modern Screen, December, 1961.

12. Hover, Helen. "We're Both As Stubborn As Mules." Motion Picture, June 1950.

13. James, Greg. "Our Hearts Were Young and Gay... And Now They Are So Sad." Movie Digest, May, 1972.

14. Kramer, Henry. "Gail Russell's Tragic Secret." QT, January, 1962.

15. Madison, Guy. "I'm Not Married." Modern Screen, March, 1949.

16. Meyer, Jim. "Gail Russell." Film Fan Monthly, May, 1971.

17. Pleck, Kaaren. "For Sentimental Reasons," Modern Screen, September, 1947.

18. "The Private Life of Guy and Gail." Movie Stars Parade, January, 1950.

19. Reid, Louis. "Ghosts of the John Wayne Divorce Case." Screenland, April, 1954.

20. Russell, Gail. "Safari To Catalina." Modern Screen, October, 1950.

21. Russell, Gail. "The Role I Liked Best." Saturday Evening Post, May 27, 1950.

22. Russell, Gail. "My Kind Of Guy." Photoplay, March, 1956.

23. Russell, Gail. "Why I Waited 4 Years To Marry Guy." Silver Screen, February, 1950.

24. Russell, Gail. "Secrets I'll Tell My Daughter." Movie Stars Parade, October, 1950.

25. Russell, Gail, as told to Helen Weller. "Secrets of An Introvert." Motion Picture, November, 1950.

26. Russell, Mrs. George. "I Am A Movie Star's Mother." Modern Screen, April, 1948.

27. Russell, Mrs. George, as told to Kate Holliday. "My Daughter's Miracle." Screenland, May, 1944.

28. Swanson, Pauline. "The Story of Guy Madison's Heartbreak Marriage." True Story, February, 1954.

29. Tildesley, Alice. "Gail Lives Alone." Modern Screen, March, 1949.

30. Vallee, William Lynch. "Movie Life Of Gail Russell." Movie Life Magazine, June, 1949.

31. Waterbury, Ruth. "Gail Russell – A Woman Reborn." Photoplay, March, 1956.

32. Weller, Hellen Hover. "Is Love Enough?" Motion Picture, May, 1950.

Index

CPSIA information can be obtained
at www.ICGtesting.com
Printed in the USA
BVOW05s0943141216

470789BV00009B/128/P